The Best of
Reader's Digest
Timeless
Favorites

Reader's Digest

New York / Montreal

Chief Content Officer, *Reader's Digest*
Jason Buhrmester
Content Director Mark Hagen
Creative Director Raeann Thompson
Editor Julie Kuczynski
Senior Art Director Kristen Stecklein
Senior Designer Anna Jo Beck
Deputy Editor, Copy Desk
Dulcie Shoener

A *READER'S DIGEST* BOOK

Copyright © 2023 Trusted Media
Brands, Inc.
485 Lexington Avenue
New York, NY 10017

ISBN 978-1-62145-997-2

Component number 116600117H

We are committed to both the quality
of our products and the service we
provide to our customers. We value
your comments, so please feel free
to contact us at TMBBookTeam@
TrustedMediaBrands.com.

For more *Reader's Digest* products and
information, visit our website:
   www.rd.com (in the United States)
   www.readersdigest.ca (in Canada)

Printed in China

10 9 8 7 6 5 4 3 2 1

Text, photography and illustrations
for *The Best of Reader's Digest:*
Timeless Favorites are based on
articles previously published in
Reader's Digest magazine (*rd.com*).

Pictured on front cover:
Anatomy of a Perfect Hand Transplant
   page 250
The Man Who Willed Himself to Fly
   page 108
The Killer Among Us page 122
The Bear Who Came to Dinner
   page 144

Pictured on back cover:
Locked in the Lion's Jaws page 196
This Is What Friends Are For page 244
An Army of Two page 216
Remembering Stephen Hawking:
   Brilliant and Funny page 276

Contents

Introduction

For more than 100 years, *Reader's Digest* has been sharing harrowing tales of adventure, inspiration, courage and humor that have no bounds of time or place. The fascinating stories told in the following pages—including a description of a special bond shared with a grandfather that lasts after his death and a riveting report about those who survived a mass arsenic poisoning in a small town—demonstrate the absolute strength of the human spirit.

We hope you enjoy the collection we've pulled together in this volume. Laugh at Mark Twain's frustration with Ben Franklin and muse on Danny Kaye's reflections on parenthood after an international trip. You'll question one man's close relationship with a bear and another's unfaltering loyalty to lions. You won't be able to stop reading about a woman's harrowing hostage situation at a convenient store or a murderer on the loose in Jerseyville, Illinois, in 1959.

There's a variety of narratives here that will pull at your heartstrings and tickle your funny bone. Some may even have you contacting an old friend or reaching out to distant relatives to reconnect. Touching and engaging, *The Best of Reader's Digest: Timeless Favorites* promises to stir conversations, provide food for thought and celebrate the resolute tenacity found within each of us.

Happy reading!

—The Editors of *Reader's Digest*

Wisdom of Bear Wood

*Who'd have thought a frail old lady
had so much to share?*

BY **MICHAEL WELZENBACH**

Originally published in December 1994

When I was 12 years old, my family moved to England, the fourth major move in my short life. My father's government job demanded that he go overseas every few years, so I was used to wrenching myself away from friends.

We rented a sprawling 18th-century farmhouse in Berkshire. Nearby were ancient castles and venerable churches. Loving nature, however, I was most delighted by the endless patchwork of farms and woodland that surrounded our house. In the deep woods that verged against our back fence, a network of paths led almost everywhere, and pheasants rocketed off into the dense laurels and bracken ahead as you walked.

I spent most of my time roaming the woods and fields alone, playing at Robin Hood, daydreaming, collecting bugs and bird-watching. It was heaven for a boy—but a lonely heaven. Keeping to myself was my way of not forming attachments that I would only have to abandon the next time we moved. But one day I became attached through no design of my own.

❖ ❖ ❖

We had been in England about six months when old Farmer Crawford gave me permission to roam about his immense property. I started hiking there every weekend, up a long, sloping hill to an almost impenetrable stand of trees called Bear Wood. It was my secret fortress, almost a holy place, I thought. Slipping through a barbed-wire fence, I'd leave the bright sun and the twitter and rustle of insects and animals outside and creep into another world—a vaulted cathedral, with tree trunks for pillars and eons' accumulation of long brown needles for a softly carpeted floor. My own breathing rang in my ears, and the slightest stirring of any woodland creature echoed through this private paradise.

Perhaps this is why the frail old lady I nearly ran into was as startled as I was. She caught her breath, instinctively touching her throat with her hand. Then, recovering quickly, she gave a welcoming smile that instantly

put me at ease. A pair of powerful-looking binoculars dangled from her neck. "Hello, young man," she said. "Are you American or Canadian?"

American, I explained in a rush, and I lived over the hill, and I was just seeing if there was a pond, and Farmer Crawford had said it was OK, and anyhow, I was on my way home, so goodbye.

As I started to turn, the woman smiled and asked, "Did you see the little owl from the spinney over there today?" She pointed toward the edge of the wood.

She knew about the owls? I was amazed. According to some unkind schoolmates, only "twitchers" (British slang for bird-watchers) like me knew anything about birds. Normal kids used slingshots.

"No," I replied, "but I've seen them before. Never close though. They always see me first."

The woman laughed. "Yes, they're wary," she said. "But then, gamekeepers have been shooting them ever since they got here. They're introduced, you know, not native."

"They're not?" I asked, fascinated. Anybody who knew this sort of stuff was definitely cool—even if she was trespassing in my special place.

"Oh, no!" she answered, laughing again. "At home I have books on birds that explain all about them. In fact," she said suddenly, "I was about to go back for tea and jam tart. Would you care to join me?"

I had been warned against going off with strangers, but somehow I sensed the old woman was harmless. "Sure," I said.

"I'm Mrs. Robertson-Glasgow," she introduced herself, extending a fine, transparent hand.

"Michael," I said, taking it clumsily in my own.

We set off, the old woman striding along at a surprisingly brisk clip. She told me how she and her husband had moved to Berkshire after he'd retired as a college professor about 10 years earlier. "He passed away last year," she said, looking suddenly wistful. "So now I'm alone, and I have all this time to walk the fields."

Soon I saw a small brick cottage that glowed pinkly in the westering sun. Mrs. Robertson-Glasgow opened the door and invited me in. I gazed about in silent admiration at the jumble of bookshelves, glass-fronted cases containing figures of ivory, ebony and carved stone, and cabinets full of fossils. There were glass terraria writhing with mosses and ferns, trays of pinned butterflies and, best of all, a dozen or so stuffed birds— including a slightly moth-eaten, glass-eyed eagle owl, tilting on its wire perch.

"Wow!" was all I could say.

"Does your mother expect you home at a particular time?" she asked as she ran the water for tea.

"No," I lied. Then, glancing at the clock, I added, "Well, maybe by five." That gave me almost an hour, not nearly enough time to ask about every single object in the room. Between mouthfuls of tea and jam tart I learned all sorts of new things—how to find fossilized sand dollars in the pebbles along the public footpaths; or that you could tell if dormice were about by the way they chiseled into hazelnuts.

The hour went by much too swiftly. Mrs. Robertson-Glasgow had to practically push me out the door. But she sent me home with two large tomes, one full of glorious illustrations of birds, and one of butterflies and other insects. I promised to return them the next weekend if she didn't mind my coming by. She smiled and said she'd look forward to that.

I had made the best friend in the world.

When I returned the books, she lent me more. Soon I began to see her almost every weekend, and my well of knowledge about natural history began to brim over. At school, I earned the nickname "Prof" and some respect from my fellow students. Even the school bully brought me a dead water rail he had found (or more likely shot), to identify.

During the summer I spent blissfully long days with my friend. I discovered she made the finest shortbread in the universe. We would explore Bear Wood,

munching happily and discussing the books she had lent me. In the afternoons we would retire to the cottage, and she would talk about her husband—what a fine man he'd been. Once or twice she seemed about to cry and left the room quickly to make more tea. But she always came back smiling.

As time passed, I did not notice that she was growing frailer and less inclined to laugh. Familiarity sometimes renders people physically invisible, for you find yourself talking to the heart—to the essence, as it were, rather than to the face. I suspected, of course, that she was lonely; I did not know she was ill.

❖   ❖   ❖

Back at school, I began to grow quickly. I played soccer and made a good friend. But I still stopped by the cottage on weekends, and there was always fresh shortbread.

One morning when I went downstairs to the kitchen, there was a familiar-looking biscuit tin on the table. I eyed it as I went to the refrigerator.

My mother was regarding me with a strange gentleness.

"Son," she began, painfully. And from the tone of her voice I knew everything instantly.

She rested her hand on the biscuit tin. "Mr. Crawford brought these by this morning." She paused, and I could tell she was having difficulty. "Mrs. Robertson-Glasgow left them for you."

I stared out the window, tears stinging my eyes.

"I'm sorry, Michael, but she died yesterday," she went on. "She was very old and very ill, and it was time."

My mother put her arm about my shoulder. "You made her very happy, because she was lonely," she said. "You were lucky to be such a good friend for her."

Wordlessly, I took the tin to my room and set it on my bed. Then, hurrying downstairs, I burst through the front door and ran to the woods.

I wandered for a long time, until my eyes had dried and I could see clearly again. It was spring—almost exactly a year since I'd met the old woman in Bear Wood. I looked around me and realized how much

I now knew. I knew where to look for bee orchids in the long grass. I knew to look for water striders, whirligig beetles and dragonfly larvae in a long-abandoned horse trough. And I knew that back in my bedroom I had a tin of the best shortbread in the universe, and I should go and eat it, savoring every crumb. And that's just what I did.

In time, that old round tin filled up with dried leaves, fossils and bits of colorful stone, a dead stag beetle, a flint arrowhead, and countless other odds and ends. I still have it.

But I have much more, the legacy of that long-ago encounter in Bear Wood. It is a wisdom tutored by nature itself, about the seen and the unseen, about things that change and things that are changeless, and about the fact that, no matter how seemingly disparate two souls may be, they possess the potential for that most precious, rare thing—an enduring and rewarding friendship.

Heist

The case of the stolen Rembrandt and the FBI agent who got it back

—

BY **SIMON WORRALL**

Originally published in December 2008

t's Christmastime in Stockholm. Dec. 22, 2000, 4:45 p.m., to be exact. Snow blankets the ground. The last visitors to the Nationalmuseum are putting on their coats, ready to leave. They're talking and laughing, but the festive mood is about to come to an end. Because just at that moment, thieves are parking a Mazda and a Ford sideways across the only two roads leading to the museum, a Renaissance-style palazzo at the tip of a peninsula, almost completely encircled by water. They douse the vehicles with barbecue lighter fluid and set them on fire. Then they strew steel spikes over the road to puncture the tires of any police cars that try to get through.

As the cars burst into flames, three members of the gang race into the museum. They wear ski masks and carry pistols and machine guns. "Everybody lie down!" shouts the gang leader, putting a pistol to the head of a guard.

Screams echo through the marble halls as two gang members sprint up the stairs. They know exactly where to go, having studied floor plans for months. Their job is made easier by the fact that there are no glass screens or cameras. Using bolt

In 2005, a little painting caused big trouble for undercover agent Bob Wittman. Here, for the first time, he tells all.

cutters, they quickly pluck a Rembrandt (*Self Portrait*, page 6) from the wall and stuff it into a bag. Then they cut the wires securing two Renoirs and race back down the stairs with their booty, past a woman who lies whimpering on the floor.

The gang leader pulls his pistol away from the head of the terrified guard and jams it into his denim jacket. Then the three masked men rush out of the building. They turn left, and left again, then sprint along the wharf behind the museum, where an associate is waiting for them in a speedboat.

The boat heads east, past Skeppsholmen Island, under Danvikstull Bridge and across a bay. At a harbor used by fishermen, the thieves tie up the boat and leap ashore, where they disappear. In less than half an hour, the most daring art theft of the century is over.

❖　❖　❖

Sweden is in mourning. Losing the Renoirs was a shock, but the Rembrandt has been a national treasure since its arrival in 1956.

To get it back, the Swedes ultimately look to the world's foremost art detective. A self-avowed keeper of the world's cultural flame, Robert Wittman is at the time the head of the FBI's Art Crime Team— a specialist force of 13 agents dedicated to hunting down stolen art. In a career stretching back 20 years, he has helped recover more than $250 million in artwork, including paintings by Norman Rockwell and Mark Rothko, gold body armor taken from a tomb in Peru, and Geronimo's warbonnet.

"Saving these things brings us closer together as human beings," says Wittman, explaining why he goes to work every day. Besides, Rembrandt's *Self Portrait* will look good on the résumé.

No artist painted himself as obsessively as Rembrandt van Rijn. In more than 90 self-portraits— from the tousle-haired youth of the 1620s to the hoary old man of 1669, the year of his death—he created a record of human aging without equal in Western art. *Self Portrait*, from 1630, is one of only five paintings he executed on copper, and one of his smallest, the size of a hardback book. But packed into this space is a work of staggering genius: a portrait of the Dutch artist as a young man, age 24, that has all the energy and pathos of a living person.

Dressed in a dark brown coat, with a black beret pushed insouciantly off his frizzy chestnut hair, Rembrandt stares out at us with an expression that is both vulnerable and steely. A costly gold leaf overlay makes the colors glow, as though lit from within. When it was first sold in Rotterdam in the 17th century, it changed hands for 35 florins, the equivalent of $35. Today you would need $40 million to own it.

Which goes a long way toward explaining why art theft is a growth industry. It's estimated that the worldwide trade in stolen and forged art is worth upwards of $6 billion annually. Only drug dealing, gunrunning and money laundering are more profitable. Some museums will pay a ransom to get the artwork back. Others aren't given that option by the

One of the stolen Renoirs,
La Conversation

thieves, says Wittman. In some cases, the robbers try to sell the work on the open market. But this rarely works—after all, a knowledgeable collector isn't going to buy a stolen Monet that he can't display publicly. So the purloined artwork tends to stay in the underworld for an average of seven years before a buyer is sought. If it's sold, it's usually for about 7% to 10% of its legitimate value. Not bad, considering some are worth millions.

The Swedish authorities don't

have to wait long to recover one of the Renoirs, *La Conversation*. Acting on a tip, police rescue the painting. Thirteen people are arrested, among them three Iraqi-born brothers. Two of them, Baha and Dieya Kadhum, are acquitted; only the middle brother, Safa, is convicted. Still, the two other works of art are nowhere to be found. And after Baha and Dieya walk free, the trail goes cold.

❖ ❖ ❖

Los Angeles. March 25, 2005, 3 p.m. Officers from the local

Jeune Parisienne, **recovered in Los Angeles**

organized-crime squad arrest a suspected member of a Eurasian crime syndicate while looking for drugs.

They don't find any dope this time. Instead they find a painting, a portrait of a woman with a soft bow at her neck. To find out who she is, they call on a local curator, as well as Bob Wittman and his FBI Art Crime Team. After photographs are scanned and databases checked, the painting is identified as the other Renoir, *Jeune Parisienne*, stolen nearly five years ago in Sweden.

When task force agents interrogate one of the thieves nabbed with the Renoir, he tells them the whereabouts of the other, far more valuable painting snatched from the Nationalmuseum: the Rembrandt. He also reveals the names and contact information of the people holding *Self Portrait*.

With phone numbers in hand, Wittman and his Swedish counterpart, Detective Magnus Osvald of the Stockholm police, concoct a sting operation to bring the Rembrandt back.

"I played an undercover art

expert for a European organized crime group in America," Wittman explains. "I flew to Copenhagen, then got into contact with the people in Stockholm who were holding the painting."

❖ ❖ ❖

The Scandic hotel, Copenhagen. Sept. 15, 2005, 10 a.m. Wittman waits in his room for a phone call. He is used to living out of suitcases. Some months, he spends more time on his cellphone than he does at home with his three kids and wife of 23 years. Besides the United States, he has worked in Brazil, Ecuador, France—18 countries in total. There are times when he wakes up and can't remember what city he's in.

Today, as usual, he has checked into a hotel under a false name, using false travel documents. Pretending to be someone else is a big part of his job. It helps that he has one of those faces that are easy to forget. No distinguishing features, no scars, no cauliflower ears. Average height, average build. A regular-looking guy. Put him in a crowded room and he would blend into the background, just like a camouflaged moth on a tree trunk.

Sometimes that can be a problem. Years ago, in a Madrid hotel, he had to throw himself on the floor as a Spanish SWAT team burst into the room to arrest Angel Suarez Flores, the head of a crime syndicate. Flores had offered Wittman one of the gems of medieval Flemish art, *The Temptation of St. Anthony* by Pieter Bruegel the Elder. It had been stolen from the penthouse of Spain's richest woman, along with paintings by Goya, Pissarro and Japanese painter Foujita—a $50 million haul. When the cops tore into the room, Wittman was worried they wouldn't know he was on their side. He got out alive by diving behind a bed, shouting, "Don't shoot! *Bueno hombre*! Good guy!"

❖ ❖ ❖

As Wittman checks the money he has brought from the States to buy the Rembrandt, $250,000 in cash, his cellphone rings. It's the Swedish police, who have been doing surveillance all the way from Stockholm. "The three art thieves came by train, with one of them holding the painting in a shopping bag," he recalls. "They switched trains at the Danish-Swedish border."

The Swedish police do not arrest the men right away. They want to catch them selling Wittman the stolen Rembrandt. Baha and Dieya Kadhum, the two acquitted Iraqi-born brothers, plus a 29-year-old Swede named Alexander Lindgren, think they are about to pull off the final move in one of the biggest art heists in history. Instead they are walking into a perfectly laid trap.

In Copenhagen, Lindgren and the two Kadhum brothers walk around the hotel a couple of times to make sure they are not being followed. Wittman, using the phone number he got from the snitch in L.A., calls them on their cellphone and arranges to meet Baha Kadhum, the leader, in the lobby.

Kadhum is in his late 20s: black hair, lean face, sallow skin, hooded eyes. He is wearing designer jeans, a T-shirt and expensive leather shoes. "We discussed how we would do the trade," says Wittman. "We would go upstairs. I would flash the money. If he's happy with that, I'll see the painting, which is outside with the two other guys."

At the heart of Wittman's job is what he calls "befriending and betraying." In every undercover operation, there is a tipping point, a moment when the bad guys move from suspicion to trust. Wittman calls this "the moment of acceptance." The period just before that is the most dangerous. A sweaty lip, an overeager smile, and he could blow his cover and end up dead. But years of practicing the art of deception ensure that, as Kadhum walks into the hotel room, Wittman looks as affable as a high school history teacher. It's Kadhum who's jumpy, while Wittman pats him down to make sure he isn't carrying a gun or a knife. "He keeps fidgeting," recalls Wittman. Kadhum's eyes dart around as though he thinks someone else is there. "Only when he has the money in his hands does he begin to relax. He trusts the money. And that is his big mistake."

❖ ❖ ❖

Kadhum says he will return with the painting in a few minutes. A half hour later and no Kadhum. What if something has gone wrong? What if Wittman's cover has been blown? What if he isn't clean?

Keeping clean is FBI-speak for making sure an agent has not been tailed. Art thieves are a cautious lot, says Wittman, which means "I usually have people following me for a while. So you don't go anywhere you shouldn't until you have been cleaned. But you always have to be aware of that possibility."

And you always practice countersurveillance. You watch the people watching you. But never alone. Wittman is always part of a team. The team is his shield, his radar. This time, the Swedish and Danish police have set up operations in a room a floor above him, as well as in the room next door. Wittman's room is wired, and there's a

miniature camera hidden in a lamp.

"After I flash him the money, Kadhum leaves the hotel room and goes downstairs," says Wittman. "The other two guys are on the street with the bag. But the three of them then go to another hotel room where a fourth guy actually has the painting." He smiles. "They are good. The other bag is just a dummy."

When Kadhum finally does come back, he's carrying the painting in a red felt bag tied tightly with cord. "I had a hard time opening the bag," recalls Wittman with a laugh, "what with there being no knives in the room!"

But untie it he does. And there it is, the Rembrandt.

"You ever take it out of the frame?" asks Wittman.

"I never touched it," says Kadhum.

"You an art lover?"

"No. I am just in it for the money."

Wittman takes the painting into the bathroom and uses a miniature ultraviolet lamp and a black light to check it for signs of forgery or damage. The end is only seconds away now, and soon all hell will break loose.

Turning off the lamp, he gives the prearranged signal. "It's a done deal!" he says to Kadhum in a loud voice.

As the door flies open and Danish police barrel in, Wittman shields the painting with his body. The five agents are encased in body armor and are toting semiautomatic weapons. "Freeze!" they scream at Kadhum.

❖   ❖   ❖

Nationalmuseum, Stockholm. Sept. 20, 2005, 6 p.m. Champagne corks pop and cameras flash as Rembrandt's *Self Portrait* is rehung. For the people of Sweden, the painting is a dear friend. Bulletproof glass and security cameras help ensure it never leaves them again.

There is no bubbly for Wittman. He is already back in America, undercover, working another case. The guests toasting the return of their beloved Rembrandt have no idea how complicated the sting operation was. Or how a quiet American with a face no one

remembers risked his life to help recover it.

But Wittman's no martyr. Just ask him what it's like to hold a Rembrandt.

"It's a eureka moment," he says, grinning widely. "It's always a eureka moment."

The Kadhum brothers and Alexander Lindgren were convicted of receiving stolen goods, but their sentences were later overturned by a Swedish appeals court, which ruled they were "provoked" by American and Swedish police.

Sergeant Erwin and the Blazing Bomb

A story of a night when the Congressional Medal of Honor seemed to be a modest award

———

BY **COREY FORD**

Originally published in July 1965

Sometimes I'm asked which I like best of all the pieces I've written. I guess the answer is something I wrote one night back in 1945, on the island of Guam. It was never published; I didn't even sign it; but it was more rewarding than anything else I've ever done.

Guam was our base in the Marianas from which the B-29s took off for their nightly incendiary raids on Japan. As an Air Force colonel, I had flown with them, and I knew what those missions were like. The seven endless hours over the Pacific to the hostile coastline. The wink of ack ack guns and the flak bursts all around us, the ground searchlights that lighted up our cabin as though an auto had parked beside us in the sky, and, after our bomb run, the red ruin of an enemy city burning. We would throttle down to cruising speed; there were 1,500 miles of empty ocean between us and home.

This particular night I was not flying. I sat in the group head-quarters tent with Col. Carl Storrie, waiting for the mission's strike report. Storrie, a lean, tough Texan, was the group commander, and he paced up and down the tent, restless as a caged animal, as the first news filtered in. The lead plane, commanded by Capt. Tony Simeral, had been forced to turn away from the target and had made an emergency landing at Iwo Jima. It was on its way back to Guam now.

We could make out the drone of its engines, see the red flares that signaled distress and hear the firetrucks rumbling to meet it as it touched down. A few moments later Captain Simeral entered the tent. His face was white; he seemed to be in a state of shock. He fumbled for a cigarette with his left hand, and I saw that the back of his right hand was pockmarked with deep ugly holes that had burned clear to the bone. He took several drags before he could trust himself to talk.

It had happened as they approached the enemy coast, he said. They were flying the pathfinder plane, which drops a phosphorus smoke bomb to assemble the formation before proceeding to the target. On a B-29 this task is performed by the radio operator, back in the waist of the plane. At a signal from the pilot he releases the bomb through a narrow tube.

The radio operator on Simeral's plane was a chunky, red-haired youngster from Alabama, Staff Sgt. Henry Erwin. His crewmates liked to mimic his soft southern drawl, and he was always with a grin, always quiet and courteous. He received the routine order from Simeral, triggered the bomb and dropped it down the tube.

There was a malfunction. The bomb exploded in the tube and bounced back into Erwin's face, blinding both eyes and searing off an ear.

Phosphorus burns with a furious intensity that melts metal like butter. Now the bomb at Erwin's feet was eating its way rapidly through the deck of the plane, toward the full load of incendiaries in their racks below. He was alone; the navigator had gone up to the astrodome to get a star shot. There was no time to think. He picked up the white-hot bomb in his bare hands and started forward to the cockpit, groping his way with elbows and feet.

The navigator's folding table was down and latched, blocking the narrow passageway. Erwin hugged the blazing bomb under an arm, feeling it devour the flesh on his ribs, unfastened the spring latch and lifted the table. (We inspected the plane later; the skin of his entire hand was seared onto the table.)

He stumbled on, a walking torch. His clothes, hair and flesh were ablaze.

The dense smoke had filled the airplane, and Simeral had opened the window beside him to clear the air. "I couldn't see Erwin," he told us, "but I heard his voice right at my elbow. He said—" Simeral paused a moment to steady his own voice. "He said, 'Pardon me, sir,' and reached across to the window and tossed out the bomb. Then he collapsed on the flight deck." A fire extinguisher was turned on him, but the phosphorus still burned.

Simeral's instrument panel was obliterated by the smoke, and the plane was out of control. It was less than 300 feet off the water when he righted it. He called to the formation that he was aborting, jettisoned his bombs and headed back to the field hospital at Iwo,

Congressional Medal of Honor

three hours away. The crew applied first aid to Erwin, gave him plasma, smeared grease on his smoldering flesh. "He never lost consciousness, but he spoke only once the whole way back. He asked me—" Simeral took another drag on his cigarette. "'Is everybody else all right, sir?'"

At Iwo, he was still exhaling phosphorus smoke from his lungs, and his body had become so rigid that he had to be eased out through the window like a log. They carried him to the hospital. When they removed the unguent pads there and exposed his flesh to the air, it began to smolder again. The airplane flew on to Guam—with 11 men who would not be living save for the one they left behind.

Simeral finished talking. A young lieutenant looked at the holes in his right hand, where the phosphorus had spattered, and said tactlessly, "You ought to put in for a Purple Heart, Captain." Simeral, his control snapping, took a wild swing at him. Then the flight surgeon arrived and gave him a sedative, and led him away to have his burns treated.

We spent the rest of the night writing up a recommendation for the Congressional Medal of Honor. It was simply worded. There was no need to speak of heroism and sacrifice; the facts were enough. It ended with the conventional military phrase "above and beyond the call of duty," but that seemed to express it pretty well. At five in the morning Colonel Storrie carried the single typewritten page to Air Force headquarters. Gen. Curtis LeMay was awakened. He read and signed it, and the recommendation

was then flashed to Washington. The reply arrived in record time: Approved.

Iwo reported that Sergeant Erwin was still alive, but no one could say how much longer he would survive. There was no Congressional Medal of Honor on Guam; the nearest was in Honolulu, and a special B-29 was dispatched to fly the Pacific to Hawaii.

The medal was in a locked display case in Gen. Robert C. Richardson's headquarters, and the key was missing. They smashed the glass, took the medal from the case and sped back to Guam. General LeMay flew to Iwo and personally presented it to Sergeant Erwin, in a ceremony at his bedside. He repeated the final line about the call of duty, and Erwin said, "Thank you, sir."

Several years after the war I heard that Erwin was back in Alabama, happily married; he had regained the use of his hands and partial vision in one eye. I hope he can read over his citation now and then. I hope it gives him as much satisfaction as it gave me to write it.

The Lost Art of Doing Nothing

Less busyness and diversions, more plain sitting around and thinking

BY **DON HEROLD**

Originally published in October 1948

If today's average American is confronted with an hour of leisure, he is likely to palpitate with panic. An hour with nothing to do! So he jumps into a dither and into a car, and starts driving off fiercely in pursuit of diversion. That may be one reason why Monday morning papers are so full of accident fatalities. Many of us set out on Friday evening to become statistics.

Even gin rummy and kindred time killers are taken up with high-powered determination. We plunge into most of our major recreations like men from Mars—motorboat speeding, nightclub skylarking, a month of touring compressed into a weekend. Even Florida and California, lands of relaxation and retirement, offer endless orgies of organized horseshoe pitchin', rumba wiggling, shuffleboard and bridge. We fly too high and whiz too fast, and can hardly wait for the advent of the private rocket plane and the jet-propelled surfboard. If we merely lie in the sun we overdo it.

Why do we thus apply the industrial ideal of high productivity even to our off moments, setting ourselves to producing *nothing* with intense efficiency? Why have we lost the fine art of beneficial floating?

19

In all nature, quietude is essential to growth.

I thank heaven I grew up in a small town, Bloomfield, Indiana, in a horse-and-buggy era, when we had, or made, time to sit and think, and often just to sit. When leisure came, we gathered in the shade of the blacksmith shop or in the back room of Cavins' drugstore and had rich and elevating conversation, not

> ## *Pascal has it that most of the evils of life arise from "man's being unable to sit still in a room."*

the empty prattle that we moderns must stomach at cocktail parties. If someone were energetic enough to dig a cellar or a cistern, we gathered round and watched his efforts and philosophized or made cracks.

Consequently, Bloomfield was full of characters, not robots. And I imagine that one explanation of Indiana's prolific production of literary figures in years past is that

there were hundreds of Bloomfields in Indiana, in which folks were talking and living literature without knowing it. Some of them just naturally got to writing it.

But where are the places and pauses for contemplation today?

Our reading, too, is on a production line. I wonder how many people now think as they read? We lap up the printed pages, with practically no pondering. The huge consumption of tabloids and the mighty movement of meretricious bestsellers prove this. In most of this fodder there is seldom even a single vitamin for the mind.

I plead for less busyness in our hours of leisure, and for more plain sitting and more contemplation.

How do you know when busynessitis is ailing you?

Well, when you get to feeling like the rabbit in a greyhound race. Or when you fume because you missed a streetcar or bus, though there'll be another one along in five minutes. Or when you play with the baby or with your grandchild with one eye on your wristwatch. When your life is too full to look up words in the dictionary and (while you are at it) to study a word or two above and below. Or when you catch yourself taking a taxi for four blocks instead of walking. Or eating lunch like a locomotive scooping up water out of a trough.

A foreign friend once talked to me about the significance of American verbs—how much they reveal our inner compulsions. We "catch" a train. We "grab" a bite of lunch. We "contact" a client. Everything has to be active and electric.

"So," you ask me, "what do you want me to do about it?"

The main idea is to achieve, somehow, a sense of leisure as you go along. Go out less, stay home more. Get bigger and better topics to think about during your slowdowns.

Even passing attempts at meditation help us to slow down. And if we loaf along we just naturally think bigger. Thoreau puts it this way: "When we are unhurried and wise, we perceive that only great and worthy things have any permanent and absolute existence, that petty fears and petty pleasures are but the shadow of the reality."

Pascal has it that most of the evils of life arise from "man's being unable to sit still in a room." He means by this not just a way of keeping out of mischief but a way of opening up the pores to life.

The only way I can lick the frenetic living of New York is to take fade-outs. I go back to my office after lunch and enjoy a 30-minute nap while Rome burns. I know other men who do this too; most of them are coronary cases. Sometimes I think we'd all be wise to play coronary—pretend we've had an attack and had the living daylights scared out of us. I've noticed that many men don't start to live until they're half dead. Somehow we've got to sneak into this life a few of the things we're planning for the next world. Somehow we've got to get more of that eternity feeling. Somehow we've got to do more of the things in our middle age, and before, that we plan to do in our old age.

We ought to do more walking with no place to go. (Walking is a lost art in America; it has become too excessively functional.) We ought to have fewer appointments and more chance encounters. When we have 10 minutes to get somewhere we should take 20, in order to loll on the way and see what we can see. We need less leg action and more acute observation as we go. Slow down the muscles and stir up the mind.

The art of loafing is not negative; it involves, rather, smarter selectivity of things worth attention. We need to change our objective—from merely getting somewhere to getting impressions and to relishing our emotions and sentiments while we are on our way.

We ought to read Thoreau about once a year. Such passages as this: "I spent many an hour, when I was younger, floating over the surface of Walden Pond as the zephyr willed, having paddled my boat to the middle, and lying on my back across the seats, in a summer forenoon, dreaming awake, until I was aroused by the boat touching the sand, and I arose to see what shore my fates had impelled me to; days when idleness was the most attractive and productive industry. Many a forenoon have I stolen away, preferring to spend thus the most valued part of the day; for I was rich, if not in money, in sunny hours and summer days, and spent them lavishly; nor do I regret that I did not waste more of them in the workshop or at the teacher's desk."

A dozen times a day we should tell ourselves that mere efficiency is not life, especially efficiency in our off moments.

We go to cocktail and dinner parties where we hope we may see somebody who will help our careers. We ought to do a lot more talking to people who aren't going to help us get anywhere: with the man who comes to fix the refrigerator, with carpenters and elevator men, with men who do the world's work—not just with those who talk about doing it.

From a workman I learned something of the inscrutable

mysteries of bees, their habits and their drives, and the beauty of a molten primitive mass of them crawling toward a new hive after the swarm in the spring. The mystery of the bee had nothing to do with the work of that man and nothing to do with my business that day. And for that reason, as well as for its inherent interest, learning about it put a new half sole on my soul—at least temporarily.

This pilfering of a little joyous living often will come from doing what we want deep in our hearts to do, instead of doing what "our set" thinks we ought to do. The party at the country club Saturday night—the heck with that! The latest novel—there are better ones 50 years old that we haven't read. Why not stay home and nibble at something else, or just sit with the family in "idle" conversation?

Minds need rotating as well as crops. Why not take up oil painting, even if you're lousy at it? It's slow, and it will teach you to look. Or photography? Or special fields of study that may lead nowhere or heaven knows where? (Somebody has said that the basis of all science is the pursuit of curiosity.)

One bad product of haste is selfishness. And one refreshing change that many of us might try is unselfishness. This takes time, but works inward magic on us. Give half an hour a day, or an hour, to going out of your way to do something for somebody else. Spend some time each week in helping in a hospital or giving of your time to some other type of social service.

So I say, somehow, if only for moments out of the 24 hours, achieve—or steal—a sense of leisure.

Soak. Nobody ever thought anything out in a shower bath. It's too fast and too efficient.

Baby in the Stream

When a neighbor pulls an unconscious toddler from an icy creek, the boy's family fears the worst. But one doctor won't give up hope.

—

BY **DEREK BURNETT**

Originally published in December 2015

t's the first warm day of spring, and the March sun pours over the ridge that borders Doyle and Rose Martin's rural property outside Mifflinburg, Pennsylvania. Yesterday it rained all day, melting the better part of the long winter's snow, and what the rain left behind, the sun is taking care of today. Water seeps and trickles down the surrounding slopes, swelling the normally humble creeks until they nearly jump their banks. The stream that runs through the Martins' yard is usually ankle deep and lethargic, but today it is so spring-riled that it courses angrily beneath the footbridge at startling speed, up to a man's waist and frigid.

The Martin boys will not squander such a lovely afternoon. After the school bus drops them off, they barge outside to ride bikes, gathering sticks to build a fire. They are what people in some circles call free-range kids; the Martins have eight in all (their youngest boy born just this April), and in keeping with their own upbringings, Doyle and

Gardell Martin, age 2, beside the creek that nearly took his life

25

Rose expect their children to learn independence and responsibility, the older ones looking after the younger. Today, Gary, 11, and Greg, 7, are playing with little Gardell, who is not yet 2. Doyle, a trucker, is out on the road. Rose is working in the kitchen, where she can frequently check on the boys through the window.

Suddenly Greg bursts through the door, his face streaked with tears. "I can't find Gardell!" he screams. "He was just with me!"

Rose and her two eldest, Gloria and Grace, charge outside, hollering Gardell's name. Just to make sure, they check the two outbuildings, but everybody is thinking about that raging stream. Rose dials 911, and the girls call their father. The property echoes with the family's frantic shouts for Gardell, as mother and children scramble along the banks of the brook, sickened by the speed of that icy gray water.

❖ ❖ ❖

Randall Beachel is washing dishes at his kitchen sink when he looks idly out the window and sees Grace and Gary Martin running alongside the stream where it exits their property. Something's wrong. Grace is barefoot, no jacket. They're yelling. He steps outside. "What's wrong?" he calls to Gary.

"We can't find my little brother!"

Randall's heart sinks. He runs back inside, tells his wife, Melissa, what's going on, and pulls on his shoes. Together they rush outside and down the road to where the stream passes through pastureland some eighth of a mile downstream of the Martin place. Randall holds the strands of electric fence wire, ignoring the shocks, as Melissa climbs through. When they reach the brook, Melissa goes downstream and Randall begins following the brook back toward the Martins', scanning the water's surface. After a moment, he sees a tiny pair of navy blue boots partially obscured by brush. A step or two farther, and he sees the whole picture: the little boy, still clad in a hooded snowsuit, hanging bizarrely on his side in the middle of that rushing stream, his face turned away from the current.

Randall plunges into the brook, gasping involuntarily—the water temperature is around 35 degrees—loses his footing and blunders into a deep hole. Recovers himself. Pulls the limp little body off what turns out to be a grassy underwater knoll. Staggers back to dry land, hollering "I found him!" even as he turns the kid over to see if he can drain the water from his mouth and lungs. An ambulance is coming up the road. Randall raises an arm, and it stops.

A paramedic comes racing across the field, and Randall hands the little boy off and stands watching as the rescuer rushes back toward the ambulance, performing CPR as he goes. When Randall reaches the road, the ambulance staff have torn off Gardell's clothes. One of the paramedics has placed a mask onto the little boy's face and is hand-pumping air into his lungs; the other is rhythmically compressing the tiny chest to force blood through the body. That's all Randall sees before the vehicle turns around and speeds toward town. As for Rose, she never gets so much as a glimpse of her son.

They're taking him to Evangelical Community Hospital in nearby Lewisburg, she learns. Within minutes, her sister and brother-in-law arrive at the house, and together they speed toward the hospital. As they rush into the emergency room 15 minutes later, Rose is told they're transporting him by Life Flight to a trauma center. Through the windows of the waiting area she can see the chopper on the heliport,

> *The CPR has gone on for more than an hour. "If he survives, it will be a miracle," a paramedic says.*

its interior illuminated, medical workers hunched over what must be Gardell's body. Her brother-in-law is an EMT, and he can tell that they're still doing CPR in there—after all this time!—but he says nothing to Rose.

Mike Lesher, the paramedic who first carried Gardell to the ambulance, heads back to the station. The CPR has gone on for more than an hour; typically rescuers give up after less than half that time. "If he survives," Lesher remarks, "it will be a miracle."

A moment later, the aircraft lifts off. Rose watches through the window, tears stinging her eyes; she has missed her little one again.

❖ ❖ ❖

Frank Maffei is preparing for his evening rounds in the pediatric intensive care unit at Geisinger Medical Center's Janet Weis Children's Hospital in Danville, some 15 miles from Lewisburg.

"I never felt hopeless," says Dr. Maffei. "I thought, *We've got a shot to save him*."

He gets a call from the ER downstairs: toddler on his way via Life Flight, full cardiac arrest. Worse: CPR ongoing for more than an hour, to no avail. Not promising.

Still, Dr. Maffei and his colleagues leap into action. Upon Gardell's arrival, they run a breathing tube down the boy's throat, and four residents line up on his left side to continue CPR: two minutes of chest compressions, move to the back of the line. It's critical to get Gardell warmed up, so even as the limp little body jiggles and jolts under the force of the chest compressions, other doctors and nurses carefully insert an IV and two catheters to send warm fluids into his body, which is at only 77 degrees.

A resident turns to Dr. Maffei. "At what point are we going to stop?"

"We'll stop if we warm him to 90 degrees and he's still unresponsive," Dr. Maffei says.

"What about a pH?"

The resident is referring to the acidity of the blood, which spikes when a person stops breathing; a pH lower than 6.8 is considered incompatible with life.

Dr. Maffei hears himself answer, "6.5." It's an outrageous threshold. A few minutes later, the pH comes back at 6.54. No heartbeat, no breathing and a low pH: The boy is dead.

Dr. Maffei has been doing this work for 25 years. Objectively, he knows that it's all over. Yet he can't shake some strange, subjective notion that Gardell is still in there. "Keep going," he says.

Now it's after 8 p.m., and Gardell remains unresponsive. The doctors move him to the operating room and prepare to put him on a heart bypass machine. They've gotten his temperature up to 83 degrees, but the machine will allow them to warm his blood externally and recirculate it, speeding the process. A surgeon stands scrubbed and ready to cut into the little boy's chest.

"Let's just do one more pulse check," Dr. Maffei says, laying his fingertips against Gardell's femoral artery. To his amazement, there is a pulse. His colleague Dr. Rich Lambert checks the brachial artery—there is a strong pulse there. Excited, they stand in the OR, monitoring Gardell's pulse for more than an hour, then transfer him to pediatric intensive care.

Dr. Maffei steps out into the waiting area to meet Rose. "Gardell's alive," he says. "However, we have to understand that he's alive after essentially being dead for an hour and 41 minutes." He needs to manage her expectations: Gardell's oxygen-starved brain will probably be forever damaged. It's anyone's guess as to when—or whether—he will wake up and what function he'll have when he does.

❖ ❖ ❖

Now it's the wee hours of the morning. Doyle Martin has gotten in from the highways, and he and Rose are sitting over Gardell's bed. "Gardell," Doyle says as he always does when he reaches home, "I came back from trucking to play with you. Do you want to play?"

And to the eternal astonishment of all, the boy opens his eyes and turns his head toward his father—

the boy who, eight hours ago, was dead.

Gardell stays in the hospital two more days, under light sedation. He's kept at a cool 90 degrees to prevent his brain tissue from swelling. He begins opening his eyes more frequently, obviously aware of his surroundings. The breathing tube is removed. He's weaned off the sedation. On the fourth day, a Sunday, he returns home. Within a week, he's playing with his siblings. "You would never know anything happened," Rose says.

❖　❖　❖

So how did a little boy who, by every objective measure, was dead for nearly two hours come back to life unscathed? To the Martins and many others, Gardell's survival was simply a miracle. Rose points out that his pulse returned just as local church groups were meeting to pray on his behalf.

Physiologically, the key to Gardell's survival was the fact that he nearly drowned in ice water. "Hypothermia imparts a degree of protection from the detrimental effects of low blood flow and low oxygen," Dr. Maffei says. The severe cold stopped Gardell's heart, but it also saved his brain, just as you might put an amputated finger on ice until you can reattach it. At a higher temperature, Gardell's brain cells would surely have died for lack of oxygen; as it was, they could wait—at least for an hour and 41 minutes. But no one involved in the rescue has ever seen such an extreme case.

Randall Beachel, the neighbor who pulled Gardell from the stream, sometimes looks over at the Martin place and chuckles at the sight of the towheaded youngster kicking dirt around in the garden or chasing his brothers. It's simple to him too. "It's truly a miracle," he says. "Truly a miracle."

He's Always Magnificently Wright

Building your first house is always an adventure. But when your architect is one of the most colorful and unpredictable in the world, well ...

——

BY **ARCH OBOLER**

Originally published in February 1958

t was raining in Southern California—one of those God's-tipped-the-bucket downpours we used to have back in 1940 before smog and spiraling tax rates dehydrated the climate. At an authoritative knock I opened the door of our rented house a crack. Through the sluicing rain I saw a soaked black Inverness cape and a water-streaming gray porkpie hat. Came a stentorian pronouncement: "I am Frank Lloyd Wright. You wrote me. May I come in?"

Those simple words signaled the beginning of a drastic change in the life of the Oboler family.

Years before, in my boyhood neighborhood in South Side Chicago, I had discovered a house which I thought was the most beautiful I had ever seen. This building was considered the neighborhood blight; its clean horizontal lines of wood and brick exasperated the surrounding owners of multistoried gingerbreaded homes. But as I grew older and the conventional houses grew uglier, the horizontal house, thanks to its simple loveliness of line and the harmony of its materials to its location, grew younger and more beautiful until it became our neighborhood's pride. And so had the designer of the house grown in esteem, the world-famous architect Frank Lloyd Wright.

When the day came that I could build my own home, I wanted that architect. In the intervening years I had been amply forewarned about the man. This was a character, the printed word told me, who strode through his world with rapier tongue and flailing Malacca cane, striking down conventionalism, hesitant clients and architectural committees with impartial gusto. Nevertheless I wrote to Mr. Wright, then in his early 70s, asking if it would be possible for him to design a California home for us.

Now, unexpectedly, he was here, eyes twinkling as he met Mrs. Oboler and obviously approved. He proceeded to rapid-fire questions at us, prefaced with the statement, "I don't build houses for *houses*. I build them for *human beings*."

From his probing it was obvious he was trying to find out what sort of human beings we were.

"So you are a writer!" he said. "What do you write?" I told him I wrote plays for radio.

"Are they good plays? I build good houses!"

The fact that we had settled in the lower end of California was definitely not in our favor. "I suppose you'll want to build in that Beverly Hills!" he snorted. "Cardboard cracker boxes anointed with pink stucco!"

We assured him that the neverland of the cinema stars was not for us. We wanted the country, the mountains.

Mr. Wright grinned. "At least you've got that much sense!" Then his face lost its laughter. "You know, of course, the banks won't advance you a dime on one of my designs."

I told him we would finance the house ourselves. Mr. Wright brightened. "And how much are you prepared to spend?"

I told him.

He sighed deeply and shook his head. "It will take at least

twice that much," he informed us.

Eleanor and I looked at each other. I got her telepathic nod, and took the plunge. "That will be all right," I said.

Hours after Mr. Wright had left, my wife and I turned to each other simultaneously. "Do you realize ... ," we both began. Before discussing a single detail of our proposed house, Frank Lloyd Wright had doubled the price!

(This man knew that over the years hundreds of his finest plans lay entombed in preliminary drawings—homes as exquisite as dream-remembered castles, glass-curtained skyscrapers prophetic of a time yet unborn, their bright hope destroyed by the harsh realities of economics. And so that our dream, too, might not end with a sheaf of drawings, he tried to dissuade us with the bitter truth.)

After a weeks-long search, we found our mountaintop. It was late afternoon. The rugged backbones of the mountains purpled down to the great blue-green sweep of the ocean, with a backdrop of sunset almost overpowering in its intensity.

Architect Frank Lloyd Wright, New York, New York, 1954

I watched as Mr. Wright stood on the cliff edge, outlined against the sky like a stern god from Olympus. I waited for him to speak.

And then his words came, strangely soft: "This is where we will build. And when I die, there will be something of me, because of you, on this mountain."

Then he sort of clutched at me and I thought, "This is too sentimental too soon, but I will go along with it for his sake." So I murmured an appropriate response and clutched right back.

Later I learned that Mr. Wright had described that scene to friends—the beautiful homesite, the dramatic sunset. Seeking to "meet each client on his own emotional level," he had decided that what Client Oboler wanted was a sense of the eternal in relation to the building in the mountains. So (as Mr. Wright put it), reluctantly, because such sentimentality was foreign to his nature, he had made the speech for my sake, and had clutched me to his bosom!

(He would have been a great actor-director-producer, this man. For the sense of the dramatic is there, not only in his person but in his creations.)

When the plans were completed, Mr. Wright had a word of advice: "During the actual building of your house, get out of town!"

Where clients wasted money, he went on to say, was in being around to make inconsequential changes in the original blueprints, to the great financial joy of the cost-plus contractor. Particularly when he would be too far away to protect the lambs from the slaughter.

The two lambs stockpiled all the materials on the building site as per the blueprints and took a boat for New York via the Panama Canal on a long-overdue vacation. I was draped over the ship's rail watching the first of the locks gurgle when the ship's radio operator handed me a message. It was from the contractor. "MR. WRIGHT HAS CHANGED MIND. WANTS BUILDING MADE OUT OF PINE. PLEASE INSTRUCT AS TO DISPOSITION FOUR THOUSAND DOLLARS REDWOOD ALREADY PURCHASED."

Eleanor watched the anger-ripped radiogram fly overboard and listened to me dictate a vigorous reply that the original plans said redwood and I wanted redwood! "Remember, dear," she soothed, "and I quote: 'Where clients waste money is in being around to make inconsequential changes in the original blueprints. Get out of town!'"

(The years have taught us one axiomatic truth: Never disagree with the man about the details of his own architecture. For here he

is magnificently Wright. Years of corrosive salt-laden winds have driven up our mountainside. Now we know that for that site the wood should have been pine.)

Back in California, we rushed anxiously to the mountain. The front elevation of the house was up in all its redwooded glory. That self-hypnosis of well-being peculiar to people viewing the birth of their first house swept over me—until I wandered out into the meadow behind. There, recumbent among the California poppies, lay what seemed to me an exact duplicate of the entire front end of the building!

The contractor dodged my first wild onrush with practiced skill. After they had finished the original framing, he told me, Mr. Wright had come by and redesigned the front end on the spot. And when the contractor had protested, "But we have it finished, Mr. Wright!" the master had spoken three words sweet to art but bitter to the exchequer: "Rip it out!"

❖ ❖ ❖

The first section of the main building was done at expensive last, and we had moved in. The guest house nearby was finished. We were entertaining our first guests with a barbecue when suddenly a caravan of low-slung imported cars curved into our driveway and stopped in a draftsman's precise line.

Out of the first car stepped the unmistakable, majestic figure of our architect. From the other small cars came 20 intense young men, his students. The master recognized our presence with a quick wave of hand, stalked forward, aimed his Malacca cane at the brand-new redwood fence that jutted out from the side of the house, and roared, "Rip it out!"

I smiled knowingly at Mrs. O. This was Mr. Wright's joking reference to the front-end-of-our-house debacle. The smile froze on my face as 20 sets of eager muscles leaped and shoved. With a crackling and crunching of timbers, the fence was down!

I found voice. "But Mr. Wright! We—we just finished that fence! You—you designed it yourself! It's on the blueprints! It cost a fortune!"

Mr. Wright transfixed me with an imperious glance. "Dear friend," he demanded, "doesn't it look better without it?" I, with my checkbook still bleeding, had to admit it did.

"Then we are in complete agreement!" Doffing his cape, he beckoned his disciples to join the Obolers and guests at the barbecue.

(He will destroy months of work on the drawing board, waive badly needed fees, turn his back on entire projects unless the work is good and true. He knows, from the experience of his amazing span of years, that the dollar is ephemeral but that the years of a building are long.)

That afternoon had another surprise. Mr. Wright strode up the hillside, followed by the long line of students. He returned shortly with the announcement that someone had made a blasted blunder. Instead of hanging our redwood-and-stone guesthouse to the mountainside, the contractor had placed it smack-dab *on top of* the mountain.

"But—but it looks all right," I stuttered hastily, visualizing 20 pairs of arms wielding house-wrecking crowbars and pickaxes.

"I designed it so you would have the house *and* the mountain," the great man thundered. "Now you've just got a house *on* a mountain. But I'll fix it—and it won't cost you a cent!" A squad of his students would camp out for a few days, he explained, and right the architectural wrong.

For 30 working days 10 young men labored mightily, erecting a tremendous native-stone-and-concrete wall just off the peak of the mountain. Soon the little cantilevered guesthouse appeared to hang rather than sit. But 10 Gargantua-appetited apprentices appeared three times a day for 30 days! I recall entering a steaming kitchen on the 28th day. A weary small wife glared at me over a Himalaya of pots and pans. She spoke with deadly emphasis. "I am not complaining," she said. "After all, it isn't costing us a cent!"

(As I write this, I can see the guesthouse peeping through an embryo cumulus cloud, and the mountaintop changed without bulldozer. Stone and cement blended the man-made structure to the very nature of the mountain, and the house and the place are one.)

❖ ❖ ❖

It was raining again in California, the first rain since we had moved into the house. A fire crackled in the fireplace, and a cocker spaniel was snoring on the hearth. As I sat down to enjoy the drumming of the drops on my very own roof, the telephone rang. A feminine voice greeted me.

"Are you the Mr. Oboler who is having a house built by Frank Lloyd Wright?"

When I said I was, she burst into tears.

She, too, was a Frank Lloyd Wright client, she told me. "I have been standing over the baby's crib with dishpans catching the water that's leaking in! Mr. Wright experimented on us with plywood. Mr. Oboler, I called to warn you!"

I mumbled words of sympathy and hung up. I looked up smugly at my own high, matched-redwood, impenetrable ceiling—and a drop of water hit me squarely on the nose!

(The flying squad of young apprentices soon descended and curbed the sprinkler tendencies of the experimental roofs. Since that time the building industry has widely copied the use of those plywood panels and so many other maligned Wright innovations.)

❖ ❖ ❖

A year ago I sat in the house Mr. Wright had built for us and my heart was low. I had written my first play for Broadway, a prophetic play in blank verse about the coming race for outer space, but the New York critics had vigorously attacked both the writing and the content. As a result, the production closed. After two years of work my message had reached only a few thousand people.

Suddenly I remembered Frank Lloyd Wright's words years before when, sitting in front of that very fire, I had asked him how he had endured those long years of unremitting attacks on his own prophetic works. He had smiled.

"The history of every artist is this," he said. "At first people discover you, and everything you do is wondrous. Then they begin to look for your feet of clay, and everything you do is berated. But if you live long enough you become an old master." Then his eyes twinkled. "Now I am an Old Master."

The English Lesson

She learned her first foreign words from an American soldier during World War II, and they have stayed with her all her life

———

BY **ELSA K. HUMMEL**

Originally published in September 2017

When I was in second grade, my friend Resi and I walked to school together every morning. We lived across the road from each other in a village in the mountains of Bavaria, Germany. We were supposed to walk to a certain corner and link up with some of the other village children. It was 1945, and I suppose this was a safety thing because of the war.

Most mornings we did as we were instructed, but sometimes Resi and I took a shortcut, a little path across a meadow. One day, on one of those detours, we saw a young man, a stranger, in the side yard of a house. He was chopping wood and whistling. We stopped and stared, then walked away quickly, wondering who he was.

The next morning, we purposely took our secret shortcut to school, curious to see whether the whistler would be there again. And there he was. He didn't seem to notice us, though we were only a few feet away, on the other side of a short fence that enclosed the yard. Again we stared at him, then ran away. We had never seen a foreigner before. To us, he was like someone from outer space.

"Do you think he is one of those Americans?" Resi asked. We had heard the adults talk of a small group of Americans being held in a vacant house in the village. During the day, the men worked around town doing chores, as most of the local men were away at war. Each night, a guard collected them and took them back to the house. Resi's older sister told her that the men

> **"You are my sunshine ..." he sang over and over, slowly, until we could repeat it.**

were prisoners of war who had been captured by the German army, waiting to rejoin the Allies at the imminent end of the war.

"Probably," I replied. "Let's keep walking, or we will be late for school."

We weren't afraid, just curious. Resi kept talking. "He looks just like everybody else," she said. The man was tall with blondish hair that stuck up all over and a big curl falling into his eyes. He looked nice. He had a friendly face, and he smiled all the time, except when he whistled.

"Well," I said, "people look the same everywhere, don't you think?"

By unspoken pact, Resi and I took our shortcut from then on. But we didn't tell anyone. It was our secret.

One morning, after about a week of us walking by, staring and scampering away, the American looked up from his woodpile. He smiled and said "Hi."

Was he talking to us? we wondered. What did he say? We had no idea; we didn't know any English. So, as usual, we ran away.

The next morning, Resi greeted me with the mysterious "Hi" and I did the same in return. We broke into giggles and continued on our way. From then on, whenever we passed by the house, we would find the American working in the yard, almost as if he was waiting for us. Every day, he waved and repeated his "Hi." We waved back and said "Hi" in return.

After another week, as we turned to leave one morning, he waved and said "Bye-bye." Another mysterious English word. We giggled and parroted it back: "Bye-bye."

I said to Resi, "Maybe we should walk the other way again." But I didn't mean it. By now, we were hooked. Having our little secret made us feel special.

After another week or so, the man came a little closer to the fence, pointed at his chest and said "Frankie."

"Frankie," we repeated. Was that his name? He laughed and went back to his work. Frankie was really nice, we decided.

Each of these encounters lasted only a minute or two before Resi and I would hurry on to school, brazen little second graders that we were, learning foreign words from an American POW. We weren't supposed to talk to strangers, and my mother would surely have walked us to school from then on if she had known our secret. I was an only child, and she was very protective, especially since my father

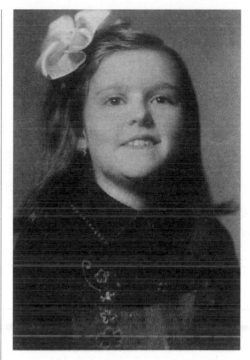

The author in 1945, around the time she met Frankie

was away in the war. He had been drafted, and we didn't know it at the time, but he was also a POW, being held by the Russians. Even after he returned home, I didn't mention these encounters with the American.

Resi and I became quite comfortable with our "Hi, Frankie; bye-bye, Frankie" morning routine. Sometimes he would be singing, and we would stand mesmerized, listening to the strange language. "You are my sunshine …" he sang over and over, slowly, until we could repeat it.

We learned one line after another, and soon we could sing the whole song, not knowing the meaning and not caring.

One morning, Resi and I arrived at the house, but there was no Frankie. We stood on the path alongside the fence, wondering if he was inside the house. No Frankie. We never saw him again. Someone said that the men had rejoined the advancing American forces, which, within days, had occupied that part of Germany. We felt sad, but we kept singing our song.

Resi and I often spoke of Frankie, hoping he was well. I wished that I knew more about him, especially after my family moved to Denver, Colorado, when I was 15. Where was he from? Did he have a sister, perhaps around our age, or even a little girl of his own? I will never know, but Frankie left Resi and me a wonderful legacy: our first English lesson and many happy memories.

Years later, at a picnic with our American relatives, someone started singing "You are my sunshine …" Of course I remembered the words, and I happily joined in. My mother looked at me, surprised. So I told her about Frankie. And to this day, I remember him whenever I hear the song he taught us.

The Hidden Message

A devotion through the years was an unexpected discovery

BY **I.A.R. WYLIE**

Originally published in January 1954

This story, which I am telling with a few necessary disguises, starts some years ago in a small hill town in southern Italy.

One of the merriest of the youngsters of the town was Lucia Gazzoni—a dark-haired, dark-eyed beauty of great charm and liveliness. Lucia amused herself by tantalizing the young men who trailed hopefully at her heels. For a few days she would choose one as her escort and then blithely discard him. But though she created despair she never aroused resentment, and none of her suitors ceased to adore her.

When adulation was for some reason withheld from her, she was herself tantalized. So it was inevitable that she would make a dead set at Giuseppe Silva, who seemed immune to her charms, and attempt to add him to her list of conquests.

In appearance Giuseppe wasn't romantic—he was rather short and heavy-shouldered, and only his bright, kindly eyes saved his swarthy face from being extremely plain. But he was the town's most eligible young man, for he was the only tailor in that region and was relatively well-to-do. A clever dress designer, he could do anything with a pair of scissors, a needle and a piece of material. The town boasted that you could go as far as Naples and do no better.

43

On the first warm days of spring the annual fair came to set up its booths in the town square. The day before it opened, Lucia went to Giuseppe's little shop, ostensibly to buy thread, but after making the purchase she lingered with an air of demure diffidence.

"Why do you stay in this little place, signor?" she asked. "Everyone says that you are so clever. You could go to Naples and make a lot of money…"

A young man did not make a formal call like that without a serious purpose.

———

"The money I have, signorina, is enough."

"You have no ambition," she said scornfully.

"It is foolish to be ambitious for things one does not really want—or for things one cannot have."

"What *do* you want?"

He went on stitching silently. Suddenly she asked gaily, "Would you like to take me to the fair?"

Any other man would have jumped at the offer, but he took his time. "I should be very pleased, signorina," he replied, and with that cool acceptance she had to be content.

At least Giuseppe had one advantage over all her other courtiers: He had money and he spent it freely. Lucia dragged him unresisting into the entertainment booths, where he bought her sweet cakes and cheap trinkets to her whim's content. But perhaps because he believed he was too old for such things, he let her ride on the carousel alone and waited for her patiently on the fringe of the crowd.

So Lucia met Roberto Bellini. He rode the wooden horse next to hers and laughed at her pretended terror, steadying her with a strong hand. She knew him by reputation. He had relatives in the town, whom he had come to visit at fair time. Roberto, a steady, successful young fellow, was a wine salesman for Italian and French vintners and had traveled throughout Europe.

Did it seem to her restless heart that Roberto was a way of escape from her drab, confining world? At any rate she was delighted when he called at her home the next day. Lucia and her parents understood why he had come—a young man did not make a formal call like that without a serious purpose.

Within a few weeks Roberto was back with a proposal of marriage. He was going to America as the representative of several winegrowers and wanted to take Lucia with him.

There was no doubt of the answer. Lucia's parents might be heavy-hearted at her going so far from them, but America was the El Dorado of an Italian peasant's dream and they were glad for her good fortune.

News of the betrothal spread quickly. When Giuseppe heard it he called on Lucia's parents and asked them to permit him to make Lucia's wedding dress. He added hastily, for fear that they might misunderstand, that it would be his wedding gift. They were thankful to accept, for they were poor and the dress would have been an expensive and burdensome item.

So almost every day Lucia, carefully chaperoned, went to Giuseppe's little shop. He knelt at her feet and fitted and snipped and pinned the lovely silk, which was so rich and heavy that everyone knew Giuseppe must have made a special journey to Naples to find it. When the dress was finished she smiled happily at herself in the mirror. She hadn't known she could be so beautiful.

The sun shone at her wedding. That night her parents kept open house and there was dancing on the square. But Giuseppe's house was closed and he had vanished. Rumor had it that he had been called out of town to visit a sick relative. Lucia, in her happy excitement, had no time to think of him. The next day she and her husband left for America.

At first, marriage was as wonderful as her dreams of it. Roberto, who was 10 years older than she, proved a good husband as well as a good businessman. They had a pleasant little house in a New York suburb, and in time they were blessed with two little girls as pretty and bright-eyed as their mother.

For a few years Lucia wrote home regularly, but then less and less often. A war intervened. The little Italian town gradually faded into the mists of her girlhood's memories. She thought of Giuseppe just once—when she laid the wedding dress away finally. It was already old-fashioned, but the material was still lovely and someday, perhaps, she would find a use for it.

Then slowly, ominously, the tide of their fortunes began to turn. Business was bad; Roberto, good salesman though he was, found himself with little but an expense account to offer his employers. After a brief illness he lost his agency. He found another job, but he had lost confidence, and illness returned—this time in disabling form. Little by little their savings were eaten up. One tragic day, suddenly, he died.

Lucia had no one to turn to except friends who had troubles of their own. Her parents were dead. Her daughters, ages 10 and 7, were far too young to support themselves.

Heartsick and frightened, she sold their home, took rooms in a cheaper locality, and earned a precarious living by teaching Italian in a New York school and giving English lessons to new arrivals from her native country. Sometimes she would lie awake at night and wonder what would become of them all if she were taken ill.

There were also minor problems. Little Lucy, the younger girl, stood on the threshold of her First Communion, the first important event in her life. "What shall I wear, Mother?" she would ask. Lucia knew what was at the back of the child's anxious questioning: would she have to be ashamed, as she was so often, of her shabby clothes?

Then Lucia remembered her wedding dress.

There it was—as rich, as lovely as ever. It was amazing to think that she had owned something so beautiful and had almost forgotten it. She began at once to rip it apart and cut it down to Lucy's measurements. Undoing the deep hem, she found, to her astonishment, a neatly folded paper. On it, in faded but strong writing, was a message that had been waiting for her nearly 15 years: "I shall always love you."

Lucia sat for a long time, remembering. She saw the dark, square-shouldered man, really, for the first time. She thought of the unspoken devotion which she had never known that Giuseppe had cherished for her. Overcome, she cried her heart out with loneliness and grief.

That night she wrote a letter. It was addressed to a man who might now be dead, and who in any case must surely have long since forgotten her. But she had a deeply felt urge to tell him that she had found his message and that she wanted to thank him at long last for a devotion she had done so little to deserve. Beyond telling him that her husband was dead she made no reference to the misfortune that had overtaken her.

Weeks passed, and there was no answer. She did not expect one. Little Lucy wore the beautiful dress at her First Communion and was the proudest, happiest girl of all her class. Watching her go up the church aisle to the altar, Lucia thanked Giuseppe for a goodness that, like the vines on their native hillside, still bore fruit.

One day soon after, she came home to find a man waiting for her in the dim hallway of her apartment house. At first she did not recognize him. The heavy shoulders had grown heavier and a little stooped; the once-thick black hair was gray. Then she heard his voice: "It is still true, Lucia!"

Though she had not written of her distress, because he loved her he had known of it in his heart. Giuseppe had come, on the brave chance that she might need him.

This story has a fitting fairy-tale ending. Giuseppe had done well for himself and was able to establish a tailoring business in the new country that had become hers, and to make a good home for all of them.

"I Stared Down Death"

Her quick stop at the convenience store turned into a 20-hour hostage ordeal

———

BY **CHRISTOPHER W. DAVIS**

Originally published in March 2006

Tammi Smith got up early and dressed in jeans and a white shirt. She had an appointment in traffic court in Shelbyville, Indiana, over a minor violation. Waking her husband, Shawn, with a kiss, she told him she was taking the van. The kids were already up, eating cereal and watching cartoons. After court, she thought she might stop to get her nails done and then pick up sodas at the Bigfoot convenience store on the way home.

Eighty miles down the interstate in Cincinnati, Ohio, Dennis McAninch and his friend Joseph G. Scalf also had appointments in court. On burglary charges. McAninch, a 34-year-old ex-con with multiple felony arrests and convictions, was currently out on parole after serving five years for burglary. But instead of showing for their court dates, the pair drove across the state line into Indiana in McAninch's 1999 white Ford compact.

In Batesville, an off-duty policeman noticed the car slowly cruising a neighborhood. There had recently been a string of burglaries there—and this guy drove like someone casing houses. The officer called in a description of the vehicle, and in minutes a

Tammi Smith stands strong.

Dennis McAninch in an Ohio Department of Rehabilitation and Correction photo; McAninch's wrecked car in front of the Bigfoot store

police car was on the scene with lights flashing.

McAninch pulled over and lifted his shirt, showing Scalf the 9 mm semiautomatic in his belt. He kept the engine running. Then, as the officer approached, he gunned it and took off.

Tammi's traffic case was quickly resolved without a fine. Leaving the courthouse, she checked her watch. She still had time to get her nails done.

McAninch reached speeds of up to 120 mph on Interstate 74, swerving around stop sticks on the highway and throwing screwdrivers, bottles, anything he could put his hands on, out the window at the police.

After leaving the manicurist, Tammi drove east on Route 44 to Bigfoot. She pulled up to the front door of the convenience store. Intending to dash in and pick up some sodas, she left her keys and cellphone on the seat.

In his frantic attempt to escape, McAninch finally crashed into another vehicle, damaging his Ford, which barely made it off the highway into the Bigfoot lot. He leaped out of the car and dashed for the store as police cars pulled up, in close pursuit. Scalf held his hands out the passenger window and surrendered. McAninch kept running, firing twice at police.

Tammi was at the register, holding a copy of *The Shelbyville News*, when a stocky man in a long-sleeved white shirt and jeans burst through the front door with a gun in his hand. "Everybody get out or I'm going to kill you!"

Two female employees rushed for the back door. McAninch leaped over the counter, cornering the clerk, a young man, at the register. Not knowing what to do, Tammi ducked behind a food rack at the back of the store.

But McAninch saw her. "You, get up here!" he shouted.

OK, Tammi told herself, *this is God's plan for me today. I might die. Don't be afraid of dying. Everybody's got their time. This might be mine.*

❖   ❖   ❖

As police cars gathered in the parking lot, McAninch ordered the clerk to lock the front door. The young man eased around the counter, locked the door and pocketed the key. Then, seeing that McAninch was focused on the police out front, he bolted for the back door.

Tammi was now alone with the gunman.

McAninch grabbed her by the hair, forced her up to the window and put his gun to her head—showing police he had a hostage.

"Please don't shoot me," Tammi said. She started to cry. "I have kids."

McAninch turned the gun away and instead fired a shot through the window at police. Then he dragged Tammi to the back of the store and into a windowless office, a cramped space with a desk, two chairs, a phone and two computer monitors, one that showed views from security cameras inside the store.

McAninch told Tammi to take a seat and then sat next to her. The wait began. Tammi knew her only chance was to stay calm, show no emotion and try to keep talking to this guy.

The office phone began to ring. One of the calls was from a reporter at Indianapolis radio station WIBC, who had heard about the police chase and called for an eyewitness account. McAninch told her he was holding a hostage, and then asked the reporter to call a woman friend. The reporter linked them on a conference call and later broadcast portions of their conversation.

"What's up, baby?" McAninch asked into the phone.

"Nothing," the woman responded. "What's wrong?"

"I'm in a gas station. There's about 50 police outside. I shot at them so … they're probably going to end up killing me."

She tried to talk sense to him. "Can't you go out with your hands up?" she asked. "Figure another way out of this."

Nothing changed his mind. In the midst of the conversation, McAninch even put Tammi on the phone.

As time dragged on, Tammi asked him if she could go to the bathroom, but McAninch said, "Baby, I just can't let you go up there. They're liable to shoot through the windows." Eventually he allowed her to relieve herself in a trash can.

At long last, police took command of the phone line. They now controlled McAninch's access to the outside world through a police negotiator.

When he first called, the negotiator asked McAninch who he was holding hostage. Was she all right? Did he or Tammi need medical attention? Then the negotiator settled into a long conversation calculated to keep McAninch calm.

Tammi was working on the same idea. When McAninch was off the phone, she took family photos out of her wallet. "Here's my daughter," she told him. "She's a cheerleader. She's 10. Isn't she beautiful?"

McAninch studied the photo. "Yeah, she's a beautiful girl."

"Do you have any kids?" Tammi asked him.

Yes, he said, one, a 13-year-old daughter, but he had no pictures.

Tammi was trying to get to know him. Win his trust. It was already obvious to her that he wasn't expecting to get out alive. She had to find a way to convince him not to take her with him.

In between phone calls, McAninch checked the layout of the store. The back entrance was a thick cold-storage door with a large metal handle. McAninch braced a stepladder against the handle and built a barricade of food boxes.

All the while, Tammi kept McAninch talking, looking for anything to engage him. He had tattoos running up the right side of his neck—his birth sign, Virgo. And on his right arm were two women's names; one was his daughter's. On his left arm, there was a poem for his parents. Tammi could make out only the last line: "Let there be no more tears." She stored it all away.

"Your daughter needs you," she said. "You know that."

"Yeah, I know," McAninch said.

"You need to give up," she said, keeping her tone even, trying not to sound bossy or pushy, more like a friend giving advice. She repeated what the police had earlier told him. "Give me the gun. Put it in a plastic bag. I'll carry it out." She kept talking. "Do your time, and you'll get out."

"I can't do that," he said.

❖ ❖ ❖

There was money everywhere. Tammi had never seen a room so disorganized. There was cash piled on the desk in the office. Checks written out to Bigfoot all over the place. Bunches of cash behind the chairs. McAninch stuffed over $1,000 into his pockets. And handed Tammi $350 out of the stack of cash on the table.

Taking a chance, Tammi walked to the front door, took the handle and pulled.

"I can't take that," she told him. "God's watching. I'm not a thief."

"Take it," he insisted. "Put it in your wallet—now!"

She tried to shake him off. "All I want is to go home and make dinner for my family."

"I can't let you go. You're my security blanket," McAninch told her. "You're what's keeping me alive."

Emergency response teams (SWAT units) from state, county and city jurisdictions were now on the scene. Police put gunmen in place. A mobile command center had been set up some 500 yards from the store near the interstate overpass. The press corps had arrived en masse.

Alerted by the radio broadcast, Tammi's husband, Shawn, his parents, and her mother and stepfather had rushed to the scene. A state police chaplain was assigned to stay with the family. Police told them Tammi was not hurt—and, in a convenience store, not hungry. They said they would do anything to keep her safe. One officer told the press, "We are prepared to talk until the last HoHo is gone."

Fifteen hours crept by. McAninch sat thinking, tapping the gun against his head and making multiple demands of the police negotiator. He wanted to visit his mother's grave before being locked up, he wanted his pal Joe Scalf set free, he wanted to talk to his daughter, he wanted a live television crew filming his surrender

so there wouldn't be any monkey business, and he wanted cold beer. "Of all places to hold up," he said, "I chose one that doesn't sell beer."

Through it all, Tammi was close enough to him to grab his gun, but even if she could wrestle it from him, she knew she'd never be able to use it. She tried to maintain an appearance of calm.

"You're a pretty cool hostage," he said, and told the police: "This bitch ain't scared at all."

Slowly McAninch began to talk to her. He confessed he was bipolar. That he used Valium. He had marijuana with him and started to smoke a joint, offering her a puff. She said no.

"At least I'm locked up in here with a beautiful girl and not some guy," he said.

Around midnight, Tammi told McAninch she was feeling sick. He let her go to the sink to throw up. Then he became concerned. "Are you all right? Can I get you some milk to settle your stomach?"

"Yes," Tammi said.

He went into the store and brought her some. Then he started to pace. A few minutes later, he went to the sink and began to vomit himself. When he returned, Tammi saw panic in his eyes.

"Are you scared?" she asked.

He didn't answer. But overhead they heard helicopters. Tammi pleaded again with McAninch to let her go. She was tired. She was sick.

"You're becoming a not-so-cool hostage," he told her.

❖   ❖   ❖

At around 2 a.m., McAninch gathered flattened cardboard boxes and put them on the floor. Then he found some Bigfoot employee uniform shirts in the back room and laid them on the cardboard to make a bed. As he stretched out, blocking the front doorway, gun in hand, he asked Tammi, "You want to do something?"

"What!" Tammi said, surprised and angry. McAninch lay there looking at her as the minutes ticked by, then said, "OK, I'm not even going to go there."

Tammi watched as he closed his eyes. *All right,* she thought. *What if he goes to sleep? Should I run for it?* In the end she decided not to. The

Tammi Smith, at home with family after her release; her mother, Cindy Hadix, is on her immediate right.

doors were locked, and he still held the gun. And as far as she could tell, he never did drift off to sleep.

The negotiator called again, offering a cellphone to McAninch because the land line had become staticky. Send Tammi out for it; they'd leave it outside.

"I'm not sending her out there till you guys back off," McAninch said.

Taking a chance, Tammi walked to the front door, took the handle and pulled. "The door's locked," she yelled to the police.

"Get back here," McAninch ordered her.

"Let me go get that phone. I'll come back," she pleaded.

After more negotiation with her and the police, McAninch finally agreed. But he wanted to make sure his "protection" would come back.

He began rummaging around in the store, searching. Suddenly he picked up a vacuum cleaner, grabbed a screwdriver and took

> **As dawn broke, police demolition experts rigged the heavy back door with explosive charges.**
> ───

it apart. He ripped the electrical cord free and came for Tammi. He tied the cord around her waist.

Holding her on a tether, he let Tammi out the front door. In the interim, working in the shadows, the police had unlocked it. Tammi moved forward, looked, but couldn't find the phone. Enraged, McAninch yanked her in.

Back on the static-filled land line, the police explained that a new cellphone had been attached to a pole just outside the door. But McAninch was in no mood to listen.

As dawn broke, police demolition experts rigged the heavy back door with explosive charges. A SWAT team was ready to blow it open and rush the store.

At the same time, around 6:30 a.m., McAninch changed his mind and decided to send Tammi out once more to get the phone. He played her out on the cord. She opened the door, stepped forward, saw the phone on the ground and reached for it.

Policemen hidden in the shadows grabbed her by the arm and tried to pull her free. For a moment Tammi was trapped in a tug of war. But McAninch reeled her back in.

"Get back!" he yelled at the police. "Get back!" He fired a shot.

Police returned fire. One SWAT unit blew open the back door. Another unit rushed the front.

"Stop shooting! Stop shooting!" Tammi yelled. "I'm right here! I'm right here!" She fell to the floor and grabbed a plastic soda tray to shield her head.

Suddenly it was silent. The shooting stopped. She looked at McAninch, who was lying motionless across her leg—bullet wounds in his arm, leg and chest.

Tammi didn't scream or cry. She didn't know whether to run or not. She thought McAninch might still be able to shoot her. But he was dying. His mouth was open and there was a gaping hole under his chin pulsing out blood. He'd shot himself—he would never go back to prison.

The police moved to scoop her up, but she was still tethered to the bloody body. An officer cut the cord, and finally she was free.

Outside it was raining. Her shoe had come off. Held between two policemen, Tammi hopped on one foot across the wet parking lot. They took her to the command trailer for her to recover and talk with negotiators. Amazingly, her only injury was to her morning manicure—a broken nail.

Her husband, Shawn, ran to the command trailer to meet her. They hugged, unable to speak, and Shawn began to cry. But

Tammi was too burned out for tears.

She didn't cry that day or night or the next day. It wasn't until around midnight of the second day that she began to weep uncontrollably.

From the time she was a child, Tammi Smith had nightmares that someone was lurking in the dark waiting to kill her with a knife or a gun. After Bigfoot, she doesn't have that dream anymore.

The Flowers Will Be There

Wind would whip at the frail stems in the garden, but the old man knew they would stand their ground. He could do no less.

—

BY **JAMES A. McCRACKEN**

Originally published in July 1982

I stood on the porch of our house one day; my grandson was at my side. Below us was the tidal cove of our coastal river in Maine. When the tide is falling, a shelf of rocks is exposed, and on bright days seals hunch their way out of the cold water to warm themselves in the sun. Such was the case as I stood with my grandson. Nearby, ducks paddled in the shallow waters. There were sea gulls and herons, crows and chickadees about; the life and activity and rebirth of spring.

All this was new and different to my grandson. He is from a city far away. I handed him my old binoculars, and he gazed at the seals and the ducks and the gulls, sweeping the glasses this way and that. Then, as kids do, he reversed them. Now things that were so near were far away. It delighted him. He laughed and pointed. "Those seals are a million miles away," he cried.

The long view. Look over the horizon. The eyes of youth see visions I no longer see. "When I grow up I'm going to be a major-league pitcher." "I'm going to be a doctor." Ah, when I grow up … 20 years, 25, 40. Old age does not grant that luxury.

We golden-agers hold the glasses and focus them so that the view of distant things is clear and close. We plan for today, for tomorrow, next month, even next year. But there is always the silent proviso: *if* all goes well.

We think of old sweet times, old frustrations. Loves that were won—and lost. We think of things that should have been done today; we'll attend to them tomorrow …

Tomorrow? How many tomorrows are left? For somewhere out there lies the unfathomable—death.

❖   ❖   ❖

It is long past midnight, and the old man who thinks these thoughts sits with a book in his lap. But he isn't reading. He stares past the lamp at his side. It is cold, and he shudders deeper into his bathrobe.

The old man finds it difficult to sleep some nights, particularly in the winter when the cold is penetrating and the footing outside is treacherous. So little chance to

Children have a different view when looking to the horizon.

exercise anymore. A fall on the ice could mean a broken hip, pneumonia, perhaps the end. As a child he looked at old people and wondered why they were so careful about their health. After all, they'd lived their lives. They'd raised their families. What was there for old people to live for?

The old man thinks about that. When there is plenty of wine in the bottle, one can afford to be prodigal with it. Give it away, waste it, drink too much of it. But life to the old is like the last few drops in the bottle—precious. *Yes,* he nods his head, *that is it*. With each passing day life becomes more precious.

The old man shifts in his chair. Like a honeybee in a garden, visiting first this flower, then that, his memory takes him to a birthday, a funeral, a Christmas Eve of long ago; then, to an evening last September, when he had stood at the edge of his flower garden.

> ## A storm might come tonight. Wind would whip at the frail stems and gossamer faces.

Not his, really. It belonged to his wife. She could make a flower bloom in soil that weeds themselves would scorn.

On that chill, late-September evening, the old man had raised his eyes to the hills in the distance. The rounded tops of the distant tiers were bathed in alpenglow, with mauve shadows blanketing the valleys. Behind and far away he heard the roll of thunder. His eyes dropped to the panoply of color at his feet. Strange, he muses now, each head seemed turned toward him. These slender, fragile things.

A storm might come tonight. Wind would whip at the frail stems and gossamer faces. But come thunder, lightning and slashing rain, these creations of some unseen Being would stand fast. They would be there in the morning!

That evening in his garden, with all the beauty of the world at his feet, it came to him. If these tiny, blessed flowers could stand their ground, he could do no less …

❖　❖　❖

"That was certainly some sigh."

"Oh, did I sigh? I wasn't aware."

We sit together in the evening; my wife there in her chair, I in mine. She is knitting me *another* sweater. How many sweaters, I wonder, has she made me through all these years? And I've worn them all, some until they've gone threadbare and disreputable. Even then it's taken my wife to discard them. Why, if it were up to me I would have a closet full of sweaters, raveled, gone at the elbow, paint stained. She made them all.

I gaze at her. Forty-seven years. Could it be 47 years that she has been there, always close by, always there like a strong reed when I've needed help?

She was so beautiful! Her hair was the color of wheat; and like a wheat field in a summer's breeze, her hair flowed back over her head, down her back to her shoulders, where it was loosely curled. Her skin was fair, but it always wore a light tan, summer or winter. She *is* so beautiful!

The needles stop clicking. She is looking at me.

"You really should write to Ben," she says. "It's been almost a month now since you had that long letter from him."

Ben. "Yes, I will write to him tonight."

"And that birch tree out back. You've been waiting to make sure it was dead before you cut it down."

"You think it's dead?"

"Well," she says dryly, "it hasn't had a leaf the last two summers."

I smile at her. "I'll do it in the morning."

"Good. And one more thing…"

I groan. "Cutting down that tree and sawing it up is all I can handle."

"I know," she says softly. "But just one more thing … you've needed a haircut for two weeks now." We both laugh.

The horizon. Don't go looking over it, I think. Take the binoculars from your grandson. Look through them the proper way. The way the Lord intended them to be used. Bring the far shore up close. Write that letter. Cut down that tree. Get that haircut. Don't feel sorry for yourself. And remember, tomorrow morning the flowers will be there!

Oh, Behave!

*The classiest ways to split a bill, send
your sympathies, say "no" and more*

—

BY **LENORE SKENAZY**

Originally published in April 2016

hen was the last time you sent a thank-you note to a friend after being invited over for dinner? Forget? You know why? Because you probably never did. No one does that anymore. The rules of decorum have changed. We polled the etiquette conundrums that vex folks most. Then we asked experts to assess the correct way to proceed. Oh, and if you like what you read, feel free to send a thank-you note. That would be nice.

Sending Condolences

Your friend's husband dies. You didn't know him that well. But still. The thing is, we all know the right thing to do when we hear of a friend's or relative's loss: Write that sympathy card and mail it already!

But what if you don't have a sympathy card around? Or what if you don't know your friend's snail mail address offhand and keep forgetting to look it up until it's 11:30 at night and you're drifting off to sleep when suddenly you

remember, I STILL HAVEN'T MAILED THAT CARD!!!? And your heart is pounding, and you are electrified with self-loathing … but still too toasty under the covers to actually do anything? If you're tempted to text a sad-faced emoji, don't. That's right up there with "liking" the news on Facebook. But here's the good news! When it comes to expressing sympathy, "there's no time limit," says Anne Klaeysen of the New York Society of Ethical Culture. In fact, sometimes it's nicer for a mourner to get a note after the initial flurry of attention, when life for everyone else has returned to "normal."

That's when dropping your friend a note—yes, even by email—will be appreciated. And the best kind of note, adds Klaeysen, includes a little story about the deceased. (So long as it doesn't end "And he still hasn't paid me back.")

For Whom the Bill Tolls

You're out to dinner with friends and order a measly hot dog— "hold the bun." Everyone else orders foie gras, lobsters and

Ketel One martinis. The check arrives. Now what?

Oh, to live in Germany, at least when it's time to pay the tab. There, says Siobhan Callahan, an American who teaches English in the town of Bremen, "the assumption is that everyone will pay separately."

In fact, Callahan says, generally the waitress comes at the end of the meal and announces to each person, "'Let's see; a coffee is 1.50, and a burger is 15—you owe me 16.50.' She does it all in her head."

This would relieve a party platter of anxiety on the part of people like … me. Those of us who have to steel ourselves before going out to dinner, knowing that the check will probably be split equally, even though we will have eaten *waaaaay* less expensively (for all sorts of psycho/social/cheapo reasons) than everyone else. I try to think of it as an entertainment tax, the price paid for socializing.

I try and try and try.

Minneapolis doctor and business-woman Archelle Georgiou has come up with the classiest way to avoid this turmoil, short of ordering three lobsters for yourself. If her friends are boozers, she says, "I'll tell the waitress at the beginning, 'We'll have separate checks for this bill.' It's between me and the waitress, but they all hear it, and that's worked out quite well."

Until America goes German, this could be your best bet. Especially for those of us who order just the soup and fill up on the crackers.

Car-Wreck Cousin

Your cousin—a notoriously lousy driver—asks to borrow your car for a few hours.

This is not a question of generosity; it's a question of what kind of damage your cousin and/or car can sustain. So don't feel compelled to fork over the keys. If you have the time or inclination, offer to chauffeur him around. If you have the money, offer Uber fare. And if you've got none of the above, fib. "Say, 'Thursday afternoon? Oh, I'm busy!'" suggests Jodi R.R. Smith, president of Mannersmith Etiquette Consulting. Whatever you do, "don't feel obligated to lend somebody something that is

incredibly valuable and important to you." Feeling obligated to do something you're opposed to is not the definition of *kind*. It's the definition of *doormat*.

"Say 'I'm sorry; it's just not possible,' with no further explanation," says psychotherapist Tina Tessina, author of *It Ends with You: Grow Up and Out of Dysfunction*.

But if you feel the crying need to utter some plausible excuse, refrain from shouting the painful truth: "There's not enough insurance in the world!" Instead, let him down easy, something kind but firm, like "I don't have the insurance to cover you," says Maggie Oldham, who blogs about modern etiquette issues at *maggieoldham.com*.

Missing Invite

You didn't receive an invitation to an event to which you expected to be invited.

It can feel like a kick in the kidneys when you hear about an event that everyone else seems to be going to—a wedding, a baby shower, even a group photo—and no one invited you. What's up with that?

If the host is not someone you know very well, don't take it personally, says Howard Forman, MD, of Montefiore Medical Center in New York City. There could be space limitations, a strained budget, whatever. Let it slide.

But if your niece is getting married and the rest of the family is already buying rice? Take it personally, then call your brother.

As calmly as you can, ask if there's some reason you weren't invited. Maybe the invite went to an old address and no one bothered to forward it. Imagine how relieved your brother will be to know your silence—to him, rudeness—was simply the result of an envelope error and not a freeze-out!

On the other hand, if there's a real reason he didn't invite you, your relationship is frayed enough that you may want to try to fix it. Explain the concept of regret insurance: If someday the two of you do reconcile, you'll both regret the fact you missed this life event. Then promise good behavior. Promise a nice gift. Promise you won't make a toast—or you will—or whatever your brother wants. This could be the beginning of a beautiful, mended relationship.

Perplexing Playdate

Your close friend's 10-year-old kid is a monster. Every time you get together, your own 10-year-old is stuck with her. You don't want her around this kid anymore.
You can try telling your friend that your kid can't see the miscreant because she's busy washing her hair from today till the day she goes off to college, but there's a good chance the friend won't buy that.

"When I was a kid, there was a child of my parents' friends who used to break my toys all the time," recalls psychotherapist Tessina. "And what my mom helped me do was hide my good toys before that person came over."

That's an unflappable mom—and kid—who totally understood the score. (Maybe that's why Tessina became a therapist.) But there are bad seeds who can bring out the worst in everyone. Faced with spending time with them, don't.

Plan events during which the kids can't interact, like going to the movies. Another technique is to sit the tiny delinquent down when she first gets to your home and have a very grown-up chat with her—in front of her parents. "I just want to make sure you know the house rules so nobody gets hurt" is how Dr. Georgiou begins. "We have a lot of glass here. If you ran into this table and the glass broke, you would have to go to the emergency room and have all these ugly stitches!"

In other words, she outlines the behavior that she wants, and by painting a vivid picture of the consequences of disobeying, she makes the kid and parents want it too. (And for what it's worth, now *everyone* is afraid of the table.)

Dinner with a Dieter

You're dining out with someone who's trying to lose weight. No one has ever failed a diet because his or her friend ordered a cheesesteak with extra grease when they got together for dinner, says psychiatrist Forman. Food is everywhere, so whether you're scarfing down that cheesesteak in front of your friend or not, he or she could always get one someplace else.

But there is one kind thing you can do when dining with a dieting friend, says Mannersmith's Smith: Do not order dessert.

Dessert is the thing with two forks. No one expects you to offer a bite of your cheesesteak, but it is rare to order the molten chocolate cake with raspberry coulis without 1) reminding yourself to look up *coulis* sometime and 2) offering a taste to everyone at the table.

The other kind thing is to refrain from offering diet tips. Duct-tape

your mouth before saying, "'Oh? You're not going to get the dressing on the side?' Or, 'Are you sure you want that?'" says Karen Yankosky, a lawyer who hosts a podcast on dating and relationships. "I don't care if you're on the cover of *Muscle* magazine; just shut up."

Entertaining Fido

Your friends from out of town are coming to visit. At the last minute, they call and ask if they can bring along their dog. While you might be tempted to tell your friends, "Of course you can bring your dog to my house if I can bring my elephant to yours," don't.

"If there's one thing I've learned in life, it's that you never want to be on the side of someone who's against a dog," says Dr. Forman. "If our friends decided to bring their dog, we'd be, 'Where would you like the dog to sleep, and what can we get him to eat?' Dogs are really important friends to people."

On the other hand, if you're allergic or your home is filled with fragile antiques, Persian rugs and cacti, you can mention this to your

friends and hope they get the hint.

"You're not running a kennel," says Crystal L. Bailey, director of the Etiquette Institute of Washington, who is not—as you might guess—a dog person.

Another effective tactic is to make it sound as if all you truly care about is the dog's comfort.

When guests asked Dr. Georgiou if they could bring along their three—yes, three—dogs, she told them, "Of course!" But added that she wasn't sure the dogs would have a great time, since she has her own temperamental dog, so the guest dogs would have to stay in the laundry room. They wouldn't get out much: "Since we have so much planned for the weekend, it'd be difficult to accommodate the dogs."

In other words, the poor, put-upon pooches!

Dr. Georgiou came off trying to make it work for the pets. She got her way without hurting feelings.

The Gold-and-Ivory Tablecloth

The impulse to be kind, even under dire circumstances, can bring about the most surprising silver linings—and even the occasional miracle

—

BY **REV. HOWARD C. SCHADE**

Originally published in December 1954

he Christmas story I most like to tell involves a young pastor. His church was old. Long ago, it had flourished. Famous men had preached from its pulpit, prayed before its altar. Rich and poor alike had worshipped there. Now the good days had passed from the section of town where it stood. But the pastor and his young wife believed in their run-down church. They felt that with paint, hammer and faith they could get it in shape. Together they went to work.

Late one December, a severe storm whipped through the river valley, and the worst blow fell on the little church. A huge chunk of rain-soaked plaster fell out of the inside wall just behind the altar. The pastor and his wife swept away the mess, but they couldn't hide the ragged hole. His wife despaired, "Christmas is only two days away!"

That afternoon, the dispirited couple attended an auction held for a local youth group. The auctioneer

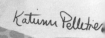

opened a box and shook out a handsome gold-and-ivory lace tablecloth. It was a magnificent item, over 4 meters long. But it, too, dated from a long-vanished era. Who, today, had any use for such a thing? There were a few half-hearted bids. Then the pastor was seized with what he thought was a great idea. He placed the winning bid: $6.50.

He carried the cloth back to the church and tacked it up on the wall behind the altar. It completely hid the hole. Its shimmering handiwork cast a fine holiday glow over the presbytery. It was a triumph.

Just before noon on Christmas Eve, as the pastor was opening the church, he noticed a woman standing in the cold at the bus stop. "The bus won't be here for 40 minutes," he called, and he invited her in to get warm.

She told him that she had come from the city that morning to be interviewed for a job as governess to the children of one of the wealthy families in town, but had been turned down. A war refugee, she spoke imperfect English.

The woman sat down in a pew, chafed her hands and rested. After a while, she dropped her head and prayed. She looked up as the pastor began to adjust the great gold-and-ivory lace cloth across the hole. She rose suddenly and walked up the steps of the chancel. She looked at the tablecloth. The pastor smiled and started to tell her about the storm damage, but she didn't seem to listen. She took up a fold of the cloth and rubbed it.

"It is mine!" she said. "It is my banquet cloth." She lifted up a corner and showed the surprised pastor that there were initials monogrammed on it. "My husband had the cloth made especially for me in Brussels. There could not be another like it."

The woman and the pastor talked solemnly. She explained that she was Viennese, that she and her husband had opposed the Nazis and decided to leave Austria. They were advised to go separately. Her husband put her on a train for Switzerland. They planned that he would join her as soon as he could arrange to ship their household goods across the border. She never saw him again. Later she heard he had died in a concentration camp.

"I have always felt that it was my fault—to leave without him," she said to the pastor. "Perhaps these years of wandering have been my punishment."

The pastor tried to comfort her, urged her to take the tablecloth. She refused. Then she left.

As the church began to fill for Christmas Eve, it was clear that the cloth was going to be a success. It had been skillfully designed to look its best by candlelight.

After the service, the pastor stood at the doorway. Many people said that the church looked beautiful. One gentle-faced, middle-aged man—the local clock and watch repairman—looked rather puzzled.

"It is strange," he said in his soft accent. "Many years ago, my wife—God rest her—and I owned such a cloth. In our home in Vienna, my wife put it on the table"—and here he smiled—"only when the bishop came to dinner."

The pastor became very excited. He told the watchmaker about the

woman who had been in church earlier that day.

The startled man clutched the pastor's arm. "Can it be? Does she live?"

Together, the two got in touch with the family who interviewed the woman. Then, in the pastor's car, they started for the city. And on Christmas Day, this man and his wife—who had been separated so many years—were reunited.

To all who heard this story, the joyful purpose of the storm that had knocked a hole in the wall of the church was now clear. People said it was a miracle, but I think you will agree it was the season for it.

How I Learned a Lesson in Parenthood

What followed from a poignant scene in a primitive hospital in India

—

BY **DANNY KAYE**

Originally published in September 1959

How many parents, I wonder, have had to learn the hard way, as I did, how delicate the relationship is between an adult and a child, and how easy it is to distort it?

Like so many other children, my daughter Dena is growing up in a family where her father is frequently away from home; and, like so many other fathers, I tried to make my homecomings compensate for these separations. I'd arrive with joyous shouts and a suitcase full of presents, sweep Dena into my arms and smother her with plans for the next day, the next week. I'd hug her close, trying to make up for the lost time, the missed love. But my exuberance just didn't seem to be contagious: At each reunion she responded to me less. And I didn't know what to do about it.

Then in the spring of 1954, when Dena was 7, I was faced with a protracted absence from home. A U.N. official had said to me, "We're trying to help some children grow up instead of dying at the age of 8 or 10, and we'd like you to give us a hand." He explained that an anti-TB vaccine costing only 1 cent per shot could mean life to uncounted African and Asian

children; that one injection of penicillin could cure the terrible ulcers of yaws; that leprosy, malaria and other ancient scourges to which millions of innocent children are heir could be defeated by modern medicine—if the world would only help.

He asked me to tour the medical and nutritional stations maintained by the United Nations Children's Fund and the World Health Organization, and with a camera crew shoot a color film to be titled *Assignment—Children*. It was hoped that this film would focus public attention on the problem and elicit the support so desperately needed. The U.N. official also thought I might be able to entertain the children and help them overcome their fears when suddenly faced by doctors and glittering medical paraphernalia. There was little I could say but yes.

I delayed telling Dena as long as I could. Then suddenly at bedtime on a Sunday evening she looked me in the eyes and said solemnly, "You're going away."

"Well …" I said. "Yes." While I had stalled and searched for the best way of breaking the news, she had seen the truth and spoken it.

"When are you going?" she asked gravely.

"Not for a whole week. And we'll have a ball during that time. A beach party every day, if you like. How about it?"

"All right," she said, but without enthusiasm. Dena had already gone away from me.

❖ ❖ ❖

We opened our tour by joining a mobile U.N. vaccination unit in India, traveling from one small village to another. The children were naturally awed and frightened when we arrived with our needles, and my job was to win their friendship and confidence. For me to be introduced to them as a movie star was obviously ridiculous. These children didn't know what a movie was. If I exploded upon them with a big fanfare, they'd see only a big-mouthed redhead who made a lot of noise in a foreign language and interrupted something much more important, such as drawing a picture in the dust or thinking secret thoughts. All children have a great sense of privacy and you violate it at your peril.

I quickly learned to move in quietly, letting them come to me. I'd wander through a village and sit down on the ground some-place, certain that curiosity would eventually lead the children to me. When they got close enough I'd make a funny face at them and there'd be giggles. Soon someone would make a funny face back and we'd have a fine contest going, with everyone laughing and relaxed. Then I'd clap hands and start a follow-the-leader game that took us down the lanes and around the temples and pagodas, to end up before the waiting doctors. The children submitted to the injections, comforted not by any skills of mine but because they saw in me a reflection of themselves. Thus the adult world was suddenly not quite so alien and overwhelming.

I remembered this lesson when I went to entertain patients in the children's ward in Mysore province in south-central India. It was a day when the very land seemed fevered. Twenty iron cots lined the walls of a stifling room, and at the far end was an upright piano. The children paid no particular attention to me as I walked down the aisle between the beds, nor did I to them. Standing beside the piano and tapping the beat out lightly, I hummed a song to myself. A couple of little boys glanced at me curiously, then turned back to the beads they were stringing.

My accompanist whispered to me, "Danny, belt one out! Wake 'em up!"

I shook my head. "Give me 'Blue Skies,' real easy."

This time I sang the lyrics instead of humming, but quietly, again as if to myself. Several children were gravely watching me now, and by the time I had started the third song a few of the more venturesome had climbed out of bed and come over to the piano. When I finished the song we stared at each other for a moment of dignified silence; then I made a face and they laughed. It was that laughter that brought every child in the room to attention and soon into the party. *Their* laughter made us friends, not mine. They came to me, and on their own terms.

But somehow I didn't see how this lesson applied to my relationship with Dena. Not until I witnessed little Kirim and his parents, and their ordeal in a primitive hospital in central India. Kirim was a delicate boy of 5, brought in for surgery. He was given an anesthetic, operated on and placed in a small crib to regain consciousness. Throughout the entire procedure his parents stood reassuringly close by, where, until the anesthetic took over, he could see their calm dignity, their outward appearance of serenity.

I was nearby when Kirim finally opened his eyes after the operation. If I'd been his father I'd probably have joked and laughed and tried to make the boy smile. But as I watched the boy look up at the familiar and loved faces of his father and mother, I suddenly realized how wrong I would have been—how deep was their wisdom. They spoke his name and touched his hand, but gave no display of their own concern and emotion. During the following hours they talked only when Kirim wished to talk, laughed only when he did, were silent when he was silent. They did not impose themselves upon him, did not use his small being to ease their own anxieties. They let *him* decide how much attention he needed, how much love he wanted displayed, and when. They were a great reservoir of strength he could dip into at will.

❖   ❖   ❖

After my tour had covered 40,000 miles, through Burma, Thailand and Africa as well as India, I turned at last homeward. Through my memory ran an endless parade of little faces. Now I wanted only to see one small face. As I stepped from the plane, my wife and daughter greeted me with the reserve that comes from a long separation. I kissed them warmly—but quietly—and the three of us left the field hand in hand. I wanted so to walk doubled over with my face thrust against Dena's, forcing upon her my attention, my love, my accumulated sense of loss. I wanted to hold her tight, literally to squeeze out of her the admission that she had missed me … I wanted it all now, this instant!

But at last I knew better. She would take her own time before accepting me again as part of her life. Usually it required about a week, and the more I bounded at her, I realized now, the slower it would be.

During the drive from the airport, Dena's mother and I talked casually about things that had happened at home during my absence. Intuitively my wife understood what I was doing, and together we tried to emphasize not the interruption in our lives but the continuity. We talked as if I had gone away only yesterday. Dena participated in the conversation, but tentatively, cautiously.

At home we had supper on the terrace, and we were sitting quietly over coffee when Dena suddenly threw her arms in the air and cried, "How about a beach party tomorrow?"

"Hey!" I cried in response. "How about that!"

I opened my arms to catch her as she launched herself at my neck. It had been but three hours since my plane landed.

Since that day I have tried never to drive my daughter from me by overwhelming her with my own moods. And I've learned that this principle doesn't apply just to long separations. Even when I'm making pictures in Hollywood—coming home each evening after the day's work like so many other fathers—I return with some calmness, holding my emotions in reserve to see what *her* needs may be. I try to be her reservoir of strength.

Someday, when she's older, I'll tell my daughter why her father changed. Then she will understand what we owe to Kirim and his parents.

Old Ben Franklin and His Miserable Maxims

This delightful—and virtually unknown—spoof was written by one of America's greatest humorists

———

BY **MARK TWAIN (1872)**
CONDENSED FROM **PROTECTION**

Originally published in June 1965

Benjamin Franklin was one of those persons whom they call philosophers.

He early prostituted his talents to the invention of maxims and aphorisms calculated to inflict suffering upon the rising generation of all subsequent ages.

His simplest acts were contrived with a view of their being held up for the emulation of boys forever. It was in this spirit that he became the son of a soap-boiler, and probably for no other reason than that the efforts of all future boys who try to be anything might be looked upon with suspicion unless they were the sons of soap-boilers.

With a malevolence without parallel in history he would work all day, and then sit up nights, and let on to be studying algebra by the light of a smoldering fire so that all boys might have to do that also. Not satisfied with these proceedings, he had a fashion of living wholly on bread and water, and studying astronomy at mealtime—a thing which has brought affliction to millions of boys since.

His maxims were full of animosity toward boys. Nowadays a boy cannot follow out a single natural instinct without tumbling over one of those everlasting aphorisms. If he buys 2 cents' worth of peanuts, his father says, "Remember what Franklin has said, my son: 'A groat a day is a penny a year,'" and the comfort is all gone out of those peanuts. If he wants to spin his top before his work is done, his father quotes, "Procrastination is the thief of time." If he does a virtuous action, he never gets anything for it because "virtue is its own reward."

A boy is robbed of his natural rest because Franklin said once:

Early to bed and early to rise
Makes a man healthy, wealthy
    and wise.

As if it were any object to a boy to be healthy, wealthy and wise on such terms. The legitimate result of this maxim is my present state of general debility, indigence and mental aberration. My parents used to have me up before nine o'clock in the morning, sometimes, when I was a boy. If they had let me take my natural rest, where would I be now? Keeping store, no doubt, and respected by all.

And what an adroit old adventurer he was. In order to get a chance to fly his kite on Sunday, he used to hang a key on the string, and let on to be fishing by lightning, and a guileless public would chirp of the "wisdom" and the "genius" of the hoary Sabbath-breaker. He invented a stove that would smoke your head off. He was always proud of how he entered Philadelphia with nothing in the world but two shillings in his pocket and four rolls of bread under his arm. Really, anybody could have done this.

Franklin did many notable things for his country, and made her young name honored in many lands as the mother of such a son. It is not the idea of this memoir to ignore that. No. The idea is to snub those pretentious maxims of his, which he worked up with a great show of originality out of truisms that had become wearisome platitudes as early as the dispersions from Babel.

I merely desire to do away with the prevalent calamitous idea among heads of families that Franklin acquired his great genius by working for nothing, studying by moonlight and getting up in the night instead of waiting until morning, and that this programming, rigidly inflicted, will make a Franklin of every father's fool. It is time these gentlemen found out that these execrable eccentricities are only the evidence of genius, not the creators of it.

I wish I had been the father of my parents long enough to make them comprehend this truth, and thus prepare them to let their son have an easier time of it. When I was a child I had to boil soap, notwithstanding my father was wealthy, and I had to get up early and study geometry at breakfast, and peddle my own poetry, and do everything as Franklin did, in the solemn hope that I would be a Franklin someday. And here I am.

Trapped in a Sunken Ship

With a loud noise, the corroded bulkhead collapsed, sealing off the diver's escape route. He could measure his life expectancy by the 25-minute supply of air in his tank.

BY **CAPT. RICHARD MIRANDA**

Originally published in December 1982

ad I known what was facing me on June 16, 1979, I would never have left the dock. As it was, preoccupied with the wreck of the USS *San Diego*, I headed my 47-foot dive boat, the *Barnacle Bill*, out of Jones Inlet, Long Island, New York.

An American heavy cruiser, the *San Diego* had met her fate in 1918 as she escorted cargo ships about 10 miles south of Fire Island. Some crew members claimed the warship struck a mine. As a professional dive boat captain, I didn't care why she sank, only that I had a good crew and 20 scuba divers aboard, all eager to hit the water in search of artifacts.

Three and a half hours later, the *Barnacle Bill* arrived at the wreck, and we dropped our grappling hook. I summoned crew members Doreen Olsen and Lars Hansen (names changed for publication), and we prepared the vessel for the dive. Since Doreen and Lars are both licensed captains, they could attend the *Barnacle Bill* while I dived.

Once the topside chores were taken care of, I suited up, hit the water with a splash and swam toward the anchor line. The water was crystal clear. Most of the divers were already at the bottom, and I could see their bubbles coming to the surface. What a sight!

Twenty feet down, I could make out the wreck's dark outline, rising off the bottom like the lonely ruins of a cathedral.

I headed toward the stern, looking for an opening in the hull that I had used on earlier dives. I knew it'd take me to the small-arms locker where I had previously located boxes of ammunition. The guns themselves should be nearby, I figured. They'd make great souvenirs, even if corroded.

Diving into a wreck like the *San Diego* can be dangerous, and definitely is not for beginners. The vessel is upside down, resting in 102 feet of water, and you can imagine the frigid loneliness that grabs you when you swim into the dark twists and turns of her interior.

I spotted the opening, moved inside and played my light around the front corridor. I knew this section of the wreck well, but as I swam deeper I saw that rusting bulkheads and decaying decks had given way during the winter, changing the shape of the interior considerably.

Suddenly I heard a loud noise. I turned and swam back 40 feet toward the first bulkhead. When I got there, I was struck with terror. The noise I had heard was a bulkhead collapsing against the gap through which I had entered the wreck.

I was trapped.

Into the Maze

My heart beat so loud I could hear it. I wanted to scream for help, pray, kick—turn all this into a nightmare from which I could awake. But it was no nightmare. Moreover, my plight was of my own making. I had gone down improperly equipped— no safety line to guide me back, no alternate air supply and, most important, no diving companion. My mind flashed back four years when my colleagues pulled the body of a diver from the same wreck. They found him 10 feet from an opening through which he might have escaped. But he had panicked, removed the equipment and made a last-ditch effort to swim to safety. His fingers were scratched to the bone by his vain attempt to tear through the ship's hull.

I tried to relax, because I knew the more excited I got, the faster I would use up my air. *Physically I'm in good shape,* I thought, *so I should be able to stretch another 25 minutes out of this tank. But what should I do?* I had to probe deeper into the wreck and find an opening large enough to escape through.

I thought of the deck guns. Often divers would squeeze through openings in the gun turrets and work their way into the vessel. *If I can get to the gun turrets, I'll have a chance.* Since the ship was inverted, however, the gun turrets might be buried under sand on the ocean's floor. Moreover, going into deeper water would cut into my precious air supply, because the more

pressure you have on your body, the more air it takes to fill your lungs.

I cringed at the possibilities, but figured I had to go for the gun turrets as fast as I dared, without getting out of breath.

I found an opening that allowed me to go lower into the ship. As I twisted through a maze of narrow corridors, a thousand ugly visions flashed through my mind. Each one reminded me that I was probably going to die.

A Few Breaths Left

I came to a fork in the corridor. On the right was a clutter of pipes and debris, so I opted for the left and went about 40 feet before coming to a dead end.

I retreated and swam carefully around the pipes and other debris in the passageway to the right. Twenty feet along it my lamp began to dim. *Without light, I'm as good as dead. Just no way I can find my way around.* So now the race was against a dying battery as well as a diminishing air supply.

In the next passageway, I caught a glimpse of light through a crack in the hull—but it was not nearly wide enough for me to get through. I knew my diving companions would be heading back to the anchor line by now, so I decided to take a chance of attracting their attention.

I found a piece of copper pipe and put one of my rubber gloves over its end. Then I pushed the glove through the opening and waved it. If someone noticed the glove, he could at least get extra tanks of air through the narrow gap. Sure enough, a diver appeared.

I stretched my arm through the opening, and with my knife scratched on the side of the hull: "Trapped … Air … Rope."

The diver headed for the surface as fast as he dared, to let the others know of my predicament.

With only a few minutes of air left in my tank, I was panicking. *I know Lars will be here … if I can just hang on.* To conserve air, I skipped every other beat in my breathing rhythm. For an instant, I considered moving on, using up the air in a last desperate effort to find my own way out. Then I heard Lars's bubbles as he approached.

Next moment he was pushing in the first of two air tanks he had brought down. I strapped it on. Each tank would give me an additional 30 minutes to work my way out of this underwater labyrinth. I felt better already.

Desperate Choice

Lars had also brought a light and a safety line. Grabbing the lamp and one end of the line, I headed back into the wreck. Now, by pulling the line after me, I could return for more air. That is, if no more bulkheads closed in behind me.

As I worked back into the wreck, Lars fastened the other spare tank to the side of the narrow opening, and then began looking along the outside of the hull for a possible way to get me out.

Pacing myself to keep from getting out of breath, I swam cautiously through a confusion of narrow corridors and cluttered spaces. I kept bumping into pipes, jabbing myself with protruding objects and taking wrong turns. Fear was squeezing the breath out of me.

Soon I came to a spot that resembled the inside of a gun turret. There was a narrow opening to it that might just accommodate my 200-pound frame if I removed my tank and pulled it through after me. I had to chance it.

But as I squeezed through the opening, the tank fell from my grasp. The regulator was jerked from my mouth, nearly pulling my front teeth out. I had a fast choice to make—either search for the tank I had dropped or try to follow the safety line 70 feet back to the other tank Lars had left for me. I doubted that I could make the swim on the air remaining in my lungs. But could I locate the dropped tank?

Perhaps I should just give up, open my mouth and fill my lungs with water. It will be over in a few seconds, and then I can rest.

This was crazy!

Something grabbed my right shoulder. I nearly jumped out of my wet suit. It was Lars. He had found a way down around the gun turret, via another opening in the wreck.

I grabbed Lars's mouthpiece and gasped in a few breaths of air. I was almost out of my jam. Lars and I could buddy-breathe from his tank and work our way clear of the wreck, following the safety line he had pulled behind him.

We wriggled out through the gun turret without too much trouble. But I had been near the bottom for 70 minutes; I'd have to spend over an hour decompressing. We followed the anchor line to the 10-foot level. There we found two sets of double tanks waiting for us, lowered by our alert shipmates.

When eventually we eased to the surface, everyone on board greeted us with sighs of relief. It seemed that a dark curtain had lifted as I gazed at the beautiful seascape glittering in bright sunshine.

Back on the *Barnacle Bill*, I pulled off my gear and thanked Lars and my other resourceful companions. Then I went down into the cabin to rest. Lars appeared in the doorway, a slight grin on his face. "What would you have done if I hadn't shown up?" he kidded me.

I considered. "When I got back to the boat," I said, "I'd have fired you. Now let me sleep."

The Ordeal of John Cali

Police thought the deaths of his wife and daughter murder-and-suicide—but he knew that couldn't be

—

BY **GERALD MOORE**

Originally published in January 1975

s soon as he walked into his big white house on "millionaires' row" in Upper Montclair, New Jersey, John Cali felt that something was wrong. Everything seemed too quiet. Renee, John's attractive, 45-year-old wife, usually met him at the door. He called her, but got no answer. He called Leslie, his 24-year-old step-daughter. Again, no answer. Then, as he started upstairs to look for the women, the doorbell rang.

Another daughter, Jonna, stood there—nearly hysterical—with two Montclair policemen. Capt. Charles Cummings stepped forward. "Mr. Cali, a terrible thing …" he said. "Your wife—Jonna found her in the basement."

Cali and the two police officers ran to the cellar. Renee Cali lay on the floor, her head and shoulders suspended a few inches above the concrete by a hemp rope knotted tightly around her neck. Stunned by what he saw, Cali thought almost immediately of Leslie— pregnant with her first child— and ran upstairs to find her. He had hardly reached the first-floor landing before Cummings called him back. Leslie was in the basement too—25 feet away from her mother, hanged in a storage bin.

John Cali required every bit of willpower that he possessed to control his emotions as he stood there on that hot evening of May 14, 1973. Yet, his ordeal had only begun. His faith in the sanity and decency of Renee and Leslie was about to be severely tested.

No Sense

Captain Cummings and a quickly assembled team of homicide detectives began sifting clues. The position of the bodies and manner of hanging was like no murder Cummings had ever seen. The rope around Renee's neck was tied with a slipknot and attached, incredibly, to a knob on a five-drawer chest. Renee was lying flat but for the few inches of elevation caused by the rope. Leslie was in a sitting position, her buttocks just inches off the floor. A rope was looped around her neck several times and tied to a vertical beam about 3 feet above the floor, within her reach.

Both women were dressed in bathing suits, and had obviously been sunbathing on the patio before their deaths. The top of Renee's suit was pulled down around her waist; the right side of Leslie's suit was also lowered. But the medical report showed that neither woman had been sexually assaulted. In fact, although Renee had a small cut on her cheek, no signs of any physical assault were found. The women had died of strangulation. The cut and the bathing-suit tops could be explained if one assumed that in the final moments of life the women had thrashed about.

There were no signs of forced entry into the house, nothing to indicate the presence of another person. A check for fingerprints turned up only those of the family. Upstairs, Renee's purse was open on her bed, $3 still in her wallet. None of the jewelry, furs and other expensive objects in the house seemed to have been touched.

To Cummings it made no sense for a criminal to commit two capital crimes for the purpose of robbery and then to leave so much behind, unless he was frightened away. But the autopsy seemed to contradict that possibility. The women had died around noon. Neighbors had seen no one around the house between noon and 5 p.m., when Jonna had come home. She had showered and changed clothes and was carrying her laundry to the basement washing machine when she discovered her stepmother's body. Shaking with fright and unable to reach Cali, who was on his way home from his office, she had jumped in her car and driven to Montclair police headquarters.

Cummings's job was made enormously difficult by the apparent absence of a motive for the killings. As he mulled over the odd case, he began to speculate. The rope around Renee's neck was tied in a slipknot. The rope on Leslie's neck was looped and tied where she could have reached it. Perhaps, he thought, Leslie was depressed over some aspect of her pregnancy, her marriage or her family situation. Perhaps she and her mother had argued. Leslie could have thrown that slipknotted rope around Renee's neck and strangled her. Then, repelled by what she had done, Leslie might have hanged herself. Or, perhaps, Leslie and

her mother had even made a suicide pact. Either theory would account for nearly all the facts on hand and supply the only motive that seemed to make sense.

Armed with Faith

John Cali received the news of Cummings's preliminary findings with astonished disbelief. "It has to be murder," he insisted. "There was absolutely no reason for my wife and daughter to end their lives." Renee, he pointed out, was an attractive, popular woman, active in community affairs, close to her family and known to be happy in her marriage. There were no financial problems—he was the head of a highly successful real-estate development firm. Leslie and Michael Grant were sharing the Cali home while searching for a place of their own. "Leslie was looking forward to the birth of her baby," Cali said. "How can anyone suggest that this is anything but cold-blooded murder?"

As the next days passed and no new evidence was uncovered, neither the police nor the county prosecutor could see any solid reason to change their conclusion of murder-suicide. It became clear to Cali that he must persuade them to his point of view if justice were to be done. He shook off the paralysis of grief and went to work.

First, he convened family meetings: son-in-law Michael Grant, a mortgage broker; Jonna, a nursing student; and Jo Ann

> ## "To me the most impressive thing about Cali was his absolute faith in his family."

Skinner, an older, married step-daughter. For literally hundreds of hours they discussed all possible motives that they could imagine for the killings. They listed the names of 64 people who had been to the house over the preceding few years. They discussed what they knew of the mental state of Leslie and Renee. Mrs. Skinner had talked to Renee on the phone the morning

of May 14. Renee had seemed in fine spirits.

Finally, Cali called on Essex County prosecutor Joseph Lordi. "To me the most impressive thing about Cali was his absolute faith in his family," recalls Lordi. "It was just too strong to be dismissed, too well reasoned." But Lordi's high regard for Cali didn't change the facts on hand. More than faith and logic were clearly required, so Cali cast about for another approach.

Unofficial Investigation

Cali had noticed several things in the basement which to him indi-cated a struggle. Needing an expert to confirm or refute his interpreta-tion, he got in touch with John Cronin, a highly regarded professor at John Jay College of Criminal Justice in New York City. Cali took Cronin through the house, pointing out what he felt indicated the presence of a killer. Renee's hair was in curlers when she died, yet several curlers were found loose on the floor. Her glasses were some distance from her body. A watering can was overturned. The assumption that Leslie had killed her mother might explain these clues, but Cronin was fascinated. The obvious conclusion, he felt, might not necessarily be the right one.

Renee's open purse was probably, Cronin concluded, an indication of robbery. There was $3 in it, but Cali insisted that his wife had cashed a $100 check just a day or two before she died. And Jonna discovered $20 in cash missing from her room. The chest that served to anchor the rope around Renee's neck had been empty; Cronin agreed that it would hardly support enough weight to strangle a person unless she was unconscious before she was hanged.

Cronin finished his unofficial investigation and told Cali he thought that the women had been victims of a very clever killer. The $3, he said, was left behind to throw police off. The differences in the knotted ropes showed that the killer had gone about his crime with terrible deliberation; it was double murder made to look like murder-suicide.

Turnabout

With Cronin's reasoning to back his own gut feelings, Cali went back to Lordi. The prosecutor decided to call his own expert: Milton Helpern, New York City's famous chief medical examiner.

In the meantime, Edwin H. Albano, New Jersey's state medical examiner, entered the case. He had not performed the first autopsy, but the strange circumstances of the deaths caught his attention. He decided to do a second autopsy. He found several previously un-noticed small bruises on Renee's upper arms, which indicated, he concluded, a "firm, steady grip"—not, significantly, the kind of grip that Leslie would have been able to apply. Then he found smaller bruises on Leslie. He, too, was inclined to a double-murder theory.

Dr. Albano's findings came to Lordi just as Dr. Helpern reported that a two-hour inspection of Cali's house had convinced him that Cronin's findings were correct.

Cali's efforts had finally paid off. The consensus of the three experts put a very different interpretation on the evidence. The cut on Renee's cheek could be further evidence of assault. The fact that both women had the tops of their swimsuits pulled down now seemed an unlikely coincidence. Lordi himself became convinced that Cali's view—double murder—was correct.

Using the list that Cali had provided, detectives began questioning everyone who had been to the Cali home in the weeks before the killings. All visitors seemed to have a solid alibi for May 14.

Tension was building in the prosecutor's office, for investigators knew that anyone who could kill so coolly might soon kill again. And the strain on John Cali was enormous. The shock of losing his wife and daughter, the intensive and continuing effort to clear their good names, and the pressures of running a competitive business were taking their toll. But constant support from his family sustained him.

Chilling Reality

On June 13, Cali noticed a small item buried in a local newspaper. Robert Petrarca, a window washer, had been arrested in South Orange, a few miles from the Cali home. Petrarca had gone to the home of an 83-year-old woman on a job and tried to strangle her with a rope.

The story sent Cali's head reeling. Petrarca worked for the Aristocrat Window Cleaning Service, and Aristocrat had billed Cali for washing windows at his house on May 13, the day before the double killing. Leslie, Jonna recalled, had showed Petrarca where to store storm windows in the basement—in the very bin where her body was later found.

"It *has* to be Petrarca," Cali insisted to Lordi.

Petrarca, 26, a powerfully built man with a substantial criminal record, freely admitted to police that he had washed the Cali windows, but steadfastly denied that he had gone back on May 14. He said he'd spent the day working, and his alibi stood up.

Because of the enormous circumstantial evidence, however, Petrarca was brought to the prosecutor's office for questioning many times in the next few weeks. But progress was nil—until Aug. 3, when for no apparent reason he abruptly confessed the chilling facts of the crime.

The day after Petrarca and a partner had washed windows at the Cali home, Petrarca said, he showed up again—alone—telling Leslie that he had lost a squeegee and wanted to look for it. She helped him in a fruitless search. Then he grabbed her from behind in a tight hammerlock and strangled her. Renee was at the washing machine, transferring clothes to the dryer, when Petrarca sneaked up behind her and grabbed her. Renee fought. She got his left ring finger in her mouth and bit hard, nearly to the bone. "Let go or I'll kill you," he growled. Renee let go, and he strangled her.

Petrarca arranged the bodies in the odd positions in which they were found, then went upstairs and searched the house. He took about $60 from the top of a dresser, $20 from Jonna's bureau.

His sordid confession finished, Petrarca told police that he wanted to call John Cali. Cali agreed to the conversation, and asked Petrarca,

"Why? *Why* did you kill two such wonderful, innocent people?"

"I don't know."

"May God help you!" Cali said and hung up.

❖　❖　❖

Petrarca was convicted and sentenced to two consecutive life sentences. John Cali's faith was vindicated, but there was no sense of triumph.

Outside the courtroom after the trial, looking drawn and tired, Cali said, "Society gives much consideration to the criminal, to his rehabilitation, his psychiatric state and his legal rights. Society might also consider the plight of the victim's family. They, too, may desperately need emotional support in overcoming their shock and outrage and sorrow, and assurance that everything possible is being done to bring the guilty party to justice."

With that, he got into his car and drove off to rebuild his life.

My Most Unforgettable Character

Dad's incredible life and lessons as a steam locomotive engineer and a man of God

———

BY **RED BARBER**

Originally published in May 1970

ecause of the red hair I had before "the grass got thin on the infield," most people call me Red. But when some old friend hails me by my real name, Walter, it gives me a warm feeling. For that's what Dad used to call me. He was my first hero and, in memory, is my favorite one. He was an engineer on those big black steam locomotives that belched smoke and fire and made the ground tremble. His uniform was the plainest: grease-stained overalls, a peak-billed cap and a bandanna at the neck to keep out the cinders. But in the game of railroading and the game of living, he was, in his quiet way, as great a champion as any I've known.

When I was 5, we were living in Columbus, Mississippi, and Mother used to take me down to the tracks by the Southern Railroad round-house to see Dad off. With a deft, sure hand on the throttle, he could get the longest train underway—not with a thunderous jerk up and down the line, but with the smooth, silken *click-click-click* of couplings that was his pride and trademark.

He could run any kind of train there was, but he explained to me, "Walter, there's nothing like the big freights." Passenger trains, with

96

their swift "through" schedules, were too easy for Dad. He preferred the rumbling power of a huge string of boxcars—the challenge of pitting his will against a mile-long monster of steel.

Railroading in those days was largely on single-track roadbeds with sidetracks for one train to pull into while another roared past in the opposite direction. This required exact schedules (10:16, not 10:15 or 10:17) to avoid head-on collisions. Dad was completely reliable, and so was his watch—a Howard chronometer, his most expensive and most important material possession. Generous as he was, he wouldn't let anyone else touch that watch. Wherever he was, he would wind it every day at precisely 6 p.m., even if he had to be waked up to do it.

Matter of Respect

Dad worked all hours, slept when he could. At any time the callboy might come to wake him and tell him what engine he'd be going out on for the next 16 hours. Because of Sunday work, he had lost the habit of going to church. Yet he was never really outside it, if church means the peace of a simple, unquestioning faith, and the living communion of a man with his fellows and his Maker. Dad didn't talk religion; he lived it.

Dad loved his fellow man—and trusted him. The tramps who came to our door always got fed. "You can't let a man go hungry," Dad would tell Mother, "and you can't take a chance that he *isn't* hungry." To Dad, the best part of railroading was waiting in the sidetracks when he had time to make coffee in the cab and visit with the people who lived and worked along the right of way.

Rugged as his work world was, and his past (Dad had been a drifter from one railroad job to another before he met Mother and settled down), you would expect him to be a rough, tough man. But he wasn't—and he loved his home.

I'd sit on the front steps until I saw him coming down the road. There was a slight roll to his gait, dating from an injury he'd received when starting out as a fireman.

Not a big man, or a particularly handsome one, he was strong, with the strength mostly in his bearlike chest, shoulders and arms. When I ran to meet him, he would put down his battered metal suitcase and swing me up in his arms.

Once we were in the house, it was my job to help him out of his overalls, so caked with grease, oil and coal dust that they could stand by themselves. Then he would scrub and scrub his blackened hands. Despite the dirty work on the big engines, he would end up with the cleanest, gentlest hands I ever saw.

Afterward, bathed and dressed, he would sit on the porch. He might read—always good books by good authors. Or, he'd ask me to play, on our old windup gramophone, selections from his favorite operas or symphonies—he didn't care for cheap music or cheap anything else. There he'd sit, rocking, smoking, letting in the enjoyment of the day.

In every yard we had, Dad spent hours planting, fertilizing, watering, pruning, enjoying. He loved the beauty and the mystery of the flowers he grew. He liked to cook too,

and often took over our kitchen to put together a stew or to simmer a country steak. He had a rich sense of humor and told stories well about his experiences on the railroad. There were a half-dozen rocking chairs on our front porch, and as often as not they were all filled with friends listening to Dad "railroad."

Mother, an English teacher, gave me an ear for grammar and pronunciation. But it was from Dad that I picked up the ability to speak and hear the earthy language of the tracks, the street, the baseball dugout. Yet I never heard my father use profanity. He respected himself, his family and the English language that much.

Rough Ride

As a boy, there was nothing I wanted so much as to ride in the cab of my father's locomotive. The first big day came when I was 12. We had moved to Sanford, Florida, and Dad was working for the Atlantic Coast Line. One day, almost casually, he asked, "How'd you like to take a little trip with me over to Leesburg?" My heart pounded as I sat on the fireman's seat and we got underway.

But, as we gathered speed, I was stunned and amazed at what life in the cab was like. The heat, the racket, the roughness of the ride, the swirling storm of cinders—unbelievable! I wondered how Dad could stand it every day, especially the violent side-to-side motion of the cab as the giant pistons on either side slammed in opposite directions. And the shrieking blast of the whistle! Up in the head end, it was like somebody running a knife in your ears.

I never told him what torture that first ride was. I was only too happy to pay the price just to be with him, to be a part of his strenuous world. Decades later, after Dad was gone and I was crisscrossing the country announcing games, I'd sometimes get permission to ride up in the newer, smoother locomotive cabs. I would watch the rails and the land rush backward, and for precious moments the strong left hand that held the throttle would again be the one I remembered so well.

"It's All Yours"

Naturally, as I grew up, I wanted to railroad too. I wanted to "go to firing"—which was then coal-shoveling, back-breaking work—for four or five years, and then take the examinations for engineer. So, when I finished high school, I went to the roundhouse and applied. Several days later, I got an answer—from my father, who said he had told

> **"Look just as far as your eyes will let you. It's a big world, and it's all yours."**

the master mechanic that if my application was accepted, he would quit.

"Walter," Dad said, "I don't care what you do in this world as long as it's honest work, and as long as it isn't railroading. The steam engine is going out. That will mean fewer crews, and less and less work. Automobiles, trucks and airplanes are going to shrink up railroading. Don't break your heart by going into a drying-up industry." This was what he said, what he saw, in 1926.

Dad never wasted words lamenting things he couldn't help. He couldn't afford to send me to college, so that was that. He never apologized for it, never mentioned it. But in a sense, he did "send" me to college after all. One afternoon when I was about 16, we were out in the front yard. It was a beautiful day. "Son," he said, "look just as far as your eyes will let you. It's a big world, and it's all yours. All you have to do is go out and get it."

Shortly after, I determined to work my way through the University of Florida. When I told him, he didn't look at all surprised. Later, when I said that I had a part-time job announcing over radio station WRUF in Gainesville, his eyes lit up with pleasure.

The Depression hit our family hard. Before I was out of college, the railroad terminal at Sanford closed down, Dad's income fell off and he lost the first home he had ever tried to own. Infinitely worse, Mother had a series of strokes that left her an invalid. Dad hid his grief,

and the face he turned to the world was stoically resolute. Railroading was still pretty good in the winter, when he "worked on his rest" (16 hours on the locomotive, 8 off to sleep). But in the summers, work was thin and spotty and, much as it galled him, he'd have to run up a grocery bill. He was too independent to tolerate financial help from me or anyone else.

Meanwhile, I was scrapping my way up in the game of sports announcing. When I eventually went to New York to announce for the Brooklyn Dodgers, he was proud. Sometimes he'd come north for a big game and sit with me in our broadcasting booth high over Ebbets Field. In return for his having let me ride in his locomotives, it was a small favor.

The Last Run

His abiding passion in his last years was to die out of debt or, as he put it, "go out even." After he was pensioned, he went to live with his sister, my Aunt Virginia, in the little North Carolina town near where they were born. He was stone-deaf from all the years of din in the cab, and ailing. Still he struggled valiantly to stretch his small pension. He insisted on paying for each delivery of medicine on the spot, and when the doctor came he was paid for the call before he left. (Dad made it, too. He not only "went out even," but left each of his three children a $500 war bond.)

However, his going wasn't easy. When at 67 he began to feel the end coming, he was afraid—the first time I'd ever seen him afraid. He wouldn't get in bed but just sat in his overstuffed chair day and night, his head sinking lower onto his chest. He was alone in his deafness, doubtless thinking of Mother, who had been gone for years, and of his youngest son, Billy, who was off fighting in Europe. But a struggle was going on inside him too.

One morning, I showed him the big newspaper headline: "V-E Day!" He smiled and said, "Billy's all right, then." Later that morning, he stunned us by suddenly announcing, "I want to see a preacher."

We called the Baptist minister. Dad didn't know him, and his

deafness was so dense that he never got the minister's name or denomination. The young man read the 23rd Psalm and said the Lord's Prayer. Dad couldn't hear the words, but slowly he raised his head, looked squarely at the young minister and—his voice calm, measured, strong again— said to him, "All my life I've loved God. That will have to be enough for now." His head sank to his chest again. He had brought forth what he felt compelled to say—the truth that his whole life had made abundantly clear.

That afternoon, he roused again briefly. "Walter," he said, "my watch—it's on the mantelpiece. You'll need it in your work. Now go on back to your job."

A few days later, in New York, the phone call came as I was on my way to a night game at Ebbets Field. It was over. I had no sooner left Aunt Virginia's house than Dad asked to be put into his bed. His fear was gone; his children were all right; he was at peace. The job was done. Dad had brought his locomotive into the roundhouse.

They Brought Home the Wrong Baby

Two sweet children, switched at birth

BY **MURRAY TEIGH BLOOM**

Originally published in June 1955

There are no outward signs that Lewis and Gladys Baughey of Fairfield, Michigan, have been through one of the most heart-chilling experiences possible to parents anywhere. Their cement-block house, their 1949 car, their dog, their TV set, their four children—all mark the average family of modest means. Gladys, 29, tall and attractive, enjoys cooking, flowers in the house and music—just like millions of other women. Lewis, 32, is a home-loving, bespectacled, sturdy 6-footer who makes about $125 a week driving a big truck-trailer.

But on this quiet plateau of everyday life, one day stands out in the Baugheys' memory like an overwhelming Everest: the day in 1950 when they learned beyond doubt that their daughter Diane, then 3½, was not their own child; that their real daughter was being brought up by another family in the same town.

In 1950 Lewis and Gladys Baughey were living in a Michigan city about 100 miles from their present home. They have asked me not to pinpoint it nor to name the other key people in this drama.

One day in May, a man I will call Pete Royer, who wanted to sell his car, stopped in front of the Baughey house; Royer's 5-year-old, Ernie, hopped out. In that moment, Lewis Baughey's quiet little world started tumbling down around him.

"Ernie," he told me, "had a happy kid's hop, full of ginger, green eyes, a little snub nose and ears sticking out, and I thought: *That's funny, the boy looks enough like my Diane to be a twin.*"

Pete Royer started talking about the car, but he could see that Lewis wasn't really listening.

"Pete," said Lewis, "your boy Ernie looks like my girl Diane."

Pete turned to look at Diane, who had now come down the porch steps. His face grew troubled, but only fleetingly. He laughed: "You're right. There *is* a resemblance. But you should see my cousin: He's a dead ringer for Red Skelton."

Now Lewis's thoughts took a spurt. He remembered suddenly that Pete's divorced wife, Laura, had had a baby girl about the same time that Gladys had—in the same maternity ward in the town's only hospital.

Where was Pete's girl now, he asked. Pete told him that since the divorce the child had been boarded with an elderly couple outside of

town. When Lewis suggested that they drive out to see the girl, Pete Royer decided to humor him. After all, a potential car buyer …

At the elderly couple's house, Royer's daughter Bernice, 3½, was playing in a sand pile. "I just sat there and looked at her and I got sick inside," Lewis recalls. "I didn't dare say a word to her. I had to get out of there until this made sense."

When they returned to the Baughey house, Lewis blurted out his fears and both men forgot the car sale. They sat and talked it over. Pete Royer began to remember things that added up.

"You know, Lewis," he said, "when Bernice was born she didn't look like anyone in my family or in my wife Laura's either. She was dark-skinned and brown-eyed; all our other kids are light and fair-haired. It made trouble …" His voice trailed off.

That evening Lewis told Gladys what had happened. At first it didn't make any sense to her. How could such a thing happen? But as he talked she recalled odd incidents.

There had been six beds in the

hospital room. Gladys had come in on the morning of Dec. 19, 1946, and had her baby at 1:50 p.m. Laura, in the next bed, had had her baby four days earlier. Gladys saw her baby for the first time that evening. The child had a lot of black hair. The next morning when the nurse brought the baby in, Gladys noticed two things:

First, the baby had practically no hair. When Gladys remarked on this, the nurse only laughed. "Oh, you probably were a little groggy last night and only *thought* your baby had a lot of black hair. Anyway, you know how babies change when they're this age."

The second thing Gladys noticed was that her baby's identity bracelet— a catgut-and-beads affair—was missing from her leg. The nurse had an answer for this too: Babies often kicked the bracelets off in their cribs. "But don't worry. We have the baby's footprints for identification."

Too weak to argue, Gladys had allowed herself to be persuaded and had not mentioned to anyone else what she later came to look

on as a mother's aberration.

After he heard this, Lewis telephoned Pete Royer. The latter recalled something too. While Laura was in the hospital, she had cried because the baby refused to take her breast. On the day she left she felt she had the wrong baby and had told her husband and her father so. The latter took it up with the hospital administration and was assured that the idea of baby mix-ups was a common one among women just after confinement, and that the hospital's identification system was foolproof. In the face of this calm and apparently scientific explanation, the Royers had dropped the matter.

Now the Baugheys were certain that Diane, whom they had brought up as their own, belonged to Laura and Pete Royer and that Bernice Royer was their own daughter.

Lewis persuaded Gladys to drive out with him to see the child. One look, and whatever doubts Gladys still had vanished.

"It wasn't just her curly hair and brown eyes and the ears which were just like mine," Gladys recalls.

"It was everything about her. That was my little girl. I wanted to run and take her in my arms, but Lewis wouldn't let me. 'Glad, if you go to her,' he said, 'we'll both break down and bawl our heads off. It won't be any good for the girl, and it won't be any good for us. We've got to be sure first.'"

But how? Looks alone didn't mean much. But there *was* one way Gladys had heard about: blood tests.

The Heredity Clinic of the University of Michigan at Ann Arbor was not far from where the Baugheys lived. Founded in 1940 as part of the university's Institute of Human Biology, the clinic was the first of its kind in the country; to it have come thousands of perplexed parents and doctors with troubling questions of heredity. Lewis asked Pete Royer if he'd bring Bernice to the clinic on the same day that the Baugheys took Diane. Pete agreed.

When the day came, the three parents drove to the house where Bernice was staying. Gladys got out with Pete, who told the little girl they were going for a ride. Gladys put on a new blue dress she had bought for her. Bernice hugged Gladys, and that made Gladys cry.

At Ann Arbor, Lewis told the story to Charles W. Cotterman, a young genetics specialist who had heard of similar cases before. A surprising number of parents think they go home from the hospital with the wrong baby, he told them. But he kept looking from Diane to Pete and from Bernice to Lewis and

"I could tell he was seeing what we'd been seeing all along."

Gladys. "I could tell he was seeing what we'd been seeing all along," recalls Lewis.

Dr. Cotterman explained that blood tests were an invaluable aid in determining parentage but were of little use if both sets of parents had very similar blood characteristics. Then he took blood samples from all of them and they drove home.

Now a nerve-wearing wait began. Dr. Cotterman had warned

that blood tests took time and often had to be rechecked by independent serologists. And soon Lewis and Gladys realized that the blood tests, even if favorable to them, would by no means solve everything.

"I almost wanted Dr. Cotterman to tell us that the kids hadn't been switched," Lewis says. "Because if they had been, we were up against something I couldn't face: We'd have to give up Diane."

Two fretful weeks went by before the first report came from Dr. Cotterman: He and the other blood experts were certain that Gladys could *not* be the mother of Diane. But he had to get a blood sample from Laura before he could be sure of anything beyond that.

This was arranged, and June 26 Dr. Cotterman completed his tests. He also received a report from Dr. Alexander S. Wiener of New York, one of the world's foremost blood experts. The Cotterman and Wiener findings agreed completely. On June 28 the Baugheys heard from Dr. Cotterman.

"We are completely convinced," the specialist wrote, "that Diane and Bernice were interchanged."

How could they be sure? As Dr. Cotterman later explained, they were fortunate. If this had happened before 1940, no blood test could have proved that the children had been interchanged. But since then the Rh factor in blood had been identified and charted, and it was by analysis of the Rh types that the case had been solved.

Diane's special Rh blood factors were found to be identical with those of Pete and Laura Royer, and Bernice's Rh factors belonged in the same blood family as those of Lewis and Gladys. The laws of heredity are quite clear on this point: These Rh blood factors *cannot* appear in the blood of a child unless present in one or both parents.

The Baugheys excitedly telephoned Dr. Cotterman. "Now what do we do?" He suggested that they talk to the doctor who had attended Gladys at the hospital. After checking with Dr. Cotterman, the doctor, distressed and apologetic, visited the Baugheys.

"Lewis," he said, "this is an awful thing. We've got to make it right somehow. Now I want you to trust me to try to straighten it out quietly—so please don't go running to lawyers."

Says Lewis today: "I suppose I could be taking it easy now instead of wrestling a 16-ton trailer, if we had sued the hospital. But we don't hold with lawsuits. Besides, we had a bug in our heads."

The Baugheys wanted *both* girls; they couldn't bear to give up Diane, whom they had brought up as their own for 3½ years.

"We had a happy home," Gladys says. "Lewis was making a good living. It was unthinkable to us that Diane should be boarded out as Bernice had been."

Pete and Laura Royer were persuaded at last that the Baugheys were right. It was the best thing to do. So the necessary papers for the release of both children were signed.

One evening in early October, the Baugheys drove to where Bernice was staying and picked her up.

"Glad drove," Lewis remembers, "and I held Bernice in my arms. We stopped at a store and I got her an ice cream cone because she was crying. When she finished the cone, she nestled close to me like she belonged there. It felt good holding her that way. When we got home, I rocked her to sleep. She looked at me as if she was going to cry again, and all I could say was: 'It's OK now, honey. I'm your real daddy, and you're always going to stay with us.' Her lips stopped trembling, and in a minute she had fallen off to sleep in my arms."

When I last visited the Baugheys, I brought along toys for the girls and a portable tape recorder. Bernice begged to talk into it and then hear herself. She held the microphone tightly, smiled at her mother and began: "My name is Bernice Baughey. I am 8 years old and I want to tell a story. This is a story about a good king and queen who went looking for their long-lost little princess who was in another castle. They looked and looked, and then they found the little girl, who didn't know she belonged to the good king and queen. She looked at them and liked them and went home with them to their castle and lived happily ever after."

The Man Who Willed Himself to Fly

When an accident rendered him nearly immobile, one man learned the meaning of true grit

BY **JACK FINCHER**

Originally published in April 1982

at Patterson, a pilot for 25 years, had never met anyone like the jut-jawed young man in the wheelchair who faced him at the Medford, Oregon, airport on July 28, 1976. Mike Henderson, a quadriplegic, wanted flying lessons.

Patterson's eyes flickered over Henderson's limbs. His legs could never operate the rudder pedals. How was he to maneuver over a ton of airplane? Henderson's hands worried the instructor most—his fingers were all but inert.

It was impossible, Patterson thought. Then what stopped him from saying so? Maybe it was the young man's obvious determination, his look of urgent desire.

Something inside the bluff and blocky flight instructor stirred in response. "Perhaps I can teach you," he said. "But under Federal Aviation Regulations, you have to be able to get in and out by yourself." He nodded toward his single-engine trainer. "I'm going to get a cup of coffee. If you're in by the time I get back, we'll start."

Mike Henderson had gone up for a plane ride three weeks before. Carried aboard and taken aloft, he

Mike Henderson preparing to climb into the cockpit of his Piper Cherokee in Medford, Oregon

had thought, *Hey, I can do this*. He certainly had the time for lessons and, with a full disability pension, the money. His first concern was whether he had the ability to handle the controls. He now realized, however, that getting into the aircraft by himself might be as tough as flying it.

Still, Henderson had grown used to meeting stiff challenges. As a 22-year-old Coast Guardsman eight years before, he had fallen off a dock and landed on a floating log, smashing his fifth and sixth vertebrae. Doctors said that he would probably never walk again. Although the sensation of touch in his lower trunk and limbs would return, he was completely paralyzed from the chest down and had little movement left in his hands and arms.

Later, a neurosurgeon bluntly told him that he would never be able to live hour to hour without somebody helping him. For reasons he has never quite fathomed, Henderson got angry.

"Here was this doctor telling me how it was going to be," he says. "But no one was going to limit my freedom to try."

After weeks of physical rehabilitation, during which, among other things, he spent endless hours forcing his fingers to pluck marbles out of one pie plate and put them in another, Henderson went home to his parents. Determined to fend for himself, he learned to drive. Before long, he met Ruth Tanner, and after a brief courtship, they were married. Eventually, he accomplished such feats as building and racing a high-speed dragster and floating down the Colorado River in an inner tube.

But Henderson's rehabilitation had barely prepared him for the challenge of a Piper Cherokee, its humped cabin and broad, low wing dazzling in the morning sun. Anchoring his wheelchair beside the plane, he put one hand on the wing's trailing edge and, with the other hand on the armrest of his

chair, propelled himself upward as far as he could go. Then he rolled to face the fuselage and, digging sharply with his right elbow, began inching his dead weight toward the cockpit.

In the flight shack, Pat Patterson watched in disbelief. "He groveled his way up that wing!" he says. "That's the only word for it. It took him 45 minutes. When I went out, he was sitting in the pilot's seat, blood from his chewed elbow all over the place. When I saw him go through that much pain, I knew nothing could stop him."

Nothing, perhaps, but a federal agency empowered to ensure that those who fly are qualified to do so. Sure enough, when Patterson sent Henderson for the FAA physical, the examining physician—a 40-year air veteran himself—balked. "My God, Pat," Dr. David Stoddard explained over the telephone, "he's got less than 10% body movement!"

Patterson persisted. If he, Patterson, vouched for his pupil's in-flight competence, would the doctor fly with Henderson and see for himself? Dr. Stoddard agreed.

Now everything was up to instructor and student, and together they set about solving each problem as it surfaced. A scrap of carpet gave Henderson traction to scale the slippery wing. A headset freed his hands from the radio microphone, and the two men developed a vertically moving tiller bar that enabled Henderson to transfer crucial rudder control from his feet to his right arm and hand.

Patterson was pleased to see that Henderson's fingers exhibited an increasing dexterity; but, as he had feared, they lacked the strength to hold back the control column in high winds or when landing and taking off. Henderson had an idea. Why not a metal hook attached to his wrist, one easily engaged or disengaged as needed? He could make it in his shop at home. The first model, a heavy steel bracelet, bit his wrist cruelly. Henderson fashioned a second one from a lightweight aluminum hospital splint sewn to a glove. It worked perfectly.

Three weeks and eight flying hours after the first lesson,

Henderson and Patterson jubilantly phoned Dr. Stoddard. At the airport, as the physician looked on, Henderson briskly wheeled himself around the airplane, doing a thorough, professional ground check. With Patterson and Dr. Stoddard on board, he went through his preflight instrument check. Minutes later, engine pulsing, the plane rolled down the runway and took off into the gray sky.

Pointing the Piper Cherokee across the wide, funnel-shaped corridor between the Cascade and Siskiyou mountain ranges, Henderson deftly put it through tight turns and stalls as Patterson, grinning at their astonished passenger, held up his hands to show that he, too, was just along for the ride. After they landed, Dr. Stoddard told Henderson to get a new evaluation from his neurologist and agreed to give him the standard flight physical. Dr. Stoddard was hopeful that they would get the FAA to issue a Statement of Demonstrated Ability.

It took several phone calls to the FAA's Aeromedical Certification

Branch, but Dr. Stoddard succeeded. An FAA flight inspector gave Henderson a medical checkout ride and approved him for solo flight. On Nov. 14, 1976, Henderson taxied the plane to a halt following his 20th hour in the air. Patterson hopped out and shouted back at him, "Make two landings and takeoffs, and I'll see you back at the office."

This was it: solo time. With just his right hand, Henderson pushed in the throttle, released the hand brake and, steering the rudder with his tiller bar, taxied out to the runway. Minutes later, he was in the air.

Aloft, Henderson experienced a thrill unlike any he had ever before felt. He was a thousand feet in the sky—and all alone! He kept thinking, *This just has to be the greatest thing I've ever done.*

Patterson was waiting on the ground. "How was it?" he asked.

"Absolutely fantastic," Henderson replied, thinking: *It's a time in your life you really take total responsibility for what's going to happen to you. And I could do it!*

In succeeding months, with the help of Dr. Stoddard, Mike Henderson became the first quadriplegic ever to get both his instrument rating and his commercial pilot's license. He began to tease airline pilots: "One of these days I'll announce over the loudspeaker, 'Ladies and gentlemen, this is your captain speaking. We'll be taking off as soon as my wheelchair is aboard.'"

"What sets Mike Henderson apart is his will," says Dr. Stoddard. "His accomplishment is truly outstanding, almost unbelievable." As he became more proficient, Henderson sought out other instructors. Patterson said some of them didn't fully understand what motivation was. He always told them, "Go take a ride with Mike—then you'll know."

Pat Patterson died in 1979, when the plane he was piloting went down at sea.

Though he continued to fly throughout his life, Mike Henderson ultimately became a social worker specializing in counseling veterans. He died of natural causes in 2014.

Why Mothers Don't Get Sick

Here is a medical miracle that virtually every family has experienced—but it takes a wise woman to recognize the real cause

BY **JOYCE LUBOLD**

Originally published in February 1967

veryone at one point in time or another gets what is known as the 24-hour bug. Doctors, of course, use the proper technical term, and diagnose the disease with exquisite precision by telling their patients, "There's a lot of it going around right now." But no matter what you call it, the one thing clear about the 24-hour bug is that *nobody* has it for exactly 24 hours.

Children can stretch the disease into three full days off from school, during which their mothers bring them meals on a tray and permit them to look at all the awful daytime television shows. One of the nicest things that can happen to a child is to get the bug that's going around.

Fathers enjoy it too. They don't have it quite so long, but they have it louder. The household revolves around the patient then, and everyone, including Father, worries for a couple of days until he's better.

Mothers, however, can catch, suffer and recover from the 24-hour bug in a flat 12 hours. Surely this is a medical miracle of some kind.

Perhaps some young doctor, as yet unknown, will one day be hailed as the man who found the cure for "there's a lot of it going around." If such a man exists, it may help him if we examine now a typical case of a typical mother who contracts a typical bug.

The first thing worth noting is that mothers react differently from other people to the first signs of fever. Children may weep, fathers get irritable. But the typical mother's reaction is pure, unadulterated joy. It is a little-known fact that many otherwise hardworking, selfless, admirable mothers are addicted to the secret vice of taking their own temperature. These fits come on them usually when winter winds are blowing, the house is a mess and their feet hurt. At such a time, a normally strong-minded woman slips quietly to the medicine cabinet, furtively puts the thermometer under her tongue and sits, owllike, on the side of the tub, her heart beating with happy anticipation. She *yearns* to be a little bit sick. She almost never is.

However, once in a long while she's lucky and, to her definite joy, the thermometer shows a fever. Not high, of course. Not much over 100 degrees—but positive proof that she actually *has* the thing-that's-going-around. Comforting memories of childhood sickness come to her mind: cool, clean sheets, bowls of hot soup, piles of books on the bedside table. What a lovely vision! And she really *is* sick. Sick enough to go to bed. Isn't that wonderful!

Let's assume that this fine moment comes just after lunch-time. The children are at school, the baby is napping, there's no reason why she can't get into bed immediately. All she has to do first is mix the meat loaf for supper, leave a note for the laundryman, find a substitute for the coffee committee that night, put in the next load of wash, carry out the trash and then … and then go upstairs and … sink … into … bed. Ah-h-h-h-h! Her aching legs soak up comfort from the cool sheets, and her eyes, which have started to burn a bit, slowly, pleasurably, close. She's asleep—in the middle of the day!

Then, too soon, the front door bangs wildly open as the children explode home from school. Their cries of "Mom! *Mom!* Where ARE you?" entirely drown out her weak answering calls, but their search is determined and very shortly they appear, reacting in their several ways to the unbelievable fact that Mother is in bed.

"Didn't you even get *up* yet?" cries the younger girl, ignoring the fact that Mom obviously was up through the breakfast bedlam.

"But how am I going to get to Bill's?" asks the boy, lurching in despair onto the bottom of the bed.

"If you're sick, what'll we have for dinner?" inquires the oldest, cutting right to the essential problem.

The point is that children are not really the unfeeling monsters they appear to be under these circumstances. It's just that the whole concept of a mother in bed, not attending to duties, is outside their picture of the way things are. A wise woman, at such a time, will

play shamelessly on their sense of the dramatic. They really *enjoy* big emergencies. They're crazy about disasters. What they *don't* like is minor disturbances, such as the one she's got. So she must throw her head back against the pillow, look pale and wan, and issue tense, whispered commands.

"I'm sick," she must say clearly. "I can't do *anything*. I'll just have to leave everything to you." Then, letting her voice trail off dramatically, but careful to mention every necessary duty, she murmurs, "Cook the potatoes ... take care of the baby ... set the table ..." So convincing a display of crisis will cause most children to rise nobly to the challenge, and for a time she will be left to the quiet of her room and the ache in her head.

But then Father comes home. Having received a breathless medical report from the children, he bounds into the bedroom without taking off his coat, drops heavily onto the side of the bed and reaches for her hand.

"The kids say you feel terrible. Have you called Dr. Murphy?

Should I go pick up the prescription? What did he say was the matter?" Suddenly she feels terribly guilty, and struggles to switch from acting sicker than she is to acting much better than she feels.

"It's nothing, darling—just this bug that's going around. I can get up and do dinner and ..." He shakes his head firmly.

"You stay right there. Don't worry about a thing. The kids and I will take over." He sounds confident, but as she looks up at him in his rumpled business suit, with end-of-the-day fatigue in his eyes, she feels a tearful remorse.

"I'm sorry, dear. It's awfully hard on you ..." she begins painfully, really wondering if she may be sicker than she thought, really wishing that he would stay and hold her for a moment. But his mind is now surging with thoughts of Efficiency-in-the-Kitchen, and Getting-the-Kids-Organized, and he has no time for bedside tenderness. "Just don't talk," he advises briskly. "We'll get along *fine* without you."

Her room is quiet again. And empty. Her lovely languor has left.

She feels scratchy and hot in the wrinkled sheets. She lies very still, straining for family sounds, feeling left out, feeling *terrible*. But everybody else seems to feel great. There seems, in fact, to be some sort of party going on, with giggling from the children and guffaws from Father, all against the clatter of plates and silverware.

Suddenly there is a dreadful crash, followed by Father's voice telling everyone loudly to get the baby out of the way for goodness' sake before he cuts himself, and where is the broom, and whatever they do they must not disturb their mother. "DON'T DISTURB YOUR MOTHER," he bawls from the kitchen, making the curtains move gently up in her bedroom.

Now the house grows quiet, and it is clear to her that the family is eating dinner while she lies there motionless, forgotten, miserable. She is not surprised that no one has thought to bring dinner to her. They've obviously forgotten about her entirely. They're obviously doing *fine* without her. There's no point in going on living.

And then there is the lovely sound of another appalling crash, and the next-to-smallest child races in breathlessly to announce, "They dropped your tray and the dog licked up all your dinner."

She dashes off and there is another period of confusing noises until, finally, all the children appear, beaming. They bring a glass of water that has spilled over onto the tray, a plate with three beans, a cold boiled potato, a tiny slab of burned meat loaf—and themselves. "Can we come up with you while you eat? Dad's kind of mad, and it's all messy in the kitchen, and nobody knows where the broom is. Is it all right if we stay here while you eat?"

Suddenly she feels marvelous! As the children watch carefully, she eats up everything in sight, assures them that dinner was delicious, and then stretches luxuriously, noticing without surprise that the vague aches and pains she felt are gone, and only a deep, marvelous, sleepy feeling remains. The children leap up alertly, solicitously, at this sign. "Go to sleep now, Mom," they chorus. And the oldest adds,

soberly, "Get better. It's no fun when you're sick."

Again the room is empty, but now it hums with comfort, and she drops into a dreamless sleep. She stirs when her husband comes in. "Go back to sleep," he says quietly. "Hope you feel better tomorrow."

And that is the great miracle. She *is* better in the morning. In fact, when she swings her legs experimentally over the side of the bed and eases to her feet, she discovers to her enormous joy that she feels great.

"I'm all better," she says exultantly to her man.

"It's about time," he replies quite succinctly.

And it *is* about time. Because some people have the 24-hour bug for 72 hours, and some have it for 48. But a mother, if she feels needed enough, can get over it in 12.

The Day I Was Fired

Most of us have had a turning point in our careers, but maybe not quite like this

BY **EDDIE CANTOR**

Originally published in October 1955

've been in show business most of my life, which, at the moment, totals 63 years. Most people find it difficult to visualize me as anything but the popeyed performer who's been around "forever." I realized this when my grandson Michael, age 15, was discussing his future. "I don't seem to know what I want to do," he sighed. "It was different with you, Gramps—you always knew you wanted show business."

The truth is that when I left school the only thing I knew about show business was that it cost the price of two salami sandwiches to go to Tony Pastor's theater on 14th Street, and while I loved vaudeville,

I loved salami sandwiches more. Show business never entered my head.

Things were a little rugged at home, and I had to go to work when I was in my early teens. I landed a steady job at a fine salary ($5 a week) as an office boy for Weir Brothers, brokers. Between chores I often thought about Surprise Lake Camp at Cold Spring, New York, where, three years before, I had been sent for a two weeks' vacation. My first day in camp was a revelation. Such trees! Such grass! Never had I seen so much green outside a poolroom! And when I read a sign on the bulletin board, "If you can entertain in any way

119

sign your name below," I was the first one in line.

Around a campfire, this kid from the lower East Side gave out with a high soprano on the big hit of the day, "Harrigan." I was completely at ease and quite unaware of the humor lent the lyrics by a little Jewish boy bellowing, "H-a-double-r-i-g-a-n—spells Harrigan—proud

> ## *Without quite realizing how it happened, my business became show business.*

of all the Irish blood that's in me!" For the next few nights I was the camp's chief entertainer. It paid off. All the other kids left after two weeks. I was held over an extra week.

But this was only a happy memory. It had no real connection with the established "Wall Street" man that I now was. True, I was only running errands and doing other menial chores. But the day

would come when I'd be somebody in the brokerage business, when I'd stride into the office with brisk authority, like Mr. J.C. Weir: in the winter, wearing a fur-collared coat; in the summer, with a boutonniere in my lapel and sporting a cane.

Destiny destroyed these dreams 50 years ago on a Friday afternoon. When the door closed behind J.C. Weir as he left the office for the weekend, something snapped in me. Grabbing a little fur jacket that belonged to one of the girls, I leaped on a long conference table, strutted, sang, danced and rolled my eyes in an exaggerated imitation of the then-current Broadway rave, Anna Held, doing her famous number, "I Just Can't Make My Eyes Behave."

Laughter burst out, then applause. All work ceased. Spurred on by this enthusiastic reception, I sang louder, danced faster and nearly swiveled my eyes out of their sockets. At the height of my frenzied efforts, I became aware of a sudden silence and a scurrying of feet. Before I could turn around, a familiar voice bellowed in my ear: "You're fired!"

J.C. Weir had returned for his briefcase. I stumbled off the table and tried to explain but, with justifiable indignation, he refused to listen. He just kept yelling: "Out! Out! Get out!"

I started to get my hat, but Mr. Weir's look stopped me. I changed course abruptly and ran through the door. I was furious! Not because of the loss of my job, or my hat, but the ignominy of my dismissal. Some day I'd show that J.C. Weir!

But the day seemed far away indeed. The only job I could get was in Coney Island, as a singing waiter. Without quite realizing how it happened, my business became show business. I forgot Wall Street and Weir Brothers.

Some years later, in June of 1917, on the opening night of my first Ziegfeld Follies, the doorman delivered a card to my dressing room. It read "J.C. Weir." I was elated. Imagine! To see me, he had to buy a ticket—a ticket that cost more than my whole week's salary when I'd worked for him.

My ex-boss was ushered into the dressing room and, before a word was said, he handed me a fine leather hatbox in which I found a high silk hat. We both laughed. "This," he said, "is to replace the hat you didn't get when you left our firm."

Although half a century has passed, I've always been grateful to J.C. Weir, who booted me from Wall Street to Broadway.

The Killer Among Us

*An arsenic poisoning sends a small
New England church into turmoil*

—

BY **MAX ALEXANDER**

Originally published in January 2004

The potato fields that roll up to the edge of New Sweden were still dusted with snow on Sunday, April 27, 2003. Even by the standards of northern Maine it had been a tough winter, and the old furnace in the parsonage of the Gustaf Adolph Evangelical Lutheran Church was giving up the ghost. The church council had gathered after services to decide who would install a new heater. Council member Dick Ruggles, a 64-year-old retired ironworker, grabbed a cup of coffee and headed into the meeting.

He lasted about five minutes. "I asked a question of one of the members," says Ruggles, "and before he could answer, I had to leave and go to the men's room." When the vomiting briefly let up, Ruggles staggered out to find his wife, who had been chatting over coffee in the kitchen with Erich Margeson. "Fran," he said, "I have to go home now!"

Home was a white clapboard farmhouse just up the road, but Fran had to stop the car twice for Dick. Once there, the violent nausea continued, and severe diarrhea added to Dick's woes. When Fran went into the bedroom

The Gustaf Adolph Evangelical Lutheran Church overlooks the town of New Sweden, Maine.

to change out of her church clothes, she suddenly felt sick herself. "I didn't make it back to the bathroom," she says. "I just could not stop vomiting."

Sometime between three and four that afternoon, the phone rang. It was Erich Margeson's wife, Alana, calling to say she'd just taken Erich to the hospital. Erich, a 30-year-old potato farmer, was also violently ill. Soon came another call: Dale Anderson, who had been at church, was sick too. When Barb Bondeson called around five, Dick and Fran were too ill to speak. Barb called Fran's sister, Julie Adler, who had skipped church that day. She raced over with her son, who had to carry Dick to the car.

With a population that hovers just over 600, New Sweden has no hospital of its own. Fortunately, an emergency room is just 8 miles away, in the town of Caribou. Staffers at the Cary Medical Center take pride in their high-tech point-of-care service. But Cary's greatest asset is its close relationship with the community. Its doctors know their patients from the local cross-country ski trails, not the medical charts. With only 37 beds and a small staff of nurses, Cary is set up for car accidents and cardiac arrests—not outbreaks of violent illness.

Yet an outbreak is exactly what Cary had by Sunday evening, as a total of 12 church members showed up retching and gasping. Patty Carson, the hospital's infection control officer, remembers, "My first thought was *Some poor old lady who made the potato salad is gonna be so upset.*" Thinking fast, Carson alerted the state's Bureau of Health to a possible food poisoning in New Sweden. Then she grabbed a notepad and headed for the patient wards, looking for answers.

It didn't take long for Carson to change her mind about the cause of the outbreak. The patients had eaten a variety of food in the church kitchen—tuna sandwiches, sponge cake, banana bread with icing— most of it left over from a bake sale the day before. The only common denominator was the coffee; every patient had sipped a cup, and they all recalled it tasted funny—"bitter," "metallic" or just plain "bad." And all got sick within an hour of drinking the brew. As a microbiologist, Carson knew that food-borne organisms typically take several hours or more to cause illness. And she doubted that any dangerous bacteria could thrive in the hot, acidic environment of a coffee urn.

Daniel Harrigan, the ER physician on duty, was coming to the same conclusion. "These people had blood pressures that were much lower than you would expect from food poisoning," he says. The most critical patient was Reid Morrill, the church's head usher and a beloved local character known for his homemade ice cream and for once hitting a hole in one at the Caribou Country Club. Morrill, 78, was still recovering from cardiac bypass surgery earlier in the year. Dr. Harrigan golfed with Morrill; now his links partner was hooked up to a ventilator. Recalls Harrigan: "I told Patty that this has to be a poisoning of some sort, and to call the poison center."

The patients at the hospital said that they all had coffee and that it tasted funny.

Arsenic was once used as a top killer by local farmers.

Morrill was one of four patients, including Fran Ruggles, admitted to Cary that night. Margeson and four others felt well enough after a few hours to go home. Convinced they were not contagious (and facing a shortage of beds), the hospital released them. Three additional patients, Dick Ruggles among them, needed more serious care but were stable enough to be transferred to the closest acute-care facility, Eastern Maine Medical Center in Bangor, 170 miles south.

As the hospital in Bangor was preparing to receive the patients, another medical team was swinging into action at the Northern New England Poison Center in Portland, 300 miles downstate. Anthony Tomassoni, the center's medical director, had been studying the charts of all the New Sweden patients. It was a little after 3 o'clock Monday morning when he called Dr. Harrigan. "I'm thinking heavy metals," he said. The toxicologist thought that some New Sweden patients were experiencing a condition known as acidosis, resulting from the body's inability to use oxygen effectively. That could be caused by lead or by antimony (an element that is in batteries), but arsenic was at the top of his list. "At the same time," remembers Dr. Tomassoni, "we thought, jeez, arsenic in northern Maine, what are the chances?"

Plenty, it turned out. Arsenic was once commonly used in potato farming as a so-called top killer. A week before the harvest, farmers would spray a dilution of inorganic arsenic on the plants' bushy green tops to kill them off—allowing the potato skins to toughen. Farmers use fewer poisonous herbicides now, but it would not be unusual to find jars of powdered arsenic in barns around potato country.

Shortly after Dr. Harrigan and Dr. Tomassoni got off the phone, Reid Morrill died. Louise Beaupre, wife of another victim, recalled that only a week before, Morrill, still ailing from heart surgery, had said, "I don't know if I'm ever gonna feel OK." She had responded, "Of course you will." The next Sunday, she says, "He was all pink cheeks, smiling and laughing. I said 'I think somebody's feeling better!' And he said 'Yep, I am.' And I can still see him standing there with a cup of coffee in his hand."

Morrill's death triggered the attention of the state medical examiner, as well as the national news media. The case was gaining urgency.

Arsenic can be identified only with specialized equipment. The nearest lab with that capability was the state's Health and Environmental Testing Laboratory in the capital of Augusta—230 miles south of Caribou. Early Monday, a state trooper left Cary Medical Center with the patients' fluid samples, his siren wailing down Interstate 95. Also in the back of his cruiser was the coffee urn from the Gustaf Adolph Lutheran Church.

The results came back at about 8 o'clock Monday night: Inconceivably high levels of arsenic were found in all the patient samples, as well as the coffee. Dr. Tomassoni was too shocked to congratulate himself on his diagnosis. "I never thought I would see something like this in my career," he says. That's when the state police were notified.

Lt. Dennis Appleton of the Maine State Police Criminal Investigation Division is not the type to jump to conclusions. Rather than assume the worst, he hoped his investigation would uncover an innocent, albeit tragic, explanation.

On Tuesday, Appleton had the church sealed off and a team of detectives on-site. The search was unsettling. "After several days of examining the church from basement to attic," Appleton recalls, "we found nothing that would have contributed to an accidental poisoning—no jar of arsenic in the cupboard that had been mistaken for the sugar bowl."

When Fran Ruggles heard she had been poisoned with arsenic, she assumed it was environmental: "We'd had a lot of rain and snow. I thought it must be in the water." Dr. Tomassoni knew otherwise, estimating the level of poison would have required "a fistful or two" of pure powdered arsenic dumped directly into the coffee urn. Detectives began interviewing patients—now victims—about possible motives. None of them had a clue. Recalls Fran, "I just could not accept the fact that this was done deliberately."

She wasn't alone. In a state famous for insular small towns, New Sweden is in a class by itself. The community was founded in 1870 by 50 Swedish homesteaders, lured across the sea by the promise of free land and a new life. New Sweden is still largely populated by descendants of those settlers; about half of the 16 arsenic victims are Swedish. With its Midsommar celebration and *fiskare frukosts* (fisherman's breakfasts), the town retains closer ties to Sweden than to mainstream America.

Even tighter than the community is the congregation at the Gustaf Adolph church, built on a hill overlooking New Sweden by the original settlers in 1880. The picturesque chapel, with its steeple rising above farm and forest, is the oldest active Lutheran church in Maine. To many, the idea that a member of the small congregation (46 people attended church that Sunday) had poisoned them was unthinkable. Fran Ruggles echoed the feeling of the group when she told detectives, "You're going to have to prove it to me."

Doctors at Cary Medical Center had little time to ponder motivation. Once arsenic was diagnosed, all the patients who were released the night before had to be called back for additional treatment. And as the day progressed, new patients started showing up—some who had sipped a tiny bit of coffee and not gotten sick (tests showed potentially fatal doses of arsenic in them as well), and others, like carpenter Lester Beaupre, 53, who initially thought he had the flu.

Beaupre, a Vietnam veteran who once spent nine weeks in the hospital with meningitis, wasn't about to go to the emergency room for a little stomach bug. He spent Sunday night at home, his wife, Louise (who has never tasted coffee in her life), keeping him hydrated with Gatorade. On Monday, says Louise, "when they called and told me about Reid's death, I said to Lester, 'OK, this is it. Put your clothes on.'" On the way to the hospital, Lester remembers, the snowbanks looked purple. "That's when I knew this was serious," he recalls.

Arsenic travels rapidly to every organ in the body, where it slows the conversion of oxygen to energy. Without energy, the heart's electrical

Lester and Louise Beaupre

activity falters, lungs fill with fluid, kidneys fail, nerve tissue is damaged and the brain starts to short-circuit. Arsenic can affect almost anything and everything in the anatomy, which is why symptoms can range from cardiac arrest to seeing purple snow.

The most effective proven antidote is a drug known as British anti-lewisite, or BAL. It attaches to the arsenic molecules, drawing them out of the bloodstream and into the urine. It's a nasty drug to administer; the only way to ingest BAL is by mixing it with peanut oil, then injecting the greasy solution directly into muscle tissue—an excruciating ordeal.

"My faith is strong, I know God pulled me through," said Ralph Ostlund, outside the Gustaf Adolph Evangelical Lutheran Church in New Sweden. He drank arsenic-laced coffee April 27, 2003.

It's also expensive, costing hundreds of dollars per dose. The price and the rarity of arsenic poisoning explain why BAL is not lying around on hospital pharmacy shelves. But with foresight that now seems miraculous, in the wake of the 2001 terrorist attacks Dr. Tomassoni had persuaded Maine's Bureau of Health to purchase BAL doses for the state's largest hospitals.

As the victims endured painful treatment and round-the-clock fluid testing, more bad news came on Friday: Church member Daniel Bondeson, a 53-year-old bachelor potato farmer, nurse's aide and high school ski coach, fatally shot himself in the chest. In his farmhouse, where he was discovered by his brother Carl, was a note in which he implicated himself in the tragedy, according to police.

The victims were stunned. "Danny was a friend of ours," says Dick Ruggles. Lester Beaupre had gone to high school with Bondeson; he still describes him as "probably the nicest person you'll ever meet."

Bondeson, a former member of the church council, was a quiet man but active in the community. Dr. Harrigan had run in races with him. Another victim, Ralph Ostlund, often skied with him. Says Erich Margeson, "Danny was always interested in helping people if they had a problem."

Louise Beaupre, who describes Bondeson as "pleasant but shy," says, "My feeling is he just snapped. There's no logical reason. It's beyond comprehension."

But why?

"We're all scratching our heads," Erich explains. Police have not released the text of Bondeson's suicide letter. But Alan Harding, an attorney representing Bondeson's estate, told local newspapers that in the note Bondeson said he wanted to give five church members a "bellyache" like they had given him. Harding also said the note indicated Bondeson did not know the poison was arsenic. Lieutenant Appleton won't comment on Harding's statements except to stress that the lawyer has not personally seen the letter. One theory is that Bondeson was angry because his family had given the church a communion table that wasn't being used. "There were some hurt feelings," says one church member. But arsenic? "It's hard to think about," says Erich Margeson.

As the community struggled to understand, police dropped another bomb: Bondeson, they said, without offering additional details, did not act alone. Church members say they have no idea why police would have come to this conclusion. Anyone could have entered the unlocked church kitchen during the Saturday bake sale or before Sunday service. When residents of New Sweden, many of whom didn't even own keys, were advised to start locking their doors, and a police guard was posted at the hospital, Alana Margeson says, "the air in the community was so heavy."

Months later, New Sweden hadn't lightened up much, and detectives were no closer to an arrest, although they said they had one or more suspects.

Meanwhile, doctors can only speculate on the survivors' long-term prognosis; elevated cancer risk is one scary possibility. Fran Ruggles had a painful outbreak of shingles that lasted weeks. Dick still has back pain that might be

"We're not innocent anymore," says one church member.

nerve-related. And many survivors deal daily with crushing fatigue. Lester Beaupre was the last victim to be released from the hospital, almost five weeks after the poisoning. The tubes that kept him alive injured his throat, and he had a tracheotomy during his hospital stay. He still feels numbness in his face and extremities.

The community is also numb. "We're not innocent anymore,"

says Louise Beaupre. Healing, in every sense of the word, will take time. On a bright summer Sunday four months after the poisoning, victims were again gathering with their neighbors to pray at Gustaf Adolph church. Fran Ruggles helped serve communion as sunlight filtered through the church's stained-glass windows. Erich Margeson, Lester Beaupre and other victims recited from the Book of Psalms: "Who among you loves life and desires long life to enjoy prosperity?" At the bottom of the day's prayer list was the simple line "For the arsenic victims." And resting on the counter of the adjoining kitchen, plainly visible from the pews, was a new coffee urn.

It is an uncomfortable reminder of the tragedy, but more visceral is the knowledge that Danny Bondeson's potential accomplice could be in the next pew. That makes worship understandably difficult, even for the most forgiving of souls. Admits Lester Beaupre, "You look around at church and wonder who did it."

Goblins, Go Home!

*Tricks and treats and a little bit of magic
is all it takes for a successful Halloween*

BY **WILL STANTON**

Originally published in October 1968

Ever notice the way Halloween is going downhill? Used to be a great time for kids. Tip things over. Throw stuff around. Not anymore. They put on costumes, collect candy bars, bubble gum. End of fun.

Decided to do something about it. Explained to Maggie, my wife. "Oh, my God!" she observed. Only harmless pranks, I told her. Soap windows. Throw rotten tomatoes. Maggie said where do you find rotten tomatoes? Good point. Told her we'd use fresh ones. She said at 49 cents a pound why not just throw money? Dropped subject.

Halloween. Offered to take boys, Barney and Pete, into town. Good place for trick-or-treat. Barney dressed as clown. Pete as pirate. Plastic pails. Identification tag on each costume. My name—address— phone number. Good thinking.

Parked car in middle of block. Let kids collect treats. Last house, man gave them pumpkin jack-o'- lantern. I told them enough treats. Time for tricks. Gave each a bar of soap to draw on windows. Skull and crossbones—scarecrows. Kids came back, said couldn't reach windows. Always excuses.

Moved on. Pete said don't forget pumpkin. I hadn't. Hoped he had. Forty pounds and slippery. Also carrying Barney's hat and Pete's mask. Stopped at house, gave boys pins to stick in doorbell. No doorbell. Next house same deal. Asked boys what they'd like to do. Said go to bathroom. Told them wait until we got home. No dice.

Problem of walking up to strange house—ask to use bathroom. Couldn't do it. Woman could. Man no. Can't explain.

Looked around. Neon light in distance. Emil's Bar and Grill. Told boys follow me. Any port in a storm. Pretty ratty-looking port. Showed kids men's room. Put pails on bar. Also hat, mask, pumpkin. Ordered drink. Hate to use men's room without buying something.

Solitary drinker couple of stools away. Red face, necktie loose. Heard him speak to bartender— Emil. Remark about big kid not satisfied with one pail, spoils it for the others. Emil brought drink. Asked which pail I wanted it in. Told him never mind the comedy. Red-faced man moved over, asked if I minded personal question. "How come you're wearing pirate mask with clown hat? What the hell you supposed to be?"

Didn't know what was keeping boys. Sounded to me like somebody outside was singing hymns. Women's voices. Emil looked at watch. Said, "Starting early tonight." He could hear them too. Glad of that. Emil explained. Group of church ladies trying to get saloon closed. Picketed place every evening. Sang hymns. Read about it in paper.

Boys came out of the restroom. Put them on stools. Ordered ginger ale for them. Reviewed situation. Ladies outside singing "Rock of Ages." Bad time to walk out of saloon with two children. Unfavorable impressions. Only one solution. Put on mask and clown hat. Gave boys pails. Picked up pumpkin. Outside, mask fell off. Singing stopped. Ladies stared. Flashbulb went off—man from local paper. More flashbulbs, comments from ladies. Left quietly.

Boys wanted more trick-or-treats. Said they'd meet me at the car. Let them go. Went around corner to car. Not there. Possibly not right place. Tried next block. Other blocks. Checked all pirates and clowns. Not many out, raining too hard. Time for decisive action. Call Maggie. Ask her what to do.

Went up to house. Rang bell. Asked man if I could use phone. Man said well he'd be son of a gun. Woman called out who was it. "Pagliacci," man called back. I'd forgotten about clown hat. "I'll hold your pumpkin," he said, indicating phone in hall.

Maggie answered. "What happened? The boys said you were supposed to meet them at the car."

I said, "You mean Barney and Pete?"

She said yes, those were the ones she meant. "When you didn't show up they telephoned and I borrowed the Jacksons' car and drove into town and picked them up."

Told her it was slight misunderstanding. Asked her where she had picked them up. Precisely. Told her I'd be right home.

Found car OK. Home. Boys still up. Maggie looked at me. Asked what caused all the foam. Told her not foam—soapsuds. "While the boys were waiting by the car they soaped the windshield. Had to drive home with head out the window. What with the rain and the soap—"

Maggie said I must be proud of the boys. Chips off the old block. Told her soaping the family windows didn't count. Supposed to play pranks on others. Barney said they did. In bar restroom. Threw toilet paper. Wrote on mirror.

Told Barney he hadn't learned to write yet. Said no, but he'd learned to print. Copied his identification tag on mirror. My name, address.

Barney said how come my face looked so funny? Glanced in mirror. Dye from wet clown hat. Orange streaks from forehead to chin. Maggie said don't annoy the tiger, and took kids upstairs. Poured myself a drink. Poured two. One might spill.

Maggie came downstairs. "You were right about Halloween," she said. "I never really appreciated it before. The way the boys were talking made me realize there was something special about it—a sort of magic."

She had a point. How else was I going to explain my photo in the paper, coming out of a bar with two kids? Wearing clown hat. Carrying pumpkin. Ladies singing.

"Magic is the only word," I said.

"Can't Anyone Hear Me?"

The patient was in a coma—all the doctors said so. The only person who disagreed? The patient.

———

BY **TOM HALLMAN**

Originally published in September 2017

ichard Marsh awakened to the rhythmic beeping of a machine. Something was lodged in his throat. He couldn't cough. He couldn't sit up. He couldn't move.

What's going on?

He tried to move his legs, arms and fingers. Even his eyeballs, he realized, wouldn't budge. He felt someone put drops in them to keep them moist, but he couldn't make out who it was.

What's wrong with me?

He could only stare in one direction—straight ahead.

With his peripheral vision, Richard could see his wife off to his right. He heard her talking to a man next to her, a man who seemed to be in surgical scrubs.

"It doesn't look good," the man said.

What doesn't look good?

"His chance of survival is very small."

They're talking about me.

Richard willed his body to respond: with his voice, his eyes, his hand. Nothing.

"You need to prepare for the worst," the man in scrubs told Richard's wife, Liliana Garcia. Though somber, she didn't cry. A registered nurse at a hospice center, she quickly turned

professional, asking the doctor clinical questions as if the man in the bed were just another patient, not the love of her life.

I'm in here.

And then his world faded to black.

❖ ❖ ❖

He hadn't felt well two mornings before. Liliana noticed he looked a little pale. But Richard didn't want her hovering and fussing over him as if he were her patient. He said he'd be fine and insisted she go to work. That was his way. Once alone, Richard relaxed on the couch before he had to leave for school. He taught forensic science and economics near his home in Napa, California, and he was considered one of the high school's popular teachers.

He stood up, ready to leave for work, when he felt as if he were on the deck of a small boat in choppy seas. He grabbed the edge of a table and made his way to the telephone. He called his wife's office and left a message for her to call him.

Richard sat back in a chair at his desk. Something was wrong

with him. He rarely drank, never smoked and really was in great shape. At 60 years old, he stood 6 feet, 2 inches tall and weighed 215 pounds. He pumped iron at the gym, a habit he'd started during his first career, as a police officer.

The phone rang—Liliana calling him back. "Come home," he told her.

All Liliana heard was a garbled voice. Then she called 911.

Minutes later, Richard was rushed to the hospital in an ambulance. Numbness had started in his feet and crept up his legs to his waist. He felt himself losing control of his muscles. He couldn't swallow. To save him, an ER team put him under and inserted a breathing tube down his throat. He was then given medication to fight a stroke that doctors believed was being caused by a clot.

After doctors did what they could, nurses wheeled Richard to intensive care. And then they waited.

❖ ❖ ❖

Once he had awakened, even though he was paralyzed, Richard

felt sensations when doctors and nurses touched him.

I don't feel sick. I just can't move.

Richard heard the blunt diagnosis: a 2% survival rate.

———

Slowly, he realized he was trapped in a prison that was his body. He heard the doctor explain to Liliana that her husband was in a coma. Richard heard the blunt diagnosis: a 2% survival rate. "If he lives, expect severe brain damage … Little hope … Best outcome is that he survives but lingers in a vegetative state … You need to consider taking him off life support," Richard recalls hearing the doctor say.

He remembered the conversation he and Liliana had had three years earlier, when they got married. They discussed end-of-life scenarios. They agreed that if, God forbid, either of them required life support for whatever reason, the other

spouse needed to pull the plug, out of compassion and love.

Richard heard his daughters' voices. Distant. Perhaps in a hallway? Liliana told the doctor she needed to discuss the issue with her husband's daughters, adult children from a previous marriage.

I guess I'm dying.

Liliana returned. The family, she told the doctor, had agreed to wait a few days to see how Richard progressed. The girls, she explained, weren't ready to let their father go. Nor was she prepared to lose her husband.

Throughout the day, friends came and stood by Richard's bed. They talked about old times. They told him they loved him and how good he looked.

His daughters came with the grandkids. As they leaned toward his face, Richard saw the tears in their eyes, even as they shared words of encouragement.

No. I'm here!

He felt lips on his forehead. A character in a macabre scene in a horror movie, Richard had only his thoughts to keep him occupied. He'd never go home again, teach or kiss his wife. He'd lie in a hospital bed—the ultimate solitary confinement—for years. Or his family would sign the papers and wait by his side as the doctors did what was necessary to let him slip away.

Richard heard the staff talking and laughing in the hallway. Life, the everyday life he'd taken for

> ## *"Has anyone checked to see if he's in there? Rich, if you can hear me, blink your eyes."*

granted, was so close and yet so far away.

Perhaps death would be a blessing, he concluded. Richard accepted the inevitable. He resigned himself to the end.

If it's going to happen, let it happen.

The next morning, a neurologist stopped in the ICU and huddled with other doctors at his bedside. Richard heard part of the

conversation: "Has anyone checked to see if he's in there?"

The neurologist leaned over, so close that Richard could feel the man's breath on his cheek: "Rich, if you can hear me, blink your eyes."

Blink … Try …

When Richard was a cop, he was trained to deal with scary events head-on. But now … What if he couldn't blink? He drew on the cop inside, the strong man, the rock. He was good with victims, those suffering tremendous loss. In this instance, Richard Marsh was the victim.

Blink!

And then … a blink so excruciatingly slow that the neurologist couldn't be sure what he'd seen.

"Rich, blink your eyes again. Can you hear me?"

A … blink.

They knew.

❖ ❖ ❖

Extensive tests revealed that Richard had suffered from a congenital anomaly in one of two arteries in his brain. One artery was fully formed but blocked. The other artery had never formed, an undiagnosed birth defect that hadn't caused Richard problems until now.

With the blood supply compromised by that blockage, Richard had suffered a brain stem stroke. The stem, which connects the brain to the spinal cord, controls nearly all bodily functions. His heart was beating, but there was virtually nothing that Richard could voluntarily will his body to do.

With Liliana by his side, doctors explained that Richard suffered from locked-in syndrome, meaning he was literally locked in his body.

They asked him questions: Blink once for yes, twice for no. It took extraordinary effort for Richard to get his eyes to work.

Up to 70% of people diagnosed with the syndrome die within a short period of time. Of those who do survive, only a handful recover enough to lead a normal life.

But before he could even hope for such an outcome, Richard would have to endure some new terrors.

❖ ❖ ❖

Richard was moved from the ICU to a hospital where specialists would let his body decide the course of the treatment. Because he could not swallow, doctors performed a tracheotomy, making an incision in his windpipe and inserting a tube so Richard could breathe and nurses could suction out the saliva that would otherwise drain into his lungs.

Horrible. But they know I'm here.

To help Richard communicate more easily, Liliana bought a letter board for the family to hold in front of him. The board had four quadrants, each containing several lines with five letters in each line, and an empty box in the middle to write his message in. Richard would look at the board. His family would have to follow his eyes to the correct quadrant.

This corner? A blink.
First line? Two blinks.
This letter? Two blinks.
Second line? Blink.
This letter? Two blinks.
Every word, slowly spelled out.

As tough as the days were, the nights, after his family had gone home, were hell. The staff didn't use the board, nor were they constantly around to take care of his every need. Trapped, Richard was alone and scared. Fluids built up in his throat, choking him, and no one was around to suction them out for him. His roommate heard him

Emotionally, Richard no longer got easily irritated or worried over the little things.

struggling to breathe and used his call button to get the nurses to help.

When his family arrived one morning, Richard looked wildly at the letter board. Slowly, he made his wishes known: *Get me out of here.*

Days later, his wife moved him to a hospital closer to their home. Physical and occupational therapists started to work with him more aggressively, trying to get his body to function fully again.

Days passed.
There's no returning to normal.
Then weeks.
Hardest thing I've done in my life.

Then one day it happened— Richard moved the big toe on his left foot. Two weeks later, he moved his head side to side. Days later, he wiggled a foot. After another day or two had passed, he could shake his legs. His family members cried, laughed and hugged one another with each new victory.

More than two months after his locked-in diagnosis, Richard did something he'd taken for granted his entire life—he raised his hand and touched his nose. And then he walked, a big toddler taking the first few wobbly steps, rocking from side to side with his walker to keep his balance as he slowly made his way from his bed to the door of his room and back, a therapist close by his side in case he fell.

Exactly four months and nine days after the stroke, after more painful and painstaking rehab, Richard Marsh walked through the front door of his home under his own power. He sat in his chair. He was back.

❖ ❖ ❖

Richard was forever changed. He'd lost 50 pounds of muscle, and when he came home he was so weak that he couldn't lift a carton of milk. Physically, he rebuilt his life. It took a year, but he returned to his fighting weight, back pumping iron at the gym.

Emotionally, Richard no longer got easily irritated or worried over the little things. He became less controlling. He even retired from teaching and took over the household duties while Liliana continued to work. He found pleasure in life's simplicity.

Someone gave him the book *The Diving Bell and the Butterfly,* the memoir of Jean-Dominique Bauby, a journalist who suffered a stroke and remained locked in for the rest of his life. Bauby dictated his story to his publisher's editorial assistant by blinking his one good eye in response to an alphabet rearranged by how often letters are used. He died two days after the book was published. Richard read two chapters and promptly gave the book away. Unlike Bauby, Richard was very much alive.

He would never forget waking up in the ICU and the long journey to escape his prison. He'd been given a second chance, a precious second chance. He vowed, daily, to never squander the gift.

The Bear Who Came to Dinner

Wild animals can bond with humans, but this 7-foot Goliath had claws that could shred a tree. He also had a remarkably understanding nature.

BY **ROBERT FRANKLIN LESLIE**

Originally published in December 1964

met Bosco in the remote wilderness near Mount Robson in western Canada. At the end of a long day of backpacking, I had made a lean-to in a clearing beside a stream and was preparing to catch supper. Then I looked up, and there he was: an enormous boar black bear, slowly circling the clearing within 30 yards.

He wasn't Bosco to me yet, and I viewed his presence with trepidation. My provisions were vulnerable if he was in a piratical mood, since I was unarmed. However, I decided to go about my fishing. The bear came along.

I've lived with wild creatures for 30 years, respecting their first fear—fast movements—so I let him see every slow, deliberate move I made. Soon he was sitting on his haunches less than 5 feet away, intensely interested in my activity. When I landed a 14-inch Loch Leven trout, I tossed it to him.

Anyone who spots a black bear should be extremely cautious.

He gulped without bothering to chew. And when I flipped out the fly again, he moved closer, planted his well-upholstered fanny on the turf beside my boot and leaned half his 500 pounds against my right leg!

When darkness set in, I was still fishing for that bear, fascinated as much by his gentle manners as by his insatiable capacity. I began to think of him in a friendly way as Big Bosco, and I didn't mind when he followed me back to camp.

After supper I built up the fire, sat on the sleeping bag under the

The author photo from *Miracle at Square Top Mountain* (1979)

lean-to and lit my pipe. All this time Bosco had sat just outside the heat perimeter of the fire, but the moment I was comfortably settled he walked over and sat down beside me. Overlooking the stench of wet fur, I rather enjoyed his warmth as we sat on the sleeping bag under the shelter. I listened to rain thumping on the tarp in time with the steady, powerful *cur-rump, cur-rump* of his heartbeat beneath his thick coat. When smoke blew our way, he snorted and sneezed, and I imitated most of his body movements, even the sneezing and snorting, swaying my head in every direction, sniffing the air as he did.

Then Bosco began licking my hands. Guessing what he wanted, I got him a handful of salt. He nailed my hand to the ground with his 4-inch claws—claws capable of peeling the bark from a full-grown cedar, claws that carried his 500-odd pounds at full gallop to the top of the tallest tree, claws that could rip a man's body like a band saw. Finally the last grain of salt was gone, and again we sat together. I wondered if this could be for real.

Bosco stood up on all fours, burped a long, fishy belch and stepped out into the rainy blackness. But he soon was back—with a message. He sat down near the sleeping bag and attempted to scratch that area of his rump just above his tail, but he couldn't reach it. Again and again he nudged me and growled savagely at the itch. Finally I got the message and laid a light hand on his back. He flattened out to occupy the total 7 feet of the lean-to as I began to scratch through the dense, oily hair.

Then the full significance of his visit hit me. Just above his stubby tail, several gorged ticks were dangerously embedded in swollen flesh. When I twisted out the first parasite, I thought I was in for a mauling—his roar shook the forest. But I determined to finish the job. Each time I removed a tick, I showed it to him for a sniff before dropping it on the fire, and by the last one he was licking my hand.

A cold, sniffling nose awakened me several times during the night as the bear came and went. He left the sleeping bag wetter and muddier

Leslie's breakthrough book

each time he crawled around over me, but he never put his full weight down when he touched any part of my body.

The next day I set off again, over a ridge, down through a chilly river, up the next crest, through thickets of birch and alder, and down a wide, north-running river canyon. To my surprise, Bosco followed like a faithful dog, digging grubs or bulbs when I stopped to rest. That evening, I fished for Bosco's supper.

❖   ❖   ❖

As the days passed and I hiked north, I used a system of trout, salt and scratch rewards to teach the bear to respond to the call "Bosco!" One evening, he walked over to the log where I was enjoying my pipe and began to dig at my boots. When I stood up, he led me straight to a dead hollow bee tree at which he clawed unsuccessfully. Returning to camp, I covered my head with mosquito netting; tied shirt, pants and glove openings; and got the hatchet. I built a smoke fire near the base of the tree and hacked away until the hollow shell crashed to earth, split wide open and exposed the hive's total summer production. For my understanding and efforts, I received three stinging welts. Bosco ate 20 pounds of honeycomb and beebread and hundreds of bees. He snored most of that night at the foot of the sleeping bag.

At campsites, Bosco never tolerated long periods of relaxation and reflection, and true to my sucker form where animals are concerned, I babied his every whim.

When he wanted his back scratched, I scratched; when he wanted a fish dinner, I fished; when he wanted to romp and roll with me in the meadow, I romped and rolled— and still wear scars to prove that he played games consummately out of my league.

During one particularly rough session, I tackled his right front leg, bowling him over on his back. As I sat on his belly regaining wind, he retaliated with a left hook that not only opened a 2-inch gash down the front of my chin but also spun me across the meadow. When I woke up, Bosco was licking my wound. His shame and remorse were inconsolable. He sat down with his ears back and bawled like a whipped pup when I put my arm around his neck and repeated all the soft ursine vocabulary he had taught me.

It is not my intention to either attribute character traits to the bear that he could not possess or exaggerate those he had. I simply studied him for what he was and saw him manifest only the normal qualities of his species, which were formidable enough without

Leslie realized afterward what Bosco was communicating.

exaggeration. Other than calling him Bosco, I never attempted human training upon him. On the contrary; I did everything possible to train myself to be a brother bear.

❖   ❖   ❖

The affection we developed for each other was spontaneous and genuinely brotherly. When it occurred to him to waddle over my way on his hind legs, grab me up in a bear hug and express an overflowing emotion with a face licking, I went along with it for two reasons. First, I was crazy about that varmint. Second, I

nourished a healthy respect for what one swat from the ambidextrous giant could accomplish.

Although his size and strength made Bosco almost invulnerable to attack by other animals, he had his own phobias. Thunder and lightning made him cringe and whine. When whisky jacks flew into camp looking for food, he fled in terror, the cacophonic birds power-diving and pecking him out of sight.

Bosco's phenomenal sense of smell amazed me. Trudging along behind me, he would suddenly stop, sniff the air and make a beeline for a big, succulent mushroom 200 yards away, to a flat rock across the river under which chipmunks had warehoused their winter seed supply, or to a berry patch two ridges over.

One afternoon when we were crossing a heath where dwarf willows grew in hedgelike clumps, Bosco suddenly reared up and let out a "Maw!" I could detect no reason for alarm, but Bosco stood erect and forbade me to move. He advanced, began to snarl—and pandemonium broke out. Every clump of willows sprouted an upright bear! Black bear, brown bear, cinnamon bear and one champagne (all subdivisions of the same species).

But these were young bears, 2-year-olds, and no match for Bosco. He charged his closest contestant with the fury of a Sherman tank, and before the 2-year-old could pick himself up, Bosco dispatched a second bear and tore into a thicket to dislodge a third. At the end of the circuit, my gladiator friend remembered me and scoured back, unscathed and still champion.

That night, we sat longer than usual at the campfire. Bosco nudged, pawed, talked at great length and looked me long in the eye before allowing me to retire. In my ignorance, I assumed it was a rehash of that afternoon's battle. He was gone most of the night.

Along toward next midafternoon, I sensed something was wrong. Bosco didn't forage but clung to my heels. I was looking over a streamside campsite when the big bear about-faced and broke into a headlong, swinging lope up the hill we had just descended. I didn't call to him as he went over the crest full steam without once looking back.

That evening, I cooked supper with one eye on the hillside, then lay awake for hours waiting for the familiar nudge. By morning, I was desolated: I knew I should never again see big brother Bosco. He left behind a relationship I shall treasure.

Robert Franklin Leslie wrote 10 books about his adventures in the wild. His most famous, The Bears and I, *was made into a 1974 Disney movie.*

"Why Don't They Pick My Daddy Up?"

A Reader's Digest Roving Editor and expert on police matters spends time with the Michigan State Police. A "routine" police patrol one summer evening turns dramatic.

BY **KARL DETZER**

Originally published in August 1956

ur state-police car purred eastward at an easy 35 mph. We were congratulating ourselves. No accidents—yet. So far we had handed out 17 tickets, mostly to fools who had crossed the yellow center line on hills or curves.

Trooper Tony Majeski (names of persons and places in this account have been disguised), with five years behind him in the Michigan State Police, was at the wheel. Trooper Pete Jordan, just six months out of recruit school, sat beside him. Traffic, which an hour ago had been a nightmare, was thinning.

We closed our eyes to the fellow who cheated the speed limit by 5 or 6 miles an hour on the straightaway, so long as he didn't weave in and out. It was the fools and speed merchants we were after.

"The fellows who are asking for it," Trooper Majeski called them. He despised them, but he remained scrupulously polite when he "wrote them up" and gave them a summons. Polite but firm. He warned each of them of death lying just around the curve, or over the hill.

The radio under the dash chatted of crime and agony in other districts across the state. Someone had stuck up a filling station somewhere, a long way off, and other police cars were setting up a roadblock. Down

One car stood squarely on the safety island in the middle of the divided highway.

near the state line a motorcyclist had hit a bridge …

"I'd like a cup of coffee," Trooper Jordan was saying when the radio began calling our car.

"Station one-one to car eleven-five." The voice was crisp. "Man injured on Route 172 at fairgrounds. May be a fatal."

Tony Majeski spun his wheel and pressed hard on the accelerator.

His partner snapped on the crimson blinker light atop the car and tipped down the siren switch.

"How far?" I asked.

"Eight miles," Tony said. "Maybe nine."

Red blinker and high-voiced siren opened the way for us. We could see cars pulling over to the shoulder and stopping a quarter-mile ahead. The speedometer showed 90, 95. We knew that traffic would be piling up on Route 172 around what the radio described as a possible "fatal." It was our job to get there before more cars crashed.

Now a clutter of headlights ahead showed us the accident scene. We slowed, and the siren moaned wearily. One car stood squarely on the safety island in the middle of the divided highway. Farther back, dark shadows of men stood in a quiet huddle, looking down.

❖ ❖ ❖

George K. Hastings was a law-abiding citizen. He was 48 years old, lived on 3 acres that he called his farm, and worked the midnight shift in a machine shop at the county seat. Five nights a week he drove his 1951 Mercury the 10 miles to town. Tonight he had taken his wife to a movie; then she had fixed his lunchbox and he left for work at 11:10 p.m. He liked to get there early.

He did not drink, had no police record—not even for a parking violation. Two miles from his own gate, 20 minutes ago, he had been doing 45 in a 55-mph zone. He was relaxed, driving almost automatically. Then from the corner of his eye he saw a blur lurching toward him from the center island. Perhaps his reaction time was a little slow. The blur shuffled into the beam of his headlights, 20 feet in front of his car. There was a jolt. George Hastings tramped the brake. Something was flattened against his radiator. We measured afterward: It was perhaps 30 feet from the point of impact to the place the brakes caught; 105 feet beyond that, the limp thing had dropped off the front of the car.

❖ ❖ ❖

Harry Field lived in a small house about a block and a half from the railroad tracks. He was 37 years old, had been married 14 years. His family consisted of his wife, Martha; his son, Charley, age 11; and his daughter, Pat, 6. There was also a dog named Frisky.

On this summer afternoon Harry stopped off after work with some of the boys at a tavern near the auto parts factory where he got $1.75 an hour as a laborer. His time sheets showed numerous unexplained absences. This evening he did not get home until seven o'clock, two hours after he had left the plant.

His family had eaten, but his wife had kept supper warm for him and he sat down at the kitchen table. It was not until he got up that Martha noticed the bottle. It was a pint of cheap whiskey.

"You promised to take Charley to the show at the fairgrounds," she reminded him.

"Sure," he said. "Goin' to take Charley. Soon's I change clothes."

Twenty minutes later he and Charley got into Harry's 1948 jalopy and headed west. Harry bought $1.50 worth of gasoline at the corner filling station, and the attendant there "didn't see nothing unusual" in his actions.

Father and son reached the fairgrounds without mishap, and went in. But Harry complained loudly about the show. Charley said afterward that "Daddy was drinking. He stopped a couple of times behind a tent."

At 11 o'clock Harry started toward the gate. Charley had found two girls from his school and was talking with them when he saw his father leaving the grounds. The boy ran after him, but outside, in the jumble of parked cars, it was perhaps 10 minutes before he sighted him again.

"Our car's over this way," Charley said.

"Over there," Harry contradicted, and headed unsteadily toward the state highway. The boy tried to argue with him, but Harry walked about 100 feet down the edge of the road, crossed through fast, heavy traffic to the center island, and once more complained that he couldn't find his car.

Charley saw the headlights approaching. He yelled at his father and started to run toward him. But Harry stepped out on the concrete and Charley heard the awful sound.

❖   ❖   ❖

We saw the boy standing in front of the half-circle of men as we piled out of our car. Harry Field's body was sprawled face upward, the head twisted grotesquely. A small, dark pool had formed under the right shoulder on the smooth white concrete. A left shoe lay some distance away.

Trooper Majeski went down on one knee. It took only five seconds to make sure. He stood up. "Anybody know him?"

"He's my daddy." The boy's voice was tight. "Is he hurt bad? Why don't they pick him up?"

Trooper Pete Jordan, getting his first taste of a "fatal," took the lad's arm and guided him toward our car.

"Yes," he said, "your daddy is hurt very bad."

Charley gave us his name and address. We put him in the car and I climbed in beside him. The troopers passed out red flares to volunteers and told them to direct all traffic around to the opposite lanes. Charley stood up, trying to see what was happening there in the road. A young woman opened the car door and said, "My husband and I were passing. Heard about the boy. Can I help?"

I moved over. She slid her arm around Charley. I backed the police car a hundred feet, slowly, and turned it to face away from the scene of sudden death. The young woman deftly turned Charley's thought from the scene, too, for a moment, with a question about the fair. The ambulance arrived. Then the coroner. More troopers with cameras to record one more "fatal" on the road. Flashbulbs popped, and Charley wanted to know what they were doing to his daddy.

Then Tony came over to the car. Charley asked, "Is ... is he ... dead?"

Tony said gently, "I don't like to tell you this, Charley. But ... yes, he is dead."

Charley did not cry. The wonderful young woman had been talking to him, about the way troubles come to all families, and the way a big boy of 11 has to stand by his mother and help her when trouble does come.

"Charles," I began—he wasn't Charley anymore—"you'll have to help us when we tell your mother."

He sat silent a moment, swallowing. We were on our way to town now. The young woman had gone,

We heard him tell his mother that some men were there to see her.

and Trooper Pete Jordan sat with his arm around the boy. At last Charley spoke.

"Yeh," he said in his thin little voice, "I'll help."

The little house was dark. We drove into the side yard, and Charley went in through the kitchen door. We followed. We heard him tell his mother that some men were there to see her. She came in a hurry, pulling on a dressing gown, and she knew when she saw our faces what message we brought. She became hysterical, but Charley stood beside her, his face streaked with tear stains, and talked gently to her.

I hurried across the street and awakened a woman neighbor, and she ran to the little house and other neighbors followed. That's how we left them, with Charley

The enormity of his misfortune seemed to press down on him, and his shoulders sagged.

suddenly taking a man's part in the shabby little kitchen. It was his arm out now, around his sobbing mother's shoulder. It was his voice urging calm.

❖ ❖ ❖

At the police station George Hastings sat sweating. He kept shaking his head as if trying to rid his mind of the picture of a blurred something flattened against the radiator of his car. He told his

story; it was a simple story and didn't take long. He signed the statement, his hand trembling.

Trooper Tony picked up the sheet and read it carefully. The small, bare room was cold with white light from the ceiling fixture. From the doorway I watched Hastings's face. It was drawn tight; his lips were dry, and he kept wetting them with his tongue. His work shirt, open at the neck, showed the way he swallowed hard, again and again.

"You may go now," Trooper Tony said quietly. "So far as we can tell now, you were in no way to blame."

Hastings stared at him. He nodded slowly, as if trying to reassure himself.

"Not to blame," he mumbled. "No, not to blame. But," he gulped, "I ... I killed a man!"

The enormity of his misfortune seemed to press down on him, and his shoulders sagged. He did not stir from his chair, and the two troopers stood uneasily, looking at him.

"What was the little boy's name?" Hastings asked.

"Charley," Trooper Jordan replied. "Nice kid, too."

"Yeh," Hastings said, getting slowly to his feet. "How did it happen to be me that did it?" He did not wait for a reply, but turned quickly toward the door.

The troopers crossed the hall to the desk corporal's office. The corporal sat with his microphone in front of him, telephones at both hands.

"Not a bad night," he said. "Only one fatal. Some drivers sure are lucky."

"Yeh," Tony agreed. "Some of 'em. Well, I got my report to finish. Seventeen summonses." He glanced at the clock. It pointed to 1:35 a.m. His tour of duty had ended at 11 p.m. "Give me a hand, Pete, and we'll knock 'em out in half an hour. Be in bed by 2:30."

"I could do with some sleep," Pete replied.

"You'll be lucky if you get to sleep tonight," Tony said. "After one of these, it's hard."

He was telling the truth. It *was* hard. I watched daylight break through my bedroom window and send the night away, but I could not drive from my memory that half-circle of men, all standing motionless, all looking down at what lay on the white concrete. I could not forget the sight of Charley's eyes or the sound of his voice, such a thin little voice, saying, "Why don't they pick my daddy up?"

Don't Do It Now!

How to be a successful procrastinator— in one easy lesson

BY **COREY FORD**

Originally published in February 1963

nybody can get things done. That's easy. The real art is in putting things off until you don't have to do them.

All it takes is a little strategy. If I notice that the bathroom faucet is leaking, for instance. I don't get a wrench and fix it. I make a note, "Fix faucet," and worry about it all day. Naturally, I can't get anything else done because the faucet is on my mind. That night I discover that someone has called the plumber, so I make a note of all the things I've put off during the day and worry about them tomorrow.

Actually my system is quite simple. Let's say I have to get my dinner jacket down from the attic and send it to the cleaner. I locate it in the cedar closet, hanging next to my old Air Force uniform. Wonder if that uniform blouse still fits? By sucking in my breath, I manage to fasten a button and beam at my reflection in the mirror. Colonel Ford reporting for duty, sir! I toss myself a brisk salute, knocking over a pile of cartons behind me and spilling their contents on the floor.

Why, here's my college annual that I haven't seen for years. Funny how everybody else has changed but me! What's this packet of letters, tied in a blue ribbon? Oh, yes, that little blonde I met in California— what was her name? I examine a faded billet-doux. Pretty hard to make it out in this light. Humming a melody of long ago, I carry the packet downstairs and pore over the letters until the cleaner has closed for the day—which solves the problem of getting my dinner jacket down from the attic.

Of course, it always helps to give yourself a logical reason for doing something later. You can't take your wife shopping today because you have to wash the car. On the other hand, you can't wash the car because the paper says rain tomorrow, and if it's going to rain tomorrow there's no point in watering the lawn right now, so the best idea is to get your golf clubs and take advantage of this nice weather while it lasts.

One excuse for postponing work is to watch someone else working. If my neighbor is painting his garage, I have an irresistible urge to drop whatever I'm doing and stroll next door to see how he's coming along. Generally he has the same urge to drop what *he's* doing, so we spend the rest of the afternoon putting things off together.

It's even more distracting when

I'm paying for the work. Last week I hired a carpenter to put up some shelves in the kitchen. I'd have done it myself, but I had to write an article. It took me several hours to go over the job with him and explain just what I wanted, and then I went upstairs to my typewriter.

The carpenter started hammering. Do you suppose he's getting those shelves the right height? Maybe I ought to go down and check. After watching him awhile and offering a few helpful suggestions, I forced myself back to my desk, only to dash downstairs again when the hammering suddenly stopped. After all, you have to keep an eye on these workmen or they'll never get anything done. It turned out that he was getting ready to saw a board, so I returned to my desk and stared at the blank page in the typewriter. Saw, saw, *crash!* No use trying to concentrate with that racket going on. Might as well go see if I can give a hand. As a result of my interruptions, it took the man all week to put up the shelves and I still have my article to write.

The trouble is that I run out of excuses sooner or later, and have to get to work. No more dilly-dallying—or is it shilly-shallying? Better look it up in the dictionary. Let's see. Shill, shillelagh, shilling— here we are. Shilly-shally, *v.i.* To be irresolute; vacillate. Well, I've vacillated long enough. I'm starting that article right now.

The first thing is to straighten up my desk, stacking papers and emptying ashtrays and untangling the string of paper clips that I linked together while I was putting off the article yesterday. The next step is to sharpen my pencils. The pencil sharpener is clogged with shavings, so I have to empty it. Might as well put a fresh ribbon in my typewriter while I'm at it too. It takes me the better part of an hour to go down to the store and buy a new ribbon, which turns out to be the wrong size. So I spend another hour threading the old ribbon back again and then scrubbing the carbon off my hands.

Now to light my pipe and get to work. Before I light it, though, I have to knock out the ashes and scrape the bowl and blow through it once or twice to see if it's clean. Doesn't seem to draw quite right. After searching in vain for a pipe cleaner, I poke one of the paper clips through the stem, wedging it firmly inside. Well, I'll clean that out later. I've got to get started.

Wait a minute, here's the postman. Might be something in the mail that would give me an idea. By the time I've gone through all the seed catalogs and advertisements for sales, it's so near noon that there's no sense in starting anything before lunch, and after lunch I have to take a nap, and after my nap I have to take a little walk to clear those cobwebs. By a strange coincidence, my walk leads me to the club, where I relax after my day's travail by shooting a little pool until it's time for dinner. I'll start bright and early tomorrow.

Here's where my system comes in. Instead of starting the article in the morning, I put it off and make an appointment with the dentist. Then I put off going to the dentist by writing my article. It's the only way I ever get things done.

Amazon Adventure

A voyage that ended with a bang this family will never forget. A Reader's Digest *"First Person Award."*

———

BY **DAVID DODGE**

Originally published in October 1955

ome years ago my wife and I, with our 9-year-old daughter, made a trip down the Amazon. We were living then in Peru, not far from the headwaters of the Amazon River system. Vacation time had come and we decided that a journey through the great South American jungle by boat would be a novel holiday.

In late June we took a plane to Iquitos, a town on the upper Amazon in the eastern Peruvian bush, and there booked passage on the river steamer *Morey* for Belém, Brazil, 2,100 miles downstream at the mouth of the river.

The ship's captain, a courteous, cordial Peruvian, was relieved to find that we spoke intelligible Spanish. "My English is very weak," he explained. "I have never carried *norteamericanos* as passengers before."

As we were soon to learn, most people who travel in that part of the world go by plane if they can afford it. Only the attraction of the *Morey*'s low fare (about $30 per person for the 10-day voyage) compensated for the ship's primitive accommodations. She was a wood-burner, old and shaky. The two dozen other passengers shared public wash basins and not-quite-so-public showers, which drew tepid, muddy water from the river whenever the ship's pumps were working. A tap with a filter provided drinking water from the same source.

Meals consisted of beans, fried bananas and dried fish, three times a day, supplemented by fruit and nuts that could be bought at the places where the vessel stopped for fuel. The ancient lighting system worked only sporadically. Amenities such as ice, hot water and mosquito nets did not exist, and the weather was too hot for the privacy of closed doors. But, despite these drawbacks, the voyage down to Belém was a rare and enjoyable experience.

My daughter Kendal took an immediate shine to the captain's two officers—the purser, a large, jolly man nicknamed Frog, and the *práctico*, or pilot. Frog let her wear his officer's cap, and the práctico had a pet dwarf monkey that liked to leap to her shoulder and snuggle against her ear. There were other pet monkeys aboard, several parrots and a tame boa constrictor.

Our fellow passengers were Peruvians, Brazilians, an Argentine couple, an old Jamaican woman, a Colombian family, a Bolivian priest, an uncommunicative German and a political deportee whose nationality was a matter of argument. He had been thrown out of his native land and told not to return unless he wanted to be promptly buried there. All these had a common bond in slim purses.

It is generally believed in South America that norteamericanos are millionaires or at least well-to-do. Since we had brought with us expensive supplies of bottled water and beer, we could not be an exception to the rule. Why, then, were we submitting ourselves to a humid 10-day river journey when we could have flown from Iquitos to Belém in a matter of hours?

The question was put to Kendal by the old Jamaican woman. Kendal was playing with the monkey and enjoying the voyage tremendously in spite of monkey fleas, mosquitos and the awful heat. She answered, "For fun. My papa and mama like to do things they haven't done before." The old woman hurried away to spread the news that the norteamericanos were making a pleasure cruise.

This raised the morale of the whole ship, from the sweating wood passers in the stokehold up to the passenger deck and the captain's cabin. The reasoning seemed to be that if we, wealthy as we surely were and able to travel in such style as we chose, had deliberately decided to take the *Morey*, there must be something about the ship that they had overlooked. Our presence, it seemed, lent the voyage a peculiar distinction, and the trip became, all at once, an excursion instead of a torment.

Because of this we were instantly immensely popular. Formalities were abandoned; we were addressed with, and invited to use, the familiar Spanish "thee" and "thou" by passengers and crew. Our best friends were Skinny, a large, swarthy man who had been manager of a remote plantation on the Upper Ucayali and was on his way to Belém to look for a job nearer civilization; two pretty Brazilian sisters; the Argentine

couple; and a dentist and his wife who were going back to Argentina for a new start.

We were drawn together because we all liked to sing. Skinny played the guitar magnificently and had a fine tenor voice. The Brazilian girls crooned lovely close harmony in the middle register, the dentist was proud of his baritone, and the rest of us could carry a tune.

The *Morey*'s lights were too dim for reading or card playing after nightfall, so we passed the evenings on the foredeck, singing songs in Spanish, Portuguese or English. Skinny could play any tune that someone would whistle for him first, and those of us who didn't know the words would hum along until we learned them. In time all the passengers and many of the crew joined the evening concerts, to listen if not to sing. In this manifestation of harmony and international goodwill, we norteamericanos basked in popularity, the acknowledged king, queen and princess of the ship.

Then came a drastic change. One evening Skinny suddenly stopped

The Amazon River near Belém

playing although the hour was early and the night too warm for sleep.

"What's the matter?" I asked.

"Too much guitar. My fingers hurt. I'll have to rest them."

This was mysterious, for the tips of his fingers were so heavily calloused from years of playing that he could have had no feeling in them. I suggested that, in any event, this would not interfere with his singing. He replied evasively that he had other matters to occupy his time, and left the foredeck. Several other passengers followed him. A few of us kept the concert going for a while, but there was a feeling of constraint, and that night the singing ended earlier than usual.

The next evening there was no singing at all. Skinny failed to show up on the foredeck. So did the Brazilian sisters and all of the regulars except the three norteamericanos. But there was some kind of activity on the afterdeck, with much serious, low-voiced talk and furtive headturnings in our direction. Since the foredeck was the only spot on the ship where a regular breeze could be hoped for, the fact that everyone was avoiding it as long as we were there made us feel like pariahs. What had we done to incur their displeasure?

"They are talking about us, I'm sure," my wife said.

"What have we done to get talked about?" I asked.

"I can't imagine. But we've certainly done something."

We could not find out what it was that had united Peru, Brazil, Argentina, Bolivia, Colombia, Jamaica, Germany and the man without a country so solidly against the United States. I approached the captain in a roundabout way and, although I could not ask him point-blank what had happened to change us into persons to be shunned, I hinted that if we had violated some obscure South American taboo it had been inadvertent. We wished to apologize.

"I don't know what you are talking about, señor," he answered formally.

The ship's lights weren't working that night, but gleams of candlelight showed from the cracks of several cabin doors. The mutter of conspiratorial voices inside the cabins was a final blow. Only an overwhelming fear of contagion could have persuaded our fellow passengers to close their doors in that humid jungle climate, for the night was like an oven. We went dismally to bed.

The next morning began with six revolver shots fired just outside our cabin door. My immediate reaction was that the people gathered on deck had come to lynch us. Then we were seized, embraced in South American bear hugs and congratulated on a happy anniversary. The captain, still holding a smoking revolver, and Skinny, Frog and the práctico led the embracing squads, all grinning at our surprise.

"What anniversary are we celebrating?" I said.

"Why, that of the independence of your United States of America! *El Cuatro de Julio, hombre.* Look there!"

"There" was a hand-drawn, hand-colored paper flag, not quite according to regulation in the number of its stars or the arrangement of its stripes but easily recognizable as Old Glory, fastened to our door. The date, which we had entirely forgotten, was the Fourth of July.

This, then, was the explanation of the mystery—the secrecy, the closed doors, interrupted conversations: For 30 hours the entire ship, planning a surprise party, had closed ranks to hide the preparations from us. The Independence Day of any South American country is an occasion for a great fiesta, and we were being honored by their observance of our own Independence Day. Because we were the only norteamericanos on a thousand-mile stretch of the river, it became in effect our private birthday party.

Kendal was presented with a gunnysack full of Brazil nuts, another of cacao pods, an enormous stem of bananas and a parakeet. All had been bought at one of the ship's fuel stops and smuggled aboard. The canopy over the dining table on the deck was decorated with wild orchids and palm fronds laboriously gathered from the jungle, and the ship's cook had been up most of the night trying to concoct something special out of his supply of beans, bananas and dried fish.

Under the circumstances I felt that I should contribute to the celebration what remained of my warm beer, along with a bottle of something stronger I had kept in reserve. Skinny tuned up his guitar, the singers all wet their whistles with a toast to the glorious U.S.A., and the *Morey* went chugging on down the Amazon to the ragged but enthusiastic strains of a song which three norteamericanos, far from home, taught that day to a most unlikely group of Fourth of July celebrants: Peruvians, Brazilians, Colombians, Argentinians, Bolivians, an old lady from Jamaica, a misplaced German and a man without a country of his own. The song began:

Oh say, can you see
By the dawn's early light …

The Christmas Present

*It was a kind of magic, the old woman
told the boy. And indeed it was: Her gift
would illuminate a novelist's life.*

—

BY **JAMES MICHENER**

Originally published in December 1967

hen I was a boy of 9 in the little town of Doylestown, Pennsylvania, I used to mow the lawn of Mrs. Long, an elderly lady who lived across from the Presbyterian Church. She paid me very little for the chore, which was not surprising, for she had not much money. But she did promise me, "When Christmas comes I shall have a present for you." And she said this with such enthusiasm that I felt assured the present would be magnificent.

I spent much time wondering what it would be. The boys I played with had baseball gloves and bicycles and ice skates, and I was so eager to acquire any one of these that I convinced myself that my benefactor intended choosing from among them.

"It would hardly be a baseball glove," I reasoned with myself. "A woman like Mrs. Long wouldn't know much about baseball." Since she was a frail little person I also ruled out the bicycle, for how could she handle such a contraption?

On my last Saturday at work Mrs. Long said, "Now remember, because you've been a good boy all summer, at Christmas I'll have a present waiting. You come to the door and collect it." These words clinched it. Since she was going to have the present in her house, and since she herself would be handling it, unquestionably she was giving me a pair of ice skates.

So convinced of this I became that I could see the skates and imagine myself upon them. As the cold days of November arrived and ice began to form on the ponds which were then a feature of rural Doylestown, I began to try my luck on the ice that would be sustaining me and my skates through the winter.

"Get away from that ice!" a man shouted. "It's not strong enough yet." But soon it would be.

As Christmas approached, it was with difficulty that I restrained myself from reporting to Mrs. Long and demanding my present. Our family agreed that the first of December was too early for me to do this. "She may not have it wrapped yet," someone argued, and this made sense. But the 15th was also too early, and the 20th, too. I argued back on the 20th, reasoning that if I was going to get a present I might as well get it now, but my mother pointed out that in our family we never opened our presents until Christmas morning.

On the 21st of December, a serious cold snap froze all the ponds so that boys who already had ice skates were able to use them, and my longing to possess mine, even though I could not open the package for a few days, became overpowering. On Dec. 22, I could restrain myself no longer. I marched down the street, presented myself at the door of the house whose lawn I had tended all summer and said, "I've come for my present, Mrs. Long."

"I've been waiting for you," she said, leading me into her parlor, its windows heavy with purple velvet. She sat me in a chair, disappeared to another room, and in a moment stood before me holding a package which under no conceivable circumstances could hold a baseball glove or a bicycle or even a pair of skates. I was painfully disappointed but so far as I can recall did not show it, because during the week my advisers at home had warned repeatedly, "Whatever she has for you, take it graciously and say thank you."

What she had was an ordinary parcel about 9 inches wide, a foot long and no more than a quarter of an inch thick. As Mrs. Long held it in her frail hands, curiosity replaced my initial disappointment, and when I lifted it from her the extreme lightness of the gift quite captivated me. It weighed almost nothing.

"What is it?" I asked.

"You'll see on Christmas Day."

I shook it. Nothing rattled, but I thought I did catch a sound of some sort—a quiet, muffled sound that was somehow familiar but unidentifiable. "What is it?" I asked again.

"A kind of magic," Mrs. Long said, and that was all.

Her words were enough to set my mind dancing with new possibilities, so that by the time I reached home I had convinced myself that I held some great wonder. "She gave me a magician's set. I'll turn pitchers of milk into rabbits."

How long the passage to Christmas was! There were other presents of normal dimension and weight. But Mrs. Long's box dominated all, for it had to do with magic.

On Christmas morning, before the sun was up, I had this box on my knees, tearing at the reused colored string which bound it. Soon the wrapping paper was off and in my lap lay a flat box with its top hinged about halfway down.

With great excitement I opened the hinged lid to find inside a shimmering pile of 10 flimsy sheets of black paper, each labeled in iridescent letters, Carbon Paper Regal Premium. Of the four words I knew only the second, and what it signified in this context I could not guess. Vaguely I remembered that the present had something to do with magic, and with this word on my lips I turned to the elders who had watched me unwrapping my gift.

"Is it magic?" I asked.

Aunt Laura, who taught school, had the presence of mind to say, "It really is!" And she took two pieces of white paper, placed between them one of the black sheets from the box and, with a hard pencil, wrote my name on the upper sheet. Then, removing it and the Carbon Paper Regal Premium, she handed me the second sheet, which her pencil had in no way touched.

There was my name! It was clean, and very dark, and well formed and as beautiful as Christmas Day itself.

I was enthralled! This was indeed magic ... of the greatest dimension. That a pencil could write on one piece of paper and mysteriously record on another was a miracle which was so gratifying to my childish mind that I can honestly say that in that one moment, in the dark of Christmas morning, I understood as much about printing, and the duplication of words, and the fundamental mystery of disseminating ideas as I have learned in the remaining half-century of my life.

I wrote and wrote, using up whole tablets until I had ground off the last shred of blackness from the 10 sheets of carbon paper. It was the most enchanting Christmas present a boy like me could have had, infinitely more significant than a baseball glove or a pair of skates. It was exactly the present I needed and it reached me at precisely that Christmas when I was best able to comprehend it. Because it enabled me to learn something about the reproduction of words, it opened vast portals of imagination.

I have received some pretty thundering Christmas presents since then, but none that ever came close to the magnificence of this one. The average present merely gratifies a temporary yearning, as the ice skates would have done; the great present illuminates all the years of life that remain.

It was not until some years later that I realized that the 10 sheets of Carbon Paper Regal Premium which Mrs. Long gave me had cost her nothing. She had used them for her purposes and would normally have thrown them away, except that she had had the ingenuity to guess that a boy might profit from a present totally outside the realm of his ordinary experience. Although she had spent no money on me, she had spent something infinitely more valuable: imagination.

I hope that this year some boys and girls will receive, from thoughtful adults who really love them, gifts which will jolt them out of all they have known up to now. It is such gifts and such experiences—usually costing little or nothing—that transform a life and lend it an impetus that may continue for decades.

Down, Boy, Down, Blast You!

There's something about a dog …

—

BY **CHARLTON OGBURN JR.**

Originally published in June 1966

**W**ould you like to carry a perpetual load of guilt, to know that no matter how much you give of yourself it will never be enough, and to take on a load of chronic harassments? You would? Then I have just the thing for you: a dog!

A devoted dog. One that will sit in front of you all evening while you are trying to read, looking at you with anxious, supplicating eyes until you feel like a brute for ignoring him. Did someone say that bestowing a few pats and affectionate words will reassure your loyal friend and enable you to go on with your reading? Only a dedicated and mindless propagandist for man's most insatiable dependent—and the country is full of just such propagandists—would venture so preposterous a claim.

A dog's need for reassurance is a bottomless well. You could devote an entire day to ministering to a dog's need to feel wanted—stroking it, romping with it, crooning over it—and the instant you desisted, the rejected creature, with an imploring whimper, would nose under your arm to confront you with an expression of bewilderment and hurt. *Don't you love me anymore?* its

173

eyes would ask. *Am I hateful to you? Do you wish I were dead?*

One way or another, a dog is a full-time proposition. Questions must be constantly in your mind. If the dog is outdoors, is it getting lost or run over, upsetting a neighbor's garbage can, mauling or being mauled by a neighbor's dog? If indoors, is it chewing up your wife's kid gloves or lying on the sofa rubbing into the fabric the stench of the decayed fish it rolled in ecstatically the day before or, seized by a sudden need, is it forgetting its housebreaking or throwing up on the rug?

To know that the dog is prevented from getting into mischief by being shut up in the cellar or tied up in the yard relieves your mind of one set of distracting concerns only to afflict it with another. The dog has nothing to do. The dog is a prisoner. You have taken on a dog and now are failing it in companionship. Here you sit and there the dog languishes, an innocent, loving creature condemned to the same punishment that would be visited upon a human criminal.

The condition of being a dog owner is that you are continually in a state either of exasperation over the dog's misdemeanors or of self-recrimination because you have let the dog down. None of this you would discover from the effervescent manuals written for prospective dog buyers. These books make much of the dog's intelligence, its desire to please its master, its responsiveness to training. Humbug! The dog is certainly intelligent, up to a point, but its intelligence is devoted to getting what *it* wants. Anyone who thinks that a dog has its master's

happiness uppermost in its mind has never eaten his meals with his devoted pet covetously watching every single forkful.

As for that longing to be trained that the books would have you believe burns in a dog's breast, that is the greatest hoax of all. To begin with, most of what you wish a dog to do, or more often not to do, is uncommunicable. "Don't wag your tail when passing the houseplant; it whacks the leaves off. Don't dig holes in the flower bed. When there are guests within hearing, don't lap water out of the toilet." How to get these ideas across, the books don't say. "Living with a dog," observed a friend of mine with a great, clumsy golden retriever, "is like having an idiot relative in the house."

Nothing is more foreign to a dog's nature than obedience. True, there are dog owners whose charges obey their commands, but these persons are all of a special sort— leathery-complexioned outdoorsmen who go around talking of bloodlines and who live more with dogs than with people. The dog knows that they will never give up until it does obey.

With you and me, it knows just the opposite. "Here, Shaughnessy!" you cry. But you know that Shaughnessy, racing madly, his face transfigured with rapture, ears flapping in the breeze, will pay no attention. Shaughnessy has got your number.

It is not as if our requirements of the dog were exorbitant. If our dog just wouldn't jump up on everybody, if he'd just obey when we say "Down!" that would be enough. But let a guest arrive— especially a woman—and up he goes, eager and possessive. If it is a small dog, he snags a woman's stockings; if a Great Dane, he licks off her makeup. Of course, you can always shut the dog up when there are guests coming, if you do not mind their being greeted by the howls of a soul in purgatory.

Leo Rosten once said of W.C. Fields that no man who dislikes dogs can be wholly bad. But outspoken honesty on this subject is rare. Dogs enjoy an idolatrous press. Have you ever heard of a dog story in which the dog was the villain? The prevailing view is that any man without a warm spot in his heart for dogs lacks the very attributes that make a dog admirable—loyalty, genuineness, capacity for unquestioning love, steadfastness.

The iconoclast might quite reasonably disagree. "Look, I've had a dog," he might plead. "There were scratch marks on our new car the first week. Every time my wife cleaned house, the dog would celebrate by galumphing through a mudhole. He would sleep unperturbed when a stranger drove up but wake the baby by barking every time our best friends came over. You couldn't reach down to tie your shoelaces without your hand closing on a cold, wet nose. Besides that, he'd want to be let in or out of the house 50 times a day."

But how often do you hear anyone talk like that? Total indoctrination—that describes the conditioning of the American mind toward dogs. It begins early in life. No boy can grow up in our country without having it borne upon him that unless he is a boy with a dog, he does not really count. And, of course, the combination does seem a natural one. Boys and dogs are much alike, similarly the creatures of impulse, equally irresponsible, alike possessed of sources of energy that are never long exhausted and also can never be harnessed to any useful end. They are equally indiscriminate in diet and devoid of any sense of hygiene, each abetting the other in his most socially deplorable proclivities.

But what about the 30- or 40- or 50-year-old boy with a dog?

Can a grown man put up with a dog? Obviously, grown men do. The reason they can is not only that they have been brainwashed but that, here again, the human and canine partners minister to each other's weaknesses. The man, buffeted by the world, consistently defeated and humiliated, as we all are, has the crutch of the dog's worshipful esteem. The most hopeless incompetent can be a god to a dog.

As may have been suspected, I did not become so overfamiliar with canine nature by observing my friends' pets. In fact, there is even now a dog in our family. We took one on at the behest of our young daughters. I was rather surprised when, some time after we had assumed the burden, my wife remarked that I'd probably be much less bothered by the dog's tagging after me if I did not make so much of her. "Leave it to the girls to pat her and rub her chest and talk baby talk to her," she counseled. "After all, she's supposed to be *their* dog."

Which, of course, is true. But the creature does show a certain attachment to me which is difficult entirely to disregard. She is a pure-blooded Dalmatian of a very distinguished line. She has—as I should be less than candid not to admit—a certain nobility. Much as you might wish to be free of her and be able to call your time your own, you do not treat such a dog unfeelingly. And another thing: I do not pretend to have those qualities that cause a person to stand out among his fellow men and command their respect and allegiance; the very idea is laughable. Still, when another living being perceives in you such qualities, it does cloak you with a certain responsibility. She may be the biggest pest in the world, but you have to show her some consideration. Don't you?

Don't Be Afraid of Your Feelings

"The ennobling difference between one man and another ... is precisely in this, that one feels more than another." —John Ruskin

BY **JOHN KORD LAGEMANN**

Originally published in July 1967

looked at a series of Charlie Chaplin one-reelers the other night and found myself laughing through tears. In just a few minutes of brilliant pantomime, Charlie expressed elation, tenderness, disappointment, joy, fear, resignation, pity and longing. By enabling me to experience these feelings with him, he made me feel kin to the whole world. There was a healing magic about it—something that is becoming harder and harder to find.

I grew up in a small Illinois city, before the emotional ice age set in. It was perfectly natural to show emotion then. When you went to a movie with a sad ending, you could hear people all over the theater blowing their noses. I remember times when my whole family would leave with tears in their eyes. We cared for things, and for each other, and we didn't hesitate to show it.

At home, my mother used to hug us when we got back from school, even before company, and the way she kissed my father goodbye in the morning you would have thought he was going off to the wars. We weren't very good at hiding our feelings—and we didn't try very hard. We could usually tell when someone had fallen in love, or done something he was proud or ashamed of, or was worried or puzzled, on top of the world, or in the dumps. If it didn't show on his face, he'd *tell* you. Feelings were a living language that kept us in touch with each other, not as mere spectators but as participants in a never-ending drama.

The wisdom of feelings became clear to me only later. After college, I joined a small-town weekly newspaper as junior partner to the publisher, who was getting on in years. He gave me carte blanche to reorganize the paper, and I pitched in with enthusiasm. But after a few weeks he began finding fault with everything I did. When I asked my father for advice, he said, "I don't know anything about the newspaper business, but I do know the old man. I think he feels left out."

That night I had a long talk with my partner. The paper was hardly mentioned. Instead, I listened to his life history, and I left with a better understanding of him, of the community and of myself. During the two years I remained with the paper, my partner gave me nothing but encouragement and support.

Since then, experience has taught me again and again that the secret of getting along with people is to *recognize how they feel*, and to let them know you know. When someone is rude or quarrelsome, it's often a way of saying "Pay attention to my feelings." When we say of someone, "He understands me," we're really saying, "He knows how I feel."

Awareness of feelings in others comes naturally, if only you let it. I saw it happen last spring just after a circus matinee as I walked by a crowd of small children waiting at a bus stop, each child holding a brightly-colored balloon. As I watched, the string of a red balloon slipped through the fingers of a 4-year-old, and his face curled up in grief at the loss. Instantly the child beside him caught his eye, extended his fist—and released his own balloon. Within seconds, a score of balloons were soaring skyward, while the 4-year-old, tears still glistening on his cheeks, laughed with the others at the spectacle.

In difficult situations, the "right thing to do" is not hard to find if you let people's feelings come through to you and acknowledge your own. Recently, the minister of our church had to carry tragic news to the parents of a 12-year-old boy: Their son had drowned on a school outing. Later, the parents told me, "Mr. Allen didn't preach or tell us to be brave. He broke into tears and wept with us. We will always love him for that."

Happiness, too, is the greater for being shared. "Isn't it a lovely day?" my wife remarked one day to a salesclerk who was humming softly under her breath and obviously pleased about something. "Is it ever!" said the girl—and then she blurted out the news that she had recently become engaged. "I just felt like telling someone," she said. "It makes it so much more real!"

"I felt like it"—that is the best reason in the world to laugh or to be generous or to applaud something. And that is what moods are—"feeling like it." Why fight them? Like the shifting of lights in the theater, moods enable you to see life in all its aspects. "I think creation comes initially out of mood," says Charlie Chaplin. In a melancholy mood you observe details that escape you in a mood of jubilation. Pensive, you filter out

Wonderful moments of joy or sheer well-being come over us now and then without warning.

distractions and concentrate on deeper thoughts. Nostalgic, you capture the flavor of past events and see meanings that had escaped you before.

We mistrust moods because they change. Yet changing moods are perhaps the surest indication of a healthy personality. It is when a mood *doesn't* change that we should be concerned. To go through life in one mood, whether cheerful or glum, would be like trying to play a trombone with a stuck slide.

Happiness itself is just a mood, and there is very little logic to it. Wonderful moments of joy or sheer well-being come over us now and then without warning; elation appears out of nowhere. It happened in our house on a lazy Saturday morning while my wife

In all the really fundamental issues of life, the final decision is best left to feelings.

and I sat in the living room reading the paper over our second cups of coffee. Sunlight streamed through the windows. On the radio the news program gave way to a concert, and the air was suddenly vibrant with the music of Mozart. Without a word my wife and I rose from our chairs, bowed to each other and started improvising the steps of a minuet. As our children, entering the room, saw what was going on,

they regarded us questioningly—and then joined in the dance.

Such moments of spontaneously shared feelings are unpredictable and fleeting. But they linger on in the atmosphere of a place. Years ago, in Paris, a curator at the Louvre glanced at a young couple and said to me, "This is a wonderful place in which to fall in love." I had never before thought of museums in quite that light, but I understood at once what he meant. The silent sharing of moods that occurs in looking at art, in watching a stirring play or in listening to great music can bring people very close.

"My feelings got the better of me," we sometimes say when we are moved to act kindly or courageously. It's almost an apology. Yet feelings welling up from the depths of our personality, shaped by a lifetime of experience, provide a reliable and almost automatic self-guidance system. They may not help much in playing the stock market or in making out your income tax. But, as Sigmund Freud once observed, in all the really fundamental issues of life, the final decision is best left to feelings. How else can one decide whom to marry, whom to trust as a friend or colleague, what to do when faced with a sudden life-or-death emergency?

Years ago, John Ruskin wrote: "The ennobling difference between one man and another ... is precisely in this, that one feels more than another." His words will always be true. I once heard the great voice teacher Rose Bampton discussing two young singers rehearsing for a Metropolitan Opera audition. Pointing to one of them, she said, "Her vocal range isn't exceptional, but her emotional range is tremendous. She gives more to her audience." Through feeling we gain self-insight, tap our creative powers, and deepen and enrich our relationships with others.

Why, then, do we so often deny our feelings? Why do we cultivate a defensive, withdrawn quality, a deadpan emotional unresponsiveness? "It's the new untouchability of today's 'cool' world," a college dean told me. "The idea is never to be shocked, surprised or deeply moved—or at least not to show it."

Feelings commit us one to another, and thus involve the risk of disappointment. They make us take sides, blurt out awkward truths, form personal preferences. "Playing it cool," on the other hand, means being "with it" until the going gets rough, then turning without regret to something else—another mate, another job, another cause. It may spare us a lot of heartache, self-searching and struggle. But when you subtract feelings from marriage, friendship or work, what is left?

You can share money, food or sex with another and still remain complete strangers. In the end, the *only* way you can mean anything to another human being is to share his feelings.

World's Dumbest Criminals

*Jewelry, gadgets, cigarettes—
and a free television—all attracted
the attention of these masterminds*

—

Originally published in April 2018 in Reader's Digest *International Edition*

**B**etter than free? One spring, an undetermined number of misguided thieves broke into a store after shop hours in Zeist, Holland, and ran off with a television set. Clearly, they did not know that they had entered a "giveaway store"—part of a recycling project—where everything is free. On top of that, the television they had stolen was broken! They have not been caught.

Vanity Did Him In

Thinking no one was looking, a 26-year-old bearded thief took a pair of headphones off the shelf in a store's electronics department, went into a dressing room—out of sight, or so he thought—and put them into his pocket. So far so good; if only he hadn't given into vanity! As he was leaving the dressing room, he looked in the mirror and, unbelievably, became concerned with how disheveled his beard was. Grabbing an electric shaver off a nearby shelf, he quickly trimmed his beard. Sadly for the thief, the clerks in the Vantaa, Finland, store had noticed his strange behavior, and he was

pulled aside when he tried to go through the checkout. The headphones were discovered in his pocket. The man has been charged with shoplifting and property crime. The shaver, having been used, could not be sold.

Very Sneaky

Suitcases belonging to passengers on buses going to Beauvais Airport outside of Paris were being pilfered. Police were baffled. When and how could a thief get into the luggage compartment of the bus, steal from suitcases and then get out again, without being seen?

Then, an observant driver noticed a passenger with a backpack and an enormous suitcase, with something inside that was moving! He alerted the authorities. Police stopped the man as he arrived at the airport and found that his rucksack contained laptops, money and valuables. His suitcase contained a "curled up individual."

The scam became clear. Once in the luggage compartment, the thief hiding in the suitcase would sneak out, steal whatever he could find, load up the backpack and get back into the suitcase before arrival at the airport. The thief and his accomplice were respectively sentenced in October 2017 to eight and 12 months in prison.

Clear Directions

After raiding a jewelry store of bracelets and rings, the thieves could have made good their getaway had they not made a series of silly mistakes. First, when police in Leicester, England, found the getaway car, they discovered the crooks' GPS device showing police where the thieves were headed. Even dumber, however, one of the men had left their address in the car. The three young thieves have been jailed for a total of 21 years.

Free Wheelin' Thief

A shoplifter seriously misjudged how quickly a supermarket's automatic doors opened in the small town of Halikko, Finland. After a burglary spree throughout the store, the thief stole a bicycle and tried to make a speedy escape. In his haste, he rode the bike smack into the store's main entrance—sliding glass doors that didn't open quickly enough as he

approached. He was apprehended by a security guard.

Smoke and Mirrors

Looking to swipe some cigarettes, three crooks smashed their way through the glass doors of a rural supermarket in Giessenburg, Holland. Heading straight for the cashier's counter, one of the men jumped over it to steal cigarettes from the shelves behind. Unfortunately for them, they tripped the store's security system, and they got more "smoke" than they had bargained on: The store's security smoke machine had been activated. Knowing that police had been alerted, they fled empty-handed.

Unlucky Friday

It was Friday the 13th when two masked men decided to rob a jewelry store outside Stockholm. But it wasn't their day. Clearly amateurs, the men filled a big bag with stolen goods, but when they returned to their scooter—their getaway vehicle—not only did it not start right away, but also the big bag of loot was too unwieldy to carry. The two were arrested mere yards from the store.

Foiled by Greed

Have you ever wondered if you could lift a bag containing 20,000 cigarettes—give or take a few? Well … after loading up with around 1,000 packets of cigarettes, three crooks were unable to get their booty up and over or around the tobacco counter, out of the store and away: It was just too darn heavy. Police arrived at the supermarket in the Midlands of England as the men fled—

empty-handed. As the presiding trial judge later commented, "This robbery was well planned out, if not well executed … You were foiled by your own greed." The men were sentenced to a total of 14 years in prison.

Go Straight to Jail

It was late one night in fall when police on patrol in Flensburg, Germany, saw a young man acting oddly. The officers approached the man and, checking his name with police files, found that he was wanted on three separate arrest warrants. Rather than hang around and await his fate, the 24-year-old ran away as fast as he could, jumped into a nearby car and told the driver to "put his foot down." The young man had gotten into an unmarked police vehicle—and not too much later, found himself in jail.

A Killer Is Loose

*The story of quiet, gentle Louis Gorman,
who, trapped with seven others by a
murderous psychopath, found the courage
to do "what had to be done"*

━━━

BY **JOSEPH P. BLANK**

Originally published in December 1961

s the residents of Jerseyville, a town of 7,500 people in southwestern Illinois, started about their daily affairs on the mild, sunny Friday morning of Oct. 9, 1959, alarming news spread among them: A cold-blooded killer was hiding somewhere in their area.

The 21-year-old killer, James Gordon Palmer, was a Jerseyville man. Police Chief Herman Blackorby described him as "a nice-looking, nice-talking boy who didn't mind killing you." In a ramble through Missouri, Illinois and Tennessee he had robbed and murdered a bait shop owner, a young waitress and a filling-station attendant. He had fired bullets into the backs of their heads—in the case of two of them, while they lay face down on the floor—until they stopped moving.

On the night of Oct. 8, sheriff's deputies had spotted Palmer as he drove up to his Jerseyville apartment. He raced them to the outskirts of town, jumped from his car and escaped into a cornfield. An hour later he shot and wounded a railroad brakeman shining a lantern near a ditch where he lay hidden.

Now more than 100 police, state troopers and sheriff's deputies had converged on Jerseyville. They put bloodhounds around the spot where Palmer had fled, but the dogs couldn't pick up a scent. They patrolled all roads and searched hundreds of buildings. Each school bus carried an armed policeman. A helicopter and four small planes kept crisscrossing the farmlands around the town. Radio broadcasters warned listeners to lock their doors. Police feared that Palmer might massacre an isolated farm family to steal a car.

As the hours passed, the people of Jerseyville grew increasingly jumpy. By afternoon sporting-goods stores had sold out their supplies of guns and ammunition. Several farm families drove into town to stay at the hotel. One woman, hearing a noise in the basement, riddled her kitchen floor with buckshot.

In the small, squat brick building that housed the two office rooms of Gorman Bros. Ready-Mix Concrete & Construction Co. on Franklin Street, business continued as usual. But when Louis Gorman went home

that evening he found his wife, Frances, and their two children frightened. Gorman, a quiet and gentle man, 52 and graying, tried to reassure them. "Palmer is probably well on his way to Mexico by now," he said.

Nevertheless, he slept restlessly. He arose before five, dressed and drove down to Sandy's Cafe, where he drank coffee and talked with two men from a posse that had searched for Palmer through the night. Then shortly after seven Gorman drove to the office. Two truck drivers, Charles Kroeschel and his son-in-law, Robert Cordes, arrived at the same time.

When Gorman put his key into the lock he found it unlocked. He made a mental note to remind his men to check the doors before leaving at night. Entering the building, Gorman went to the washroom. He saw that the glass pane in the rear door had been broken and covered with cardboard, but he assumed that one of his men had broken the window on the previous day.

Meanwhile, Charlie Kroeschel walked around the service counter in the outer office, stepped into the inner office—and was confronted by a man pointing a .22-caliber semiautomatic rifle. Kroeschel's mouth fell open. He backed away, repeating incredulously, "Louie, he's here. That guy is *here*."

Palmer, tall, lean, blond, with a boyish face, said, "Do as I tell you and you won't get killed. Sit down on the floor of the inside office and don't move." Kroeschel and Cordes obeyed.

Gorman, in the washroom, had heard Kroeschel's astonished words. Quickly he locked the door and opened the washroom window, but he couldn't push out the jammed screen. Palmer banged on the door with his rifle butt and said, "Are you coming out or will I have to shoot you through the door?" Gorman came out.

"Sit down with your buddies," Palmer directed, then asked the trio if the owner of the business was among them. Gorman answered. The killer nodded toward him and said, "Open the safe, brother."

"I can't," Gorman said. "It's a tricky combination lock and our office manager, Ernie Pohlman, is the only one who knows how to open it."

"Brother, you're lying," Palmer said evenly. "I've got a notion to kill you right now." He moved his rifle.

"I'm not lying. Ernie will open the safe when he comes in." Gorman admits he was scared. He had no way of knowing at what point a twisted whim might prompt the killer to start shooting.

At that moment truck driver Edward Fitzgibbons drove his pickup to the back of the building and parked it. Palmer crouched behind the 4-foot-high service counter. Fitzgibbons, noticing the broken pane in the rear door, ambled into the office saying, "Hey, it looks like somebody broke in here."

Palmer rose from behind the counter, his gun leveled. "And I'm still here," he announced. "You just sit down on the floor there with your buddies." Fitzgibbons did so.

The next captive was William Kuehnel, a railroad engineer for the local freight line, who dropped in to tell Gorman that a car of cement had arrived for him. The engineer was followed by Herschel Andrews, a construction-equipment operator, and then truck driver Darrell Smith.

Ernie Pohlman was a little late that morning. Reluctant to leave his wife and three children in the house 6 miles out in the country, he had stayed to show his wife how to fire his shotgun. His first sensation when confronted by Palmer was relief: At least he knew his family was safe.

When Pohlman identified himself, Palmer said, "Just the man. Open the safe, Ernie."

Pohlman knelt before the safe, which for a long time had been difficult to open. He twirled the knob. He failed on the first try. He failed again. In a warning tone Palmer said, "Ernie!" Again Pohlman muffed the combination. Palmer said, "Ernie, I'll give you one more minute. If you don't open that safe, you're a dead man."

"Take your time, Ernie," Gorman urged. "A minute's a long time."

Pohlman's face was white and wet with sweat. He carefully turned the dial again, heard the tumblers click and slumped with relief.

He dumped the contents of the money box onto the floor. Palmer nodded to Bill Kuehnel and said, "Now, sir, I want you to get the bills from the wallets and put all the money into that paper bag."

When Kuehnel had completed his task, Gorman said to Palmer, "You've got all we can give you. Why don't you take off?"

Palmer ignored the suggestion and stared at the men for a minute. "Brother," he said to Gorman, "write out a sign saying 'Closed till 1 p.m.' and put it on the window of the front door." Palmer seemed to have a plan in mind.

Gorman penciled the words on a rectangle of cardboard. As he taped the sign to the door window he saw a man step onto the porch of the house across the street. He kept rubbing the sign, hoping to attract the man's attention. But Palmer grew aware of his excess motions and said, "Brother, you're having a hard time with that sign. Get away from there." Each time Palmer gave an order he moved the rifle decisively.

He then addressed the group: "Do any of you have a knife?"

Nobody answered. To Kuehnel, he said, "Take a piece of glass, sir, and cut that telephone wire." Palmer seemed to enjoy using the word "sir" in giving orders.

After Kuehnel had cut the cord Palmer asked, "Is there any rope around here?"

Again nobody answered, although Gorman and his employees knew there was rope in the shed behind the building.

To Gorman, Palmer repeated, "Is there any rope?"

"On top of that elevator outside." Gorman pointed to the elevated sand-and-gravel bin and cement chute about 40 feet away. A wood ladder rose from the ground to the top of the bin where two lengths of rope dangled.

Palmer spoke to Kuehnel. "You, sir, get up that ladder and bring down a rope." As Kuehnel started out, Palmer said, "Wait! It might not look right unless it was the owner." He nodded at Gorman. "Better if you did it, brother."

He ordered the seven other men to lie on their bellies, face to the floor and hands behind their backs.

"Not a false move out of any of you," he warned, "or your boss'll get it." He posted himself at the door and told Gorman to climb the ladder and get the rope. "And if you try anything funny, there are going to be a lot of dead men in here."

Gorman climbed the ladder. As he began fooling with the rope he stood close to the top edge of the sand bin. He wanted terribly to be free of Palmer. *I could roll into the sand bin and Palmer could never hit me*, he thought. *Then I'd yell for help. Maybe when the men heard me they could make a break for it. But, no, Palmer would start shooting.* Gorman gathered up the rope and climbed down.

In the office, Palmer told Gorman to tie the men's hands behind their backs as they lay face down on the floor. First in line was Kuehnel. As the railroad man felt the rope go around his wrists he resigned himself to death. "I figured this was my time," he later recalled. "I knew he was going to shoot us."

Palmer tested the knot and said, "Brother, you tie a loose knot. If I find another knot like that, I'm going to shoot the man through the head."

Gorman retied the knot. Then he bound Fitzgibbons's wrists. "As the seven of us lay there," Fitzgibbons says, "I swear I felt the floor vibrate from our heartbeats." Gorman was feeling sick that he was tying up the men so that Palmer could shoot them while helpless. This was the killer's pattern, he knew.

After Gorman tied the wrists of the next man, Darrell Smith, Palmer said, "Three down and four to go. When they're all tied up I'll have to shoot them through the head." On the floor the silent men lay tense as boards, listening to the blood pound in their ears, waiting for the shots.

"I was never more scared in my life," Gorman said recently, "but I knew I had to do something. If I lunged at Palmer I'd probably get a bullet in the head. If I simply obeyed him, I'd still get the bullet in the head and so would the seven other men."

Palmer sat alertly on his haunches, his rifle muzzle following Gorman's every move. Gorman,

about 7 feet away, knew that if he tied up the fourth man he'd be a step farther away from the killer. He had to get closer.

During his 75 minutes of captivity, Gorman had noticed that whenever Palmer rose from his haunches he invariably pointed his rifle at the ceiling before bringing it to bear on his victims. If attacked, would Palmer stick to this habit, giving his assailant an added fraction of a second—or would he fire from his haunched position?

Gorman said, "Their legs are too jammed together for me to step between them."

"Then step on their legs, brother. They won't be hurting for long."

"I'll be able to do a better job if I can work from around their heads," Gorman said. This would put him a little closer to Palmer.

"You have my permission," Palmer said.

Then Gorman had a sudden idea, felt his guts twist in fear, and acted. He stepped between the second and the third man and, without haste, pretended to stumble. He tottered, then, in a seeming effort to regain his balance, stepped over the second man, moving closer to Palmer. To make the action seem innocent he stepped *backward*, giving the killer a clear shot at his back. Again, Gorman took a step backward, over the remaining man between him and Palmer.

The killer hesitated a moment, then—following habit—rose from his haunches, pointing the rifle toward the ceiling. In the split moment it took Palmer to bring the rifle down, Gorman was next to him and felt the gun barrel on his shoulder. He swung his left fist at the trigger guard, scraping the skin off his knuckles as he knocked the gun from Palmer's hands. Then, with all his power, he shot his right fist at Palmer's jaw. The killer went down, and Gorman fell on him. Palmer groped for the gun 6 inches away. Gorman jammed a knee on his wrist and hit him again, yelling, "Come on, boys!"

Galvanized into action, the four free men dived at Palmer. As they subdued him, contractor Ralph Russell came in the door. Hearing the scuffling and exclamations, he peered over the counter and said, "What's going on, a crap game this time of the morning?"

One of the men looked up and grunted, "Palmer!" Charlie Kroeschel ran to the nearest telephone. In three minutes the sheriff's car skidded to a halt in front of the office. Deputies handcuffed Palmer, now meek and whimpering a little, and hauled him away. It was all over.

Gorman and the seven men stood staring at one another. The thought of what might have happened was coursing through each of them like an electric shock. Gorman looked at his bloody hand. Then, in a dazed but businesslike tone he said, "OK, boys, we've got concrete to haul."

That broke the spell. Almost in chorus, the four truck drivers demanded, "Who the hell is going to haul it?"

Gorman felt a flush of relief, and grinned. "This morning," he said, "I guess nobody is."

For his action, Louis Gorman received the Carnegie Hero Fund Commission's Silver Medal.

Locked in the Lion's Jaws

As the enormous lion bit down hard, Tony Fitzjohn felt sure he had only a minute to live. Then he realized that another lion was entering the fray.

—

BY **ARNOLD SHAPIRO**

Originally published in May 1977

he 18-month-old lion cub, already bigger than a Great Dane, leaped out of the thick underbrush, put his furry front paws up on Tony Fitzjohn's broad shoulders and rubbed heads joyously with his friend. It was Thursday, June 12, 1975, and in lion fashion Freddie was welcoming Tony back to Kora Camp from a two-day supply trip.

Kora is an isolated huddle of tents protected by a high wire fence in northern Kenya, where 70-year-old naturalist George Adamson rehabilitates lions in a unique conservation project. Orphaned cubs or young zoo lions—lions that would otherwise remain in captivity—grow up, reproduce and live free in an area the Kenya government has designated a national game reserve.

Conditions at the camp are rugged: intense heat and biting

There is a rule in the bush: Never sit on the ground outside of camp.

tsetse flies, no electricity or plumbing, and a six-hour drive to the nearest settlement. But 31-year-old, English-born Fitzjohn had read the *Born Free* books as a teenager and had been captivated by the story of Joy and George Adamson raising the orphaned lioness, Elsa. Living in Africa and working with Adamson for the past three years was a dream come true for Tony.

His glasses were smashed and he saw flashes of the camp he had thought close.

One of his regular jobs was a monthly trip by Land Rover to buy supplies at the tiny outpost of Garissa. This morning, before his return, he had stopped to see the district game warden and to thank him for evicting a gang of armed poachers that had been leaving poison traps for rhinos inside the reserve.

The warden had asked about Freddie, the abandoned lion cub he had found in the bush some 17 months earlier and turned over to Tony. "That was the first cub I'd known," Tony recalls. He had taken the frail, fluffy animal in his arms, driven him home to Kora and given him the name Freddie.

Later, three more cubs were brought from zoos. But Freddie always held a special place with Tony. Freddie was not only good-natured, but he was also the bravest of the cubs, scrappier and more inclined to take liberties with the fully grown wild lions that prowl around the fence. He and Tony had slept in the same bed until Freddie outgrew it. Tony's girlfriend, Lindsay Bell, who lives in Nairobi, has said that Tony is completely relaxed only when he is with his lions.

❖ ❖ ❖

After two days of rough driving, Tony was exhausted and glad to be back at Kora. He was dressed only in shorts and sandals, his tan skin glistening with perspiration in the 97-degree heat. It was time to gather the cubs—the other three had joined Freddie now in welcoming Tony—

and take them inside the fence for the night. To gentle the frisky Freddie, Tony sat down, his arms clasped around his knees, his back to the underbrush a few yards away, and began talking quietly. One rule in the bush is *never* to sit on the ground outside camp because of the possibility of unexpected contact with animals. But Tony felt safe within shouting distance of the tents.

It was 5:10 p.m. The camp, 50 yards away, was quiet. Then, without warning, Tony felt a giant creature pounce on him from behind. He crashed forward to the ground and momentarily lost consciousness. When he came to, it was to the terrifying awareness that his head was locked between the jaws of an enormous lion.

The attacker clamped down hard, then released the headlock and began a barrage of biting and clawing—sharp bites to the neck and head, deep bites to both shoulders, slashing claws to back and legs.

To Tony this horror was a "series of jerky slides separated by periods of blackout." His glasses were smashed and he saw flashes of the camp he had thought close; it seemed to be moving farther and farther away, getting smaller and smaller. Which lion was attacking him? One of George's? He knew only that the beast was fully grown and powerful—400 pounds and 8 feet long.

Tony didn't have a chance. He covered his genitals and closed his eyes. More blows from mighty paws struck his head; more deep gashes from razor-sharp claws opened his face. Because of shock and concussion, he felt no pain and heard no sounds. Paralyzed by injuries and bewilderment, he was experiencing his own death as a silent movie.

Now the lion grabbed Tony's neck and bit down. Tony couldn't breathe through his nose and couldn't open his mouth. He remembered that lions often kill by strangulation, holding their viselike grip until the prey stops breathing. It takes no more than a minute.

During this minute, Tony suddenly realized that there were

two lions in the battle. As he forced his bloody eyelids open, he saw Freddie charging toward him. *Oh, no, not Freddie too!* he thought.

But little Freddie wasn't attacking Tony; he was after the mighty lion, four times as big as he. Proper juvenile behavior is to submit to adult lions; to attack an enraged adult was suicide.

Freddie kept charging, however—snapping and snarling and biting at the flanks of the lion who stood astride Tony's torso. And for an instant it worked. The lion released his grip on Tony's neck and charged after Freddie, who ran for his life. Tony lay in a pool of blood, gasping for air. The attacker could have caught Freddie and torn him apart on the spot. But he stopped his pursuit and ran back to the victim. Again, he clamped down on Tony's neck in the fatal strangulation hold. *God, I'm dying! I can feel it,* Tony thought. In seconds, he lost consciousness again.

But Freddie returned to the fray and bit the surprised beast's rear, then circled with snarls and yelps, bold charges and nips. Freddie

withdrew only when the bigger animal swiped at him with his powerful paw. But he could not stop the foe.

Throughout the attack, Tony was a silent victim and the lion a silent killer. The only sounds were Freddie's unrelenting growls and piercing yelps that Tony could not hear.

❖ ❖ ❖

But Freddie's shrill cries *were* heard by Erigumsa, the compound's cook. At first, he thought two cubs were fighting, but Freddie's distant voice sounded too desperate. The cook ran to the gate—and saw Tony being mauled to death. Erigumsa raced to the dining tent, 75 feet away, where George Adamson was having tea.

"*Simba ame kamata Tony inje! Anataka kuua yeye!*" he cried in Swahili. ("The lion has caught Tony outside! He's trying to kill him!")

George believed the cubs' playfulness had unintentionally got too rough. So he took only a walking stick, bypassing a loaded rifle, when he ran from the tent.

Outside the gate, George saw Tony's neck locked between the jaws of a full-grown lion. There was no time to return for the rifle—he had to act instantly. Without a second thought, he charged the lion, frantically yelling and waving the walking stick.

Now George was vulnerable to attack. But the beast released Tony and retreated to stare at George. The lion prepared to spring, but George kept moving forward, shouting and brandishing the stick. It worked! The lion hesitated, then slunk off into the bush, splotched with Tony's blood.

❖ ❖ ❖

The next thing Tony realized, he was stumbling back to camp, supported by George. "George, I think I'm dying. Whatever you do," Tony pleaded, "don't shoot the lion. My fault … Caught unaware … Shouldn't have happened."

The minute he got Tony into his tent, George rushed to the shortwave radio to call the Flying Doctor Service in Nairobi. It was too late—the 135-mile flight would take an hour and a quarter, and

Tony Fitzjohn in Mkomazi, Tanzania, in 2012

regulations firmly prohibit landing on a bush strip after dark, even for a critical emergency.

The nurse assured George that the plane would come first thing in the morning and advised him on first-aid treatment for Tony's myriad deep wounds. George signed off, staring at the setting sun. Could Tony make it through the long night ahead without a surgeon and blood transfusions?

Drifting in and out of consciousness, Tony fought for breath—and life. "I've got to live—for Lindsay, George and the lions. I know if I just think about living, I'll make it."

At dawn, outside camp, George and Erigumsa managed smiles; 13 hours after his mauling, Tony was still alive.

Tony had been literally eaten by a lion, which had chewed the flesh off his face and neck.

Lindsay was the first one out of the Flying Doctor aircraft when it touched down—George had radioed her the night before about Tony's condition. "I was expecting bad wounds, but not all over his head," she recalls. "He could hardly breathe. The right side of his neck was completely open and his wounds were oozing. It was horrible." During the flight back to Nairobi with Tony, Lindsay broke down and wept. "I knew how much he loved his work," she says. "If he lived, would he ever want to return to the lions?"

Tony spent two hours in surgery when they got him to the hospital. There were three dozen wounds—some so deep and dangerous they couldn't be stitched at that time. His trachea had been squeezed but not broken. Miraculously, the lion's teeth had not severed any nerve, artery or vein. Tony would be one of the few people ever to survive a lion mauling.

❖ ❖ ❖

The day after the attack, a large lion appeared outside Kora with dried blood on his chest and muzzle. It was a 2½-year-old wild lion George had known since infancy, a creature so placid that he'd been named Shyman.

Now the cubs wouldn't go near Shyman, and he, uncharacteristically, began growling menacingly at them. George drove outside the compound and positioned the Land Rover between Shyman and the frightened cubs. Then he observed

Shyman carefully. His movements were erratic and unusual. The once-gentle lion had probably eaten from a poisoned carcass left by the rhino poachers. Since he had attacked once, he could do it again. The lives of humans and other lions were in jeopardy. After an hour of watching Shyman's behavior, George sadly raised his rifle and put a bullet into the lion's brain.

Such a mauling as Tony had received would make even the bravest soul reevaluate the risks of work in the bush. Tony had been literally eaten by a lion, which had chewed the flesh off his face and neck—the scars will be with him always. But Tony remembered how a lion cub whom he loved had tried to save him.

Two months after the accident, Tony returned to Kora, wondering what kind of greeting, if any, he'd receive after his absence. As he reached camp, he saw the cubs atop a large rock. And when they saw him, they rushed toward him, Freddie in the lead, making woofing sounds all the way. Typical lion

greetings last less than a minute—this one lasted close to 10, the excited cubs leaping all over Tony.

"I never had any thoughts about not going back," Tony told me when I visited him. "We're creating an animal reserve. People from all over the world can eventually come and see our lions, and the lions can live free and unmolested in nature. I belong here."

203

"Charlie Would Have Loved This"

If people were just a little more dreamy!

BY **J.P. McEVOY**

Originally published in June 1954

She was sitting beside me on the beach at Waikiki. Sounds romantic, doesn't it? But it wasn't really. There were many ladies just like her—tourists from everywhere—white-haired, restless, lonely. On a small stage, flaming with tropical flowers, a colorful group of Hawaiian singers and dancers were broadcasting their weekly sun-kissed program of synthetic romance to the frostbitten unfortunates on the mainland.

"This is your Isle of Golden Dreams, calling to you from across the sea," crooned the announcer. His assistant ran a few yards down to the lapping waves with a microphone.

"Listen, folks! The waves of Waikiki. Can't you see the surfboard riders? Can't you just picture those hula girls swaying under the palms?"

The white-haired lady beside me said, "Charlie would have loved this. It's just like we used to hear it on the radio back in Illinois. Saturday nights when Charlie came in from the fields, he'd turn on this program *Hawaii Calls* and we'd listen, and Charlie would say 'Mary, we're going there someday,' and I'd say 'When?' and he'd say 'Soon as we've saved up some money and get some time,' and I'd say, 'You've been saying that for years, Charlie, but every time we get a little money ahead you buy another 40 acres. Are you trying to buy up the whole state of Illinois?' That was a joke we had, and Charlie would laugh and say, 'No, I just want the piece next to me.' So Charlie never did get out here."

"You are listening to the Singing Surfriders," purred the announcer, "but unfortunately you cannot see the lovely Lani dancing her famous hula under the palms. She is wearing a green ti-leaf skirt and a red hibiscus in her long black hair."

The little white-haired lady said, "We had such good times together. If only Charlie was here with me now."

Every Sunday night, in the High Talking Chiefs Long House on Waikiki Beach, Don the Beachcomber puts on a luau for the tourists. This is a Polynesian-type clambake where only the barbecued pig comes fully dressed, while the guests sit on the floor, kick off their shoes, and drape leis of white gardenias or pink carnations around their necks, and the ladies stick a red hibiscus over their ear— the right ear if they have a man, the left if they want one.

Tourists milled around the bar, carrying bamboo tubes filled with rum concoctions playfully labeled Missionary's Downfall, Cobra's Fang and the Vicious Virgin. I spotted my white-haired friend, timid and alone but bravely sporting a man's aloha shirt that looked like an explosion in a paint factory. But the conventional black skirt and high-heeled shoes were definitely out of place in this Technicolor jungle of muumuus, holokus, sarongs, bare torsos and coconut hats.

I walked over and said, "Are you with anyone?"

"No," she said. "Is it all right to come alone?"

"You're not alone," I told her and hung a flower lei around her neck and kissed her cheek. "Let's go sit down. They're bringing in the barbecued pig."

I introduced her to my party and they moved over to make room for her as she looked around a bit helplessly. "But everybody's sitting on the floor."

"That's right," I said. "Those creaking noises you hear are just old mainland joints like yours and mine." She sat down on the floor beside me. "Now kick off your shoes and dive in," I told her.

Wooden platters were set before each guest but no knives or forks. My friend watched as we old-timers dug in with bare hands and licked our fingers. Then she followed suit, embarrassed at first, but quickly getting into the spirit of the occasion.

"What are we eating?" she asked. "Not that I care," she added quickly.

"This is pig baked underground with heated rocks. And this is laulau—butterfish wrapped in ti leaf. And this," I said, dipping it up with my fingers, "is the poi they sing about. It looks and tastes like paperhanger's paste. If you can scoop it up with one finger, it's one-finger poi. If you need two fingers, it's two-finger poi."

Don came over and tucked a red hibiscus into my friend's white hair over her right ear. I explained the difference and she moved it to her left ear.

"Charlie would have loved this," she said.

And then the jungle drums started and a beautiful young Polynesian typhoon, wearing a crown of plumeria blossoms and a grass skirt, exploded into a dance.

"Wouldn't it be wonderful if people could live like this all the time," she said. "Kick off your shoes and sit on the floor and eat with your fingers and wear flowers in your hair and listen to music like that and watch dancers like what's-her-name there."

"Johnny," I said. "She comes from Pukapuka in the South Seas."

"Charlie always wanted to go there," she said. "There was a book, *White Shadows in the South Seas.* He used to read it aloud to me and once we saw a movie by the same name and he said, 'Someday I'll take you there.' But he kept putting it off. And when he died I wouldn't have been able to make this trip if it hadn't been for the insurance money he left."

A troupe from Samoa took the floor and did a dazzling fire dance. My friend sighed.

"I guess we waited too long." She shook her head a little, bewildered. "There's something wrong somewhere. What's the use of working yourself to death if you don't live to enjoy it?"

"Maybe we don't have to," I said. "When we want homes we don't wait until we're too old to get them. We borrow the money and live in the houses while we pay it off. Lots of us do the same about cars. We don't walk our legs off until we need wheelchairs. We get the cars and manage somehow to pay for them. Suppose Charlie had added a few hundred more to the mortgage and brought you out here while you both could enjoy it. Wouldn't that have made a lot more sense than buying another 40 acres? Practical people would be a lot more practical if they were just a little more dreamy. Then they wouldn't put off living until they were dead. Someday we may even be practical enough to invest in our dreams first."

"Aloha!" cried Don the Beachcomber. "Let's sing the song we all know—

"One fond embrace
Before we now depart,
Until we meet again ..."

There's no sweeter, sadder song. Even in broad daylight you feel like crying like a baby when perfect strangers sing "Aloha" and wave farewell to you from Honolulu piers and airports. As the party ended we started out into the street in our bare feet.

The little white-haired lady from Illinois had forgotten her shoes under the table, but her red hibiscus dangled jauntily over her left ear and there was a brave swing to the flower lei around her neck.

"You know what?" she said.

"Yes," I said. "Charlie would have loved this."

"That's for sure," she said, and she walked across the street to her lonely hotel room.

Granddad

A love story such as this can come only to the very young and the very old. A Reader's Digest *"First Person Award."*

BY **PEGGY MAPES TATE**

Originally published in October 1965

My granddad's house was 50 yards nearer the road than ours, but neither was really close to anything but the Texas land. Our rambling two-story had many gables and chimneys, but Granddad's was a simple structure, gabled only on the ends. A single stovepipe jutted from the center of the roof.

His front door opened onto a small screened-in porch. He called it his gallery, and it was his link with the world. Often he would sit there gazing out over the open prairie. His eyes could pick out a cow about to calve in a herd almost a mile away. Sometimes he would read aloud from the battered Bible on his lap, the old-fashioned round spectacles placed precisely midway down his nose. He had never gone to school. Some of the passages he read with such authority and drama that you knew he'd memorized them many years ago. Less familiar passages would find him seeking out the syllables one by one with his fingers.

So far as I was concerned, the one big room inside Granddad's house contained all the important treasures of the world. Along one wall squatted a large humpbacked trunk. On the oilcloth-covered table, under a spotless white cloth reposed a large pitcher of "lick," a black, thick molasses with a matchless, pungent taste.

In the center of the room sat a potbellied stove. During a cold norther its sides would glow red. There was no heat in the world so pervading, so comforting.

The dry sink in the corner was no planter for greenery, as in modern suburbia, but performed its intended function with dignity. Atop it sat the water bucket and the big china pitcher and washbasin that served for washing hands and dishes. Concealed behind its doors were a big bar of homemade lye soap, a solitary black skillet and the dry ingredients that could make a one-dish meal seem like seven courses.

The straight-backed chair at the table and the captain's chair by the stove offered the only conventional seating, but there was always the trunk or the tarp-covered bed. Granddad had ridden too many years with a tarpaulin tied behind his saddle to use anything less efficient for a bedspread. Two saddle blankets were a bright spot of color at the foot of the bed and furnished extra foot warmth on a cold night. Besides, you could bury your face in them, and the faint smell of horseflesh gave reality to the stories Granddad told by lamplight. The scrubbed, barren room was only a bachelor's cow camp moved in closer to civilization, but to a small child it offered a feeling of strength present in no other place on earth.

When I was barely 4, Granddad began teaching me the old folk songs of the cattle trails. There was no accompaniment, but his high-topped shoes would beat a solid bass rhythm, our clapping hands the offbeat. His aged, croaky voice and my squeaky soprano would fill the air and rattle the stovepipe, and in our heads the fiddlers played an accompaniment livelier and more wonderful than any ever played in real life.

It was that year, just before I turned 5, that he bought me a piano. I never knew what secret dream he gave up to throw down a fortune of $150 for the best instrument in town. For years he had existed on a paltry pension and the little he could earn in wages for odd jobs. From his only living child, my father, he would accept nothing except for services rendered. It wasn't that they weren't friendly. Granddad had a fierce independence that no one infringed on.

From the day I got the piano, self-discipline entered my life. An hour of practice is an endless corner of eternity for one so young, but to have done less would have been insult to the priceless gift. Granddad would seldom come in to listen, but he usually managed to make a trip to the well house for water while I practiced. I didn't need to look to know when he came. I could hear the cane, the bad foot dragging behind the other like a child skipping in very slow motion. Two or three cats usually stepped daintily in his wake—he seemed to commune directly with all animals.

One bright summer morning, I went to the well house to wait for him. It took my eyes a moment to adjust to the dim interior, to identify the bright stripe of white in the corner. When Granddad finally peered in the door, I was standing in hypnotic horror facing a skunk—a frightened, cornered animal with tail high in the air.

"Back very slowly out the door," Granddad said. He handed me his cane as I backed past him, and he began humming a Native American dirge in a low, soothing voice. When

> ### "Same principle as rubbing your wart away; as the Bible says, faith can move a mountain."

he came out, he held the skunk high on its tail, walked toward the pasture with the skunk hanging quietly. He set the animal down gently, facing him, then turned and walked slowly toward me without looking back. The skunk blinked in the bright sunlight, turned and humped his way across the prairie in the opposite direction, as if being carried by a man were something that happened every day.

Granddad never told me how he did it. When I asked him he said, "Same principle as rubbing your wart away; as the Bible says, faith can move a mountain."

The years went tumbling by. The year I made his first birthday cake, I was 8 and he was 88. The cake sank in the middle and was rock-hard on the sides. It said

> *"God gave us something special," he went on, "a closeness he gives to few of his creatures."*

"Happy Birthday" in red coloring that slipped crazily in too-soft frosting, but I believed him when he said he had never tasted anything so wonderful.

The year I was 12, he nearly died with erysipelas. His swollen face was a purple blotch on the pillow before he would allow us to call a doctor. By the time he sat on his gallery again, he no longer had the strength to lace his heavy shoes. Going to tie Granddad's shoes became my first morning duty.

He spoke disparagingly of "that budget-bustin' medicine man," and when his hair had grown beyond the bounds of decency I finally realized he had no money for haircuts. He seemed delighted when I showed up with hand clippers, shears and comb. It never occurred to me to doubt that a 12-year-old kid could cut hair, because he never by so much as a look expressed a lack of confidence.

He had no nickels and dimes to reward me with now, but he often insisted on fixing me something to eat. While the home-cured bacon was crisping in the skillet, he would prepare the scrambled eggs. Into the bacon grease he would dump a handful of cornmeal to brown before the eggs were added. There is no more delicious aroma in the whole world.

Just before I left to catch the train that would take me away for my second year of college, I went to say goodbye, as I always did before going away. For years he'd been saying, "I may not be here when you get back," and it had come to be part of the routine.

This time he said, "I won't be here when you come back," and the tone of voice had something of premonition in it that had not been there before. "God gave us something special," he went on, "a closeness he gives to few of his creatures."

I sat tense and intent. He'd seldom lectured seriously, always showing by action or story what he wanted me to be.

"You'll not always be happy," he said. "You have the spirit of a wild mustang and the willfulness of a mule, and you'll always be a maverick in the herd. Being a maverick is not a bad thing, but it can get awful lonely."

He wiped his glasses carefully, and I couldn't say a thing for the lump in my throat. "When I die and they call you to come, don't do it," he said. "I'll never be far from you, but you might not believe that if you saw me dead. Anyway, the ones cryin' the loudest at a funeral is usually the ones that cared the least." He grinned at his own observation and went on. "We won't say 'bye this time. Just walk straight out of here, and I'll be 'round if you ever need me."

I touched his cheek lightly with my fingertips and walked out without a word. All the time I felt like two people, one wanting to run back, the other marching straight ahead with shoulders back and chin up—the way he liked you to look when you had to step off into something taking a lot of courage.

A few weeks later, the phone call came just as I was leaving for class.

"I can't come to the funeral," I lied. "If I miss those tests, I'll have to repeat a whole semester." Just as I hung up, my roommate came in.

"What *is* that odor?" she asked, wrinkling her nose and sniffing the air. "If I didn't know cooking was against the rules, I'd swear I smelled cornmeal and something frying!"

She wasn't mistaken at all.

Clams Are Not My Dish

*Let's talk and make our mistakes early,
for which we can either love each other
or part company soon*

—

BY **DON HEROLD**

Originally published in November 1960

nce I loved a girl to whom I bared my soul (talked my head off). She bounced me in favor of a mono-syllabic Tarzan whom she described as "the strong, silent type." Since then I've been astonished at how frequently people who keep their mouths shut are praised.

What's so wonderful about being a clam?

I prefer people who speak up, people who volunteer information, people with conversational careless-ness. They may make some errors, but they *give.*

I am totally unimpressed by cagey men with poker faces, or bankers with glass eyes, or doctors who say nothing but "Hmm!" and will not tell me my temperature, or by movie cowboys who just say "Yup." Many times I have finally succeeded in getting them to talk, and it has been worth something less than the effort.

I like people who wag injudi-ciously like a dog, not people who pussyfoot through life. Chatterers, spouters, blabbers and kidders—they constitute 95% of the spirited, kindly and sympathetic people of the earth. It's among these that you'll find the philosophers, the poets, the appreciators and the stimulators.

And if some of them should happen to be bores, I thank them for helping me find it out all the sooner. People who never talk nonsense never say anything profound. People who are afraid of being inconsequential are of no consequence.

Generosity—or the lack of it—is often the key. I've found that the silent individual is often hostile. The man who so politely conceals his knowledge is usually overestimating its extent. And a man who never interrupts isn't listening to you. But the man who talks about himself trusts you. And the man who "talks shop" likes his job.

I know that most of life's aphorisms counsel silence, such as "He who does not open his mouth will never put his foot in it." But how much more lively the world would be if we saw more people with their feet in their mouths!

An Army of Two

*A judge sentences a fellow vet to jail—
then joins him in his cell for the night*

BY **ROBERT KIENER**

Originally published in April 2018

The minute Joe Serna walked into the Veterans Treatment Court in Fayetteville, North Carolina, he could feel his shoulders tense up, hear his stomach growling. He had come to turn himself in. Six months earlier, Serna had been arrested for impaired driving. As part of his sentence, he was required to report to Judge Lou Olivera's court every two weeks to take a urine test and prove he hadn't been drinking.

Serna had passed every biweekly screening—until the week before. Positive. He decided to try to bluff his way out of trouble. "I never had a drink, Judge," he told the court. "Honest."

If Judge Olivera suspected anything, he didn't let on. Both men were veterans, and Olivera had come to know and admire Serna as he participated in the court's program to help vets with drinking and addiction problems. Though their lives had gone in opposite directions since they'd left the military, they were still connected by their service. And

Judge Lou Olivera (left) with fellow vet Joe Serna

that was what ate at Serna, what had brought him back to Olivera's court a week after his lie. *This guy is a fellow soldier*, he told himself. *I need to make this right*. So Serna stood before Olivera and admitted quietly, "I lied." As beads of perspiration rolled down his forehead, he said, this time a bit louder, "I lied, Judge. I was drinking."

❖   ❖   ❖

After three tours of duty in Afghanistan, countless combat missions, two Purple Hearts and the memories of way too many "best buddies" losing their lives, 39-year-old Joe Serna left the Army in 2013 with 18 years of service. By 2016, he was living in Fayetteville with his wife and three children and studying for an accounting degree at nearby Methodist University. But in truth, he had never really left the Army, and it certainly had never left him. The memories would lie low for a while, like a hidden enemy, only to reemerge in a nightmare or a tormenting flashback.

His wife, Rocio, had learned the warning signs: his cold sweats, the way he would tense his shoulders or cry out in the night. She was rarely surprised when he woke her up, thrashing in bed and whispering, "Bad guy … bad guys." Sometimes he'd kick and shout "IED!" Then, "No! No!"

The flashbacks emerged, seemingly, from a thousand points of darkness. There was the time during Serna's first tour in Afghanistan, in 2006, when his convoy was ambushed. Or the time when he threw a wounded comrade over his shoulder and carried him through heavy fire. As he would later explain, "He was my brother in arms. We never leave each other behind."

Once, while he was interrogating a local Afghan with an interpreter,

he suddenly heard a metallic click, followed by a telltale ping as something hit the floor. A suicide bomber had detonated a grenade that sent shrapnel through much of Serna's body and face and knocked out his teeth. "If I had been a foot closer to the grenade, it would have killed me," he recalls.

Yet it was another incident that caused most of his nightmares. As part of a convoy, he and three other Special Forces soldiers were inside a 19-ton RG-31 mine-resistant truck, driving through Kandahar, Afghanistan, to recover a fallen brother who had died after stepping on a mine. Just after midnight, as they were driving along a pitch black dirt road that was flanked by a canal, the narrow road gave way. The massive armored vehicle fell sideways, slipped down the bank and toppled into the canal.

"The truck started filling with water, and I couldn't release my seat belt," Serna remembers. Helpless, he felt the water rising over his feet, then up to his knees, then his chest. His heart pounding, he heard his team members screaming for help as the water swallowed them up. *This is it*, he thought as he struggled to free himself. *I'm going to die.*

But then one of his brothers came to the rescue. "When the water had reached my chin, I felt a hand come down and unfasten my seat belt and release my body armor," Serna says. "Sergeant James Treber picked me up and moved me to a pocket of air."

> ## *Doctors suggested to him that he was suffering from post-traumatic stress disorder (PTSD).*

The truck's hydraulic system had been knocked out, so the doors wouldn't budge. The soldiers were trapped. Because there was not enough space for both of them in the small air pocket, Treber dived into the water to find a larger one. Suddenly some fuel cans broke and contaminated Serna's air pocket with gasoline. He passed out.

"I thought I'd died," says Serna. "Someone pulled me out of the truck. When I came to, I saw three bodies lying on the ground. Everyone else in the truck, including Sergeant Treber, had died." To this day, being stuck in a confined space can trigger flashbacks for Serna.

He was still in the military when doctors suggested to him that he was suffering from post-traumatic stress disorder (PTSD). He wanted to keep it quiet. He was a Green Beret, among the best of the best, and Special Forces types don't like to admit weakness.

In truth, he was scared, afraid that the diagnosis could end his career. He turned to drink to quiet his demons.

❖　❖　❖

Still, he never gave up the fight, and Judge Olivera knew that. On the day when Serna stood in the courtroom to admit he had lied about drinking, the judge wasn't angry. He was moved.

"One of the main aims of the Veterans Treatment Court is to build trust and relationships with the veterans who appear before us,"

Olivera says. "We are one big team—we are all veterans—and when one of us screws up, the rest of the team says, 'You have to square yourself away.'"

He listened to Serna's confession that day and decided on the punishment: one night in the Cumberland County jail.

The next afternoon, Olivera got a text telling him, "FYI, Joe Serna is reporting to jail today." Olivera crossed the street to wish Serna luck. He found him highly agitated, his white T-shirt soaked with sweat.

"You OK?" asked Olivera.

Serna, his eyes locked on the floor, mumbled an answer. Suddenly Olivera remembered the story of Serna's rollover and the lingering claustrophobia it had caused. The judge asked the jailer whether he had an open cell, one with bars instead of cinder blocks and a door. He didn't.

The judge turned to Serna and asked him, "Do you trust me?"

"Yes, sir," said Serna.

"Then get in my car," Olivera said to him.

He drove Serna to nearby Lumberton, North Carolina, where he knew the local chief of police.

An hour later, Joe Serna, dressed in a jail issued orange jumpsuit, walked into a 10-by-7-foot one-person cell in the Robeson County Detention Center. As the heavy steel door slammed behind him, Serna sat on the hard steel cot. He felt his shoulders tightening, his heart beating faster. He tried to fight the familiar feeling of dread, but as his body tensed, the gunmetal gray walls began to close in on him.

He knew he would soon be flashing back to that armored truck, feeling helpless as the water rose up to his chin, reliving the horror of that night. His mind was racing. *How do I get out of here?* he thought. *There is no way out!*

Then the door jangled as the jailer unlocked it. Standing in the open doorway was Judge Olivera, carrying two dinner trays.

"OK, Joe, are you ready?" Olivera asked.

Serna looked at him and asked, "Where are we going?"

"We aren't going anywhere," Olivera said. "*We* are staying here."

Serna was confused. But a few minutes later, after the jailer brought in a 2-inch-thick foam mattress and once again locked the heavy steel door behind him, Serna understood. The judge, a fellow veteran, realizing that this cell was no better than the first

> ## "And I have slept on the floor before," the judge said. "In fact, you and I have slept in worse places."

one, had decided to spend the night with a comrade in arms.

Olivera's compassion nearly drove Serna to tears. But he managed to regain his composure enough to beg Olivera to take the cot and let him sleep on the floor.

"Judge, I can't give you the floor," he said.

"Call me Lou, Joe. And I have slept on the floor before. In fact, you and I have slept in worse places."

They traded war stories as they tucked into jail-issued meat loaf and mashed potatoes. "Nasty stuff, isn't it?" joked Olivera, cutting the tension in the cell. Serna told the judge about the day he was almost blown to bits by the Afghan suicide bomber, and he found himself actually laughing as he described the ping he'd heard when the grenade pin had hit the floor. Olivera laughed too, sharing in a shade of black humor only a fellow veteran would understand.

The two talked for hours about their service, their families and their hopes for the future. At around one in the morning, Olivera heard Serna's breathing get deeper, and he eventually began to snore. *He will be OK now*, the judge said to himself as he rolled up his shirt into a makeshift pillow. *He'll be fine.*

❖ ❖ ❖

Serna is due to graduate from Methodist University. Afterward, he will move to California with his wife and their children, Matthew, Efrain and Andrea, to run his father's construction company. (Matthew is named after the man

who saved Serna's life: Sgt. James Matthew Treber.)

For his part, Judge Olivera insists that any veteran would have reacted to Serna's plight just as he did. He is fond of telling a story he once read about a veteran who was suffering from PTSD: "The veteran was in a deep hole. First his family threw down a rope, but he wouldn't come out. Then his therapist threw down a rope, but again he didn't come out. Then his minister, with the same result. Finally, a second veteran came by, and he too threw down a rope. But this time, he climbed into the hole with the first vet. 'What are you doing down here with me?' the vet with PTSD asked. The second vet answered, 'I'm here to climb out with you.'

"I've never forgotten that story, and I know that there are many veterans who would have done the same. These are our brothers. We never leave each other behind."

The Wreck of the *Guinevere*

*The saga of four days in a hurricane,
with death never more than a wave away.
A* Reader's Digest *"First Person Award."*

—

BY **RODNEY STRULO**

Originally published in July 1965

Monday, March 5, 1962, brought with it the ever-new miracle of dawn after a night at sea. I was at the wheel of *Guinevere*, our 40-foot ketch, with Heather, my wife, beside me. Astern, in the thinly lightening sky, lay Charleston, South Carolina.

We were headed back to St. Thomas, in the West Indies, after a vacation in the United States. The year before, I had been a teacher in London, my wife a nurse. But we both hated living in cities and had left London to sail our own boat across the Atlantic to St. Thomas, where I found another teaching job.

The rising sun colored our sails pink as they filled to the light breeze. Duke, the only other member of our crew, poked his head out of the companionway. "I've been making a radio check," he said. "The Weather Bureau reckons it'll stay this way."

We had met Duke only two days before on the dock at Charleston and had taken to him at sight. A tall, husky ex-Navy diver, he was headed for the Caribbean. An extra

hand would be welcome; so, here he was, his youthful face almost lost in the fur collar that topped the worn remains of an old waterproof jacket.

The wind freshened all day, confounding the forecast, until by nightfall it was drumming the rigging. I went below to cook our supper of ham, eggs and peas on the tiny gas cooker in the heaving cabin. With the wheel lashed, we ate together under the swinging shadows of the kerosene lamp. It was our last meal for three days.

"No Sweat"

Back on deck, we found *Guinevere* thundering into the waves, hurling back sheets of spray. Duke and I lowered the mainsail and lashed it down; I clambered into the cockpit for my watch at the wheel. The seas were growing increasingly rough. Out of the inky black world beyond the circle of light from our compass, a hissing white-topped wave would emerge, lift our decks through creaming foam and race on.

When I called Duke for his watch, he came awake as soon as I touched him.

"Barometer's still dropping," I said. With difficulty we lowered our tiny mizzen sail. Before we could get to the jib it blew out with a crack, leaving ropes snapping in the wind.

"No sweat," Duke said as Heather and I turned in. "Tomorrow we'll be in trade winds."

Wave crests breaking on the boat woke me about midnight. Standing in a foot of water, Heather was wrapping the radio in plastic bags. "The only dry place is the 'fridge," she said. "I've already put in matches and the sextant. I was going to call you, but I thought you needed the sleep."

I made a quick inspection. We were leaking badly. The electric pumps were working, but they couldn't keep up with the deluge. I passed Heather a life jacket, then dug out others for Duke and myself.

"Better put these on," I said. "And let's bail."

I scooped water from the foot of the companionway into a bucket. Heather, perched above me on the ladder, reached down for the bucket and tilted it out the hatch. She didn't have to empty it—

the wind tore the water away.

When I relieved Duke at the wheel, he took my place below, bailing. After a time, Heather noticed that he was stumbling. "You feeling all right?" she asked.

"Not too good," he admitted.

"OK, swap jobs. You come up here and chuck."

In everything he did after that, Duke was fighting the nausea and weakness of seasickness.

A Howling Desert

On Tuesday the sun didn't rise. In that terrible dawn, a gray light seeped through the storm clouds, revealing mountainous seas. Duke and I watched with awe as a wave built up high above the mizzenmast— over 40 feet. When its crest reared over us, *Guinevere* rose to it, her stern flying into the sky. From the top we saw a fog of driven spray and spindrift covering the howling desert of the ocean. In a moment we were falling before the next wave.

"This is a freak hurricane, Rodney," Duke said. "We had one once in the Pacific."

Heather hung on to the wheel, a frail figure, yet emanating strength and assurance. If you asked Heather to hold on to a line, she'd do it, even if it pulled her off the deck. We hunted out all the ropes on board and trailed them astern to check our speed and quiet the boiling heaps of water alongside. I looked at the sea streaming by. If one of us went over the side, it would be impossible to stop *Guinevere* to make a search.

As a precaution we unpacked the rubber life raft, and Duke screwed on the carbon-dioxide cartridges. They didn't inflate the raft enough to give it shape. Duke threw the cartridges overboard in disgust. Then he put his mouth to the valve and blew. Human lungs weren't powerful enough to do the job. Our expensive life raft was worthless.

"We can always swim for it," Heather said.

"You've forgotten," I said. "*I can't swim.*" We burst out laughing.

Half Under

Back we went to our routine—one steering, two bailing. At 7:30 a.m. there was a lull. We hoped that this was the eye of the hurricane, but the wind came back stronger from the same direction, with hail squalls. Half an hour later I heard Heather scream. Suddenly I was lying face down; the cabin was full of water.

When I reached her, Heather sobbed. "The wave … we didn't rise to it. It broke right on top of us."

I held her tight in my arms. Duke grabbed the wheel. "It's dead," he shouted. "Bail!"

We worked desperately. Half-filled with water, the boat rolled like a log, unable to lift to the seas. For a few minutes the waves held off—and slowly the boat grew buoyant. The wind took hold, she picked up speed and now we could steer again.

But from this point on, everything was changed. None of us thought about finishing the voyage. We thought only about getting off alive. *Guinevere* looked derelict. Her decks were swept clean, hatches gone; planking was torn off. The sides of the cockpit were smashed; the sea swirled into the bilges.

"Mayday! Mayday!"

Down in the cabin I tore the plastic bags off the radio, hoping that it had kept dry. The ammeter swung slowly over. Soon, with a burst of twittering, we were linked with the world beyond the storm.

"Mayday! Mayday!" I began. "Yacht *Guinevere* calling Coast Guard. Position approximately 110 miles east-southeast of Charleston. My boat is sinking."

It was like the moment of trying to avoid an auto accident: Your foot hard on the brake, you can only wait and see what happens.

I repeated the distress call, and again, slowly. Suddenly a voice, matter-of-fact and reassuring, came through: "Charleston Coast Guard calling *Guinevere*. Your message received. Your position: 110 miles east-southeast of Charleston." I shouted up through the driving hail to Heather and Duke. "They know we're here!"

"No Regrets"

For the next three days death was with us constantly, never more than a wave away. A freighter passed near us, seemed to veer our way, then passed on in the blinding spindrift. Our radio went dead.

But we fought back. With canvas and broken planks, we patched the holes in *Guinevere*'s hull. We bailed and steered. Hour after hour our belief in life was tested. In the effort and pain of every action we had to reaffirm our will to survive.

One afternoon a plane passed over, low enough for us to read USCG on the wings. We waved and shouted, but the aircraft was visible for only a few seconds. We doubted that we had been seen.

I began to give up hope. I said to Heather, "I'm sorry I got you into this."

"It's a chance we both took," she answered. "We've had a lot of happiness together. I've no regrets."

We fought on through day and night, no longer aware of our bruises, the cold and the wet. We no longer heard the never-ending howl of the storm. We were beyond exhaustion, beyond thought. After hours of fighting the desire to drop down in the water and sleep, the desire itself died.

The wind was so strong it tore at pieces of the Dacron sails lashed to the booms and ripped them away.

From the Spout

Cooking was impossible, so we got by on sips of water and canned milk. As *Guinevere* broke up, however, her water tanks were broached and we had no more fresh water. It was Thursday afternoon. Heather reached out a teapot to Duke and me. "This is dinner," she said. "It's raw eggs beaten up with ketchup."

Duke and I suddenly realized how hungry and thirsty we were. We all gulped from the spout.

Duke commented, "This is my girl Betty's day off. I always ate at her place Thursdays …"

In the stark, ruined cabin that had been our home we felt curiously tranquil. We talked gently and with affection; we felt at peace with the world. The peril in which we lived washed away inessentials. When we prayed, it was not for a miracle but for the strength to go on fighting, to enjoy for another hour the grandeur of being alive.

Thursday night, Duke turned on his pocket transistor radio, hoping for music. A voice announced: "Search for the yacht *Guinevere* has been abandoned.

She is now considered lost …"

We drowned the rest of the bulletin with our laughter. "We're lost! They're telling *us*!"

Broken Bones

On Friday, the wind dropped back. I got a sight of the sun and worked out a position line. We were about 240 miles off the coast. Then …

Heather saw it first. It was a tanker, half a mile astern. We heard Heather's sob of relief and looked. We could see the name on the bow: *Esso Greenville*. She seemed to be headed for us.

"They see us this time," Duke said.

We had thought our lives were over, and now we were being offered another chance.

The tanker maneuvered slowly, giving us a lee in the heavy seas. Her crew was waving from the rail. They threw us a line. I made it fast to the samson post, the strongest point on the boat. At the first tension, the post pulled out. *Guinevere*'s bones were broken. She smashed against the tanker.

From the bridge they saw what had happened. Men worked feverishly to swing out davits. Another line came down; this one had a bosun's chair slung on it.

One of the officers shouted, "Get that woman off."

"She's a sailor," Duke shouted back. "As good as any of us."

He pulled the chair over Heather's head. As the crew hauled her up, he held the line taut so she would not swing against the ship's side. Then I held the line for Duke.

There was no one to do the same for me. My responsibility had driven me; now it was over. I felt drained of will. As I hesitated, *Guinevere* gave her final roll. I caught at the chair. They dragged me up fast. I struck the side of the ship once, then I was on solid deck.

With Heather and Duke, I watched silently as *Guinevere* dived into a wave for the last time. The tanker's crew crowded around to offer their hands or to put an arm around our shoulders. We had escaped death, and we had learned how simple, precious and fragile life is. We resolved not to waste a moment of our lives thereafter.

Forget and Forgive

An odd situation causes a young married couple to reconsider their outlook

BY **ROBERT ZACKS**

Originally published in October 1954

n World War II, I was stationed as a medic at the Army's Halloran General Hospital on Staten Island, New York. To be near me, my wife got a job as a medical stenographer in Halloran's neurosurgery department. Her work was to take notes on the operations from the surgeons for insertion in the medical record.

Sometimes the surgeons would reminisce about their experiences. This story about a wounded soldier named Steve and his young wife, Laura, is the strangest one my wife passed on to me. For obvious reasons all names have been changed, including the surgeon's, a medical corps captain we'll call Dr. Paul.

Dr. Paul said, "I saw by Steve's record that he was married. I knew he hadn't had any visitors. I thought perhaps his wife hadn't been notified that Steve had been wounded and brought here, so I hunted down her address and asked her to come."

Halloran is in the isolated area of Staten Island, and to reach it from New York City means a ferry trip and two long bus rides. When Laura finally showed up she seemed fatigued and annoyed.

"I know it's a long trip here," Dr. Paul said, "But after all …"

The woman's eyes flamed. "It isn't that," she said. "It's just … well, what's the point of calling me down here? We're getting a divorce. Why should I be tortured this way? Why don't you mind your own business?"

"I'm very sorry," Dr. Paul said. "I had no idea that things were like that between you."

There was a moment of awkward silence and Laura said nervously, "How is he? Is he hurt badly?"

"His head wound has healed."

Suddenly the woman began to weep. She looked so forlorn that

> ## "There was no excuse for me. Then word got to Steve about what I'd done."

Dr. Paul said, cautiously, "Do you still care for him?"

"What's the use of talking like that?" she said. "It's finished." She controlled herself with an effort, then looked up at Dr. Paul and told him the story.

She had been unfaithful to Steve while he'd been overseas. They had been just a couple of kids when they'd married, and after a few months Steve had

been sent away. She felt terribly alone. She had no family and after a while got the frightening feeling that she didn't even have a husband, and that it was all a dream.

"I was stupid and shallow, too young and too flighty," she whispered, staring at the floor. "There was no excuse for me. Then word got to Steve about what I'd done."

She said Steve had then written her such a letter that she nearly died of self-loathing. He said that he'd never forgive her and that he never wanted to see her again. "When I got that letter I prayed. Isn't that a joke?" She got up abruptly. "Well, I'm glad Steve is all right now."

"He isn't," said Dr. Paul. "It's true his head wound is healed, but actually Steve is quite ill. You see, he has amnesia."

"Amnesia?" said Laura, dazed.

"That's right. He has lost a large part of his memory. He doesn't even know how to read. He'll have to be taught all over again. He's forgotten his past, his identity. I'd hoped that seeing you would bring it all back."

When they brought Steve in to face Laura he stared at her with eagerness but obviously did not remember her.

"This is your wife," said Dr. Paul quietly, and left them.

Afterward Laura came to Dr. Paul, her eyes full of mingled fear and hope. "Doctor," she said, "when he's discharged I'm going to live with him again. I'll support him, and help him get on his feet. I'll teach him to read. But will he ever get his memory back?"

"Very probably he'll recover from amnesia in time. He'll remember ... everything. What then?"

"Until then, I can help him," Laura said.

Steve was discharged from the hospital and from the Army. He went away with Laura.

A year later Dr. Paul received a letter from Laura. Steve had finally recovered from amnesia. There had been a bad hour while he sat staring out of the window, suffering with the memory. Then he had taken her in his arms and told her how much he loved her.

"In that year," Dr. Paul said, "she had made up for her mistake with such love and unselfishness that it outweighed the bad old memory that returned. It's really a pity more of us can't get an amnesia that will help us forgive."

The Most Nerve-Shattering Word in the Language

It's a word you never want to hear your mechanic, dentist or doctor utter

———

BY **H. ALLEN SMITH**

Originally published in April 1967

ullaby. Golden. Damask. Moonlight. Do these words seem esthetically attractive to you? They have appeared with some regularity on lists of "the 10 most beautiful words in our language." Along with *luminous*, and *hush*, *anemone*, *mother* and various others. These lists appear from time to time in the public prints. But I can't recall ever seeing a list of the 10 ugliest words in the language.

Almost every literate person has in his head an agglomeration of words that can cause him to wince, and even shudder, such as *agglomeration*. I lay claim to several hundred of the uglies. *Mulcted* almost nauseates me. I cringe in the face of *albeit, and/or, yclept, obsequies, whilom* and *tinsmith*. Want to hear a *real* ugly word? *Ugly*.

But my own nomination for the meanest and low-downest and ugliest word of them all is *oh*. Said twice, with maybe a hyphen, this way: *oh-oh*. In its maximal ugliness, it is customarily spoken softly with inflections that would curl the toes of a sandy-land mule.

Something is wrong, let us say, with the engine of your car. You take it to the garage. The mechanic lifts the hood and pokes around a bit and then you hear him murmur "oh-oh." The wretched creature says it in such a quietly dramatic manner that you know instantly that your whole motor has to be derricked out and thrown away and a new one put in.

Consider our friends the dentists. Most of them have enough gumption (beautiful word!) to conceal their opinions and judgments, but sometimes you'll run across one who forgets his chairside manner. He'll be inspecting a big molar in the back, and suddenly he'll say "oh-oh." Or he'll come out of his darkroom carrying an X-ray taken a few minutes earlier, and he'll put it up against the light, and he'll look at it briefly, and then his head will give a jerk and he'll say "oh-oh." You know at once, without ESP, precisely what is meant. Out. All of them. From now on, plates. No apples. No corn on the cob. No a lot of things.

Physicians as a general thing have schooled themselves carefully to conceal any sinister condition they may find during an examination. Yet I have run across one offender in my checkered medical career. He was giving me the annual checkup. He took my blood pressure and tapped me for knee jerks and scratched me on the bottoms of my feet for God knows what and stethoscoped me front and back and had me blow into a machine to test my "vital capacity" and then he turned the electrocardiograph loose on me. As he studied the saw-toothed dossier on my heart, his brow crinkled and I heard him say, quite softly, "Oh-oh." Everything inside of me suddenly bunched together in one large knot.

"What is it?" I demanded. "Whad you find there?"

"It's nothing, really," he said.

Nothing! Cancer of the heart is *nothing*? It had to be at least that.

"I heard you say 'oh-oh,'" I told him. "Come on. Tell me.

I'm a man. I can take it. Let me have it straight."

"OK," he said, and I steeled myself and began to turn chicken. "I said 'oh-oh' because," he went on, "I just happened to think that I haven't made out my tax return yet, and the deadline is tomorrow."

I quit him the next day. I can't use a doctor who is mooning over his income-tax return while he is looking at the record of my frightful heart disorders. I don't want a doctor *ever* to say "oh-oh" in my presence, unless perhaps he has dropped his sphygmomanometer on the floor and busted it. Even in that contingency I think he should employ a more masculine expression. I would.

"Oh-oh" is the most frightening, nerve-shattering locution to come into general usage since Noah Webster's day. It should surely be forbidden by federal statute.

One of America's Worst Disasters

The Johnstown flood in a few brief hours killed hundreds, made thousands homeless

---

BY **JO CHAMBERLIN**

CONDENSED FROM **THE AMERICAN LEGION MAGAZINE**

Originally published in January 1942

he Johnstown flood of 1889 was one of America's worst disasters. Johnstown was destroyed in less than a quarter of an hour. More lives were lost than in the San Francisco earthquake and fire, the Iroquois Theater fire in Chicago, the Dayton flood and the 1937 Mississippi flood combined.

For years the people of Johnstown, Pennsylvania, had lived complacently below the dam that gave way. In 1889 Johnstown was a bustling city of 30,000, built along the flats of the Conemaugh River—a turbulent stream, flowing swiftly down a narrow gorge until it widened out to join the Stonycreek River. The town was prospering, with its new steel mills. New streets were added by filling in river land, thus further narrowing a channel already too small. Every spring the Conemaugh would overrun its banks and fill workmen's homes with mud. Johnstown folk were used to moving to upper floors and taking their livestock to hill pastures during high water. But town officials denounced those who expressed the fear that some rainy spring the dam might go.

Johnstown disaster damage piled on itself

The dam, built in 1853, was a huge earthwork structure, 90 feet high and 930 feet long, impounding Conemaugh Lake 16 miles above the city. The lake, one of the largest reservoirs in the United States, stored water for the Pennsylvania Canal, an important commercial route to the West until the coming of the railroads. The canal was abandoned in 1857, and there was no further need for the reservoir. The dam deteriorated, and seepage drained the reservoir to half its normal level. A small break occurred in 1862, but only the lower part of Johnstown was flooded.

In 1879 the site was leased as a fishing club by a group of Pittsburgh millionaires. The club repaired and heightened the dam. The job looked fine, but stumps, sand, leaves and straw had been dumped in the breach. The dam itself was rotten at the core.

During the last week in May 1889, there was unprecedented

rainfall in western Pennsylvania. Storm after storm drove across the mountains until the overflowing Conemaugh, aided by the torrential Stonycreek, had flooded Johnstown streets to a depth of 3 to 6 feet.

At the dam, water rose steadily until Friday, May 31. An official of the fishing club, alarmed at the water seeping through, set men to work with shovels. It was no use—more leaks appeared. At noon, a civil engineer, John G. Parke, inspected the dam and realized it would not hold. On horseback he rushed to the village of South Fork, 2 miles below, to warn its 2,000 people. They took to the hills.

Telephones were not then in wide use, and washouts had cut service. Parke sent two men to a nearby telegraph office with telegrams of warning for Johnstown. But the wires were down and the messages never got through.

Jets of water spouted from leaks in the dam, and then water began to trickle over the top. Frantic workmen watched with sickening hearts as small stones began washing over the top, then larger and larger stones, in an alarming, fate-filled crescendo. Soon a notch 20 feet wide opened in the dam. At 3:30 p.m., with a rumble and roar, a great V-shaped section gave way completely.

Through the breach rushed over half a million cubic feet of water in less than an hour. At 40 miles an hour, the flood roared toward Johnstown, 400 feet lower. An avalanche of water 75 feet high, it overturned huge trees, picked up great boulders, and crushed homes and barns like matchboxes. In actual volume it was as though Niagara Falls had been turned into the valley. And the results were the same: annihilation.

A railroad ran along the riverbank. Ahead of the oncoming flood a freight locomotive engineer tied open his whistle and tried to race the waters. The flood overtook him before he could reach Johnstown. Miraculously, he escaped to higher ground, with the waters churning around his legs. The whistle suddenly stopped. The train was swept off the tracks and into the current.

Other communities between South Fork and Johnstown—Mineral Point, Conemaugh and Woodvale—all met destruction.

Just above Johnstown the valley is very narrow; there the waters rose to a wall 100 feet high. Over 250 houses were crushed. A wire-and-steel works was demolished, its machinery and stock loosed into the boiling current. Barbed wire and steel fencing became ensnarled with the floating rubbish, dragging people under. Careening timbers crushed those clinging to other timbers. Swimming was impossible.

A train stopped and its passengers headed for the nearby hills. One of them records, "As I jumped off the coach I looked up the valley and was almost paralyzed by the sight. Not over 300 yards away was an advancing rotary wave of black water. Huge tree trunks lolled in the air as they turned endwise and disappeared. I sprinted up the steep grade of one of the streets. The advance wave of the flood rushed by, carrying the houses away at the lower end of the block I was on, covering ground I had left less than five seconds before."

With no warning, the flood rolled down upon Johnstown at 4:10. Water in the streets was already 6 feet deep in places. There was no time or chance for mass flight. The water swept to the hills in the western part of town, then turned and drove through the flats of central Johnstown. Tree trunks, heavy boulders and debris battered down the city's houses.

Just below Johnstown, the Pennsylvania Railroad bridge spanned the Conemaugh, a massive structure arching 32 feet above the river. The arches filled with wreckage, forming a leaky but immovable dam. Johnstown was thus covered with an immense and swiftly moving whirlpool, 25 feet deep and three quarters of a mile wide. Thousands who had survived the first onslaught floated around helplessly in the whirlpool, "most of them on roofs, some clinging to wreckage, shrieking and praying for help, while frantic groups of survivors rushed about the shore, powerless to render aid except

People clung to debris as the waters surged around them.

to those few who, by accident, chanced to float near."

Most of those who clung to wreckage were thrown into the flood or pitched into the mass of debris in front of the bridge. At 6 o'clock, fire broke out at the bridge. Several carloads of petroleum had been overturned, saturating driftwood and houses. To refugees on the hills above, it must have seemed as if the Biblical Deluge had been loosed in hell. Rafts would drift nearer and nearer

the pyre and then be thrust into it. The crackle of burning timbers would suddenly still the screams of the dying. The fire burned for four days, consuming hundreds of bodies imprisoned in the debris.

Through Friday night the floodwaters gradually receded.

On Saturday morning, dazed survivors began wandering about, seeking loved ones. Drowned mothers and children were found locked in one another's arms. Nearly 3,000 were dead. No food or dry clothing was to be had. No communication. No shelter. What had been a thriving city was now a vast muddy plain. Every surviving Johnstown citizen had lost a brother, sister, relative or friend. Whole families were wiped out.

A 5-month-old baby was rescued uninjured at Pittsburgh the next morning after floating the entire 75 miles on the floor of a house. A mare standing in an alley was submerged by the waters; whole buildings were seen to pass over her. However, she was found later in a cellar, a half mile away, muddy but unhurt. Rescuers found a stable buried under two wrecked freight cars. It contained a small dog, five angry wet hens and a cow, calmly chewing her cud.

One of those who miraculously escaped the flood, Victor Heiser, lived to record his delivery in *An American Doctor's Odyssey*. A boy of 16 at the time, he had been sent to the barn on an errand. As he started toward the house he heard the terrifying noise of the flood and saw his father frantically motion him toward the top of the barn. He had hardly reached its roof when he saw his home crushed. The barn was ripped from its foundations. Clinging to a piece of the roof, he was borne headlong toward a jam where wreckage was piling up before a stone church and a three-story brick building. Into this hurly-burly he was catapulted.

"The pressure was terrific," he records. "Huge trees would shoot out of the water and come thundering down. As these trees drove booming into the jam, I jumped them desperately, one after another. Then suddenly a freight car reared up over my head; I could not leap that. But just as it plunged toward me the brick building gave way, and my raft shot out from beneath the freight car."

In the whirlpool below the city his raft was swept behind a hill. As it passed a brick building he was able to jump to the roof and join a small group of people stranded there. The building held while others about it were smashed.

The biggest problem after the waters subsided was the burial of the dead.

Bodies were jammed in debris, covered with muck, thrust in strange places. Many were never found. There was grave danger of disease, for by the time many bodies could be recovered, decomposition had set in. Six thousand men were kept busy for six weeks, cleaning up the city, dynamiting, burning, salvaging.

Eight morgues were set up. Anxious relatives walked for hours between the rows of dead, seeking loved ones. Only clothes and jewelry could identify some of the battered bodies. Nearly 800 victims were never identified. Three men cutting off fingers and ears of dead persons for their jewelry were beaten unmercifully by vigilantes. The National Guard was called in to maintain order and would let no one into town without good reason. Crazed survivors caused much trouble. One man, who had lost his four children, walked into a store, bought a revolver and shot himself on the spot. Other bereaved parents had to be restrained from throwing themselves into the waters.

Reporters dramatized the flood to millions. America, deeply moved, came through generously. Nearby farmers and residents housed victims until they could rebuild their homes. Cities rushed clothes, food and money. Gifts came from England, Germany, Turkey, Italy, Persia and Mexico. The YMCA, fraternal organizations and the Red Cross all sent men with cash.

After 1889, other communities examined their dangerous dams, and doubtless other disasters were prevented. Standards of dam building were improved and margins of safety increased. Johnstown continued to have trouble with its rivers, culminating in the flood of 1936, which caused property damage of $40,000,000 and made 9,000 homeless. Not until 1937 was a large-scale flood-control project launched. The major part of the work is now complete.

This Is What Friends Are For

If you're lucky, you'll find one person who brightens your day, lends an ear and inspires you. Reader's Digest *readers share stories of their best buds.*

——

Originally published in May 2017

I grew up in a family that didn't show affection. I knew I was loved, but it was rarely expressed, either in words or with a hug. Then, at the age of 40, I met Judy. I quickly noticed how often she told her kids she loved them and how she hugged everyone hello and goodbye. As with any habit, I picked it up, and the more I did so, the easier it became for me. Now I never fail to hug friends or family members, and it has completely changed how I relate to them.

It's an awesome feeling! Oh, I love you, Judy!

—**BETTY PLOUGH**, *Traverse City, Michigan*

When I was 9, I had a friend with the unusual name of Westa Joy. I can still picture her wild, naturally curly hair, her porcelain skin and her sparkling hazel eyes. I, on the other hand, was overweight and shy. We used to walk laughing and holding hands down a sandy dirt road in southeastern New Mexico. She would tell me the plot of the latest Nancy Drew book she was reading. I had never read a book,

and I didn't want to. Reading was much too difficult for me because I was dyslexic. But thanks to Westa's storytelling, I eventually bought all the Nancy Drew books. Thank you, my dear childhood friend, for giving me the joy of reading.

—ESSIE BOWDEN,

North Kingstown, Rhode Island

Five months after my husband, my 2-year-old daughter and I moved 2,000 miles from home, I gave birth to a beautiful baby girl with severely clubbed feet. This marked the

Meghan (right) with her BFF, Melissa Doyle

beginning of a long series of doctor appointments. Taking care of two young children, one of whom required constant medical attention, meant that I was always tired and behind on my household chores.

One day, we came home from yet another doctor's visit to find the front door ajar. I cautiously proceeded into the house, only to find the floors spotless, the dishes cleaned and dried, and the dirty laundry washed and folded. Upstairs, the beds were made, and there were even flowers in a vase beside my bed. It turns out that my friend Joy was driving by my home and noticed my car was gone, so she took the opportunity to help me out. I learned an important lesson that day about compassion. And this friendship was sealed for life!

—JUDITH HEICKSEN, *Santa, Idaho*

I came down with a horrible stomach bug when my husband was out of town. My best friend showed up with saltines, Sprite, essential oils and—the best part—her Netflix password.

—MEGHAN SIMECEK, *Friendswood, Texas*

My fiance walked out on me three days before our wedding. Now every year on the anniversary of the day I would have been married, my best friend texts me a hilarious (and completely inappropriate) picture, reminding me I dodged a bullet. His humor makes a hard day better.

—**JASON WOODS**, *via Twitter*

Because we are all over the country, my three closest friends—Miranda, Rachel and Johlandi—and I keep in touch via group texting. We share daily struggles, complaints, triumphs and, most of all, laughs. These special ladies respond nonjudgmentally to whatever I tell them, allowing me to be as vulnerable as I please. Conversely, it's a blessing to help them through their difficult times. Having such receptive friends has taught me that life is more fun and meaningful when I share myself with others.

—**LAUREN YOUNG**, *Rockingham, Virginia*

After my wife of 44 years died, I didn't feel the urge to socialize. But that didn't stop my friend Tony from inviting me to join a group of guys who got together every Thursday for dinner. I told him I wasn't ready. He called again the next week, and again I said no. He kept calling every week, and finally I said, "OK, I'll go. Anything to keep you from calling me every week." It has now been six years since my wife died, and thanks to Tony, I have been going to dinner every week with the gang we've dubbed ROMEO—Retired Old Men Eating Out.

—**DAVID FENWICK**, *Ocean Township, New Jersey*

Today is my birthday, and I know my friend Linda is making me a cake. Sometimes when you're an adult, no one thinks to do that for you.

—**TAMARA CASTELLARI**, *Parachute, Colorado*

My best friend and I are both trying to lose weight, so we text each other every day to check in. He encourages me to work out when I don't want to or to put down the ice cream. It really helps me stay on track.

—RICK NELSON, *via Twitter*

When I was pregnant, I felt— and acted—as if I had PMS for the entire nine months. My best friend, Laura, told me she was calling me every other day to make sure someone was still speaking to me. That is true friendship.

—GAIL BUA, *Nutley, New Jersey*

Whenever I visited Ruth at the rest home, I'd always greet her with "Good morning, sweetie." She, in turn, would say, "Heeeyyyyy! I've been missing you." For as long as I knew Ruth, she greeted me with "I've been missing you," even if I'd just seen her that morning. And when I'd leave, it was always "Come back!"

Ruth was my first friend in South Carolina. Our house was built on her property. I went over and introduced myself one day and told her that I was out every morning and if she liked, I could bring her newspaper to her door. She said, "Well, I suppose that

would be all right." It wasn't long after that I started bringing her the afternoon mail and cookies too. And soon I started taking her to the library, doctors and the store.

At the rest home, if Ruth's breakfast tray was ready, I'd pick it up. I knew how she liked her grits, with just a bit of butter and salt, and that she really, really liked orange juice and always got two glasses. After a bit, it would be time to go. She'd give me a kiss and tell me to "come back!"

I am ashamed to admit that at one time, both my grandmothers were in convalescent homes and I rarely visited them. I cannot change the person I was, but I can try to be a better person today. Ruth is no longer with us, but I wish to God that I could "come back" and visit with her again.

—JANET ALDEN, *Inman, South Carolina*

My friend Lisa comes over, and we do each other's nails while we lie in bed watching TV like high school girls.

—SHANNON HAGEN,

Minneapolis, Minnesota

In my senior year of high school, my mother passed away. Dad, who lived in Seattle, wanted me to live with him. But my friend Joy invited me to stay with her and her father until I graduated. Joy's mother had passed away a few years earlier, so Joy understood my terrible loss and depression. Because of her generosity, I was able to complete my last year of high school with all my friends, affording me a bit of normalcy.

—LORRAINE MORROW,
Bonney Lake, Washington

I met Mary Lou 14 years ago, while tending the grave of my 34-year-old son Kevin just weeks after he passed. Mary Lou was visiting her son Gary. She smiled, and soon we were sharing our stories—not only about our sons but about life in general. On my next visit with Kevin, I saw a piece of paper sticking out from under a rock—an inspirational note from Mary Lou. I wrote her back and put my note under the same rock. A week later, I returned to find another note from Mary Lou.

Lorraine (right) and Joy on graduation day

We went back and forth like this for years. Today, we still see each other, but usually over a hot fudge sundae. We talk and laugh and rarely feel the need to discuss our deep pain. That's why we are friends for life.

—PATRICIA COLER-DARK,
Concord, California

Anatomy of a Perfect Hand Transplant

A mysterious illness cost a healthy, athletic man parts of all four limbs. But thanks to one doctor's groundbreaking surgery, the patient got a piece of himself back.

BY **AMY WALLACE**
FROM **LOS ANGELES**

Originally published in October 2017

On Monday, Jan. 26, 2015, Jonathan Koch awakened feeling awful. *God, I'm sweaty*, he thought. *Even my knees are aching. And what's up with my freezing-cold feet?*

Jonathan was supposed to be on the day's first flight from Los Angeles to Washington, D.C.; as the co-runner of a reality TV production company, he was expected at an important conference that afternoon. Instead, he headed not to the airport but to Providence Tarzana Medical Center, where doctors—finding no cause for his discomfort—gave him a shot of morphine and sent him on his way. He made it to D.C., checked in to his hotel and fell into bed by midnight.

The next morning, he could barely get up. *Why does my body*

Jonathan Koch prior to receiving his new hand

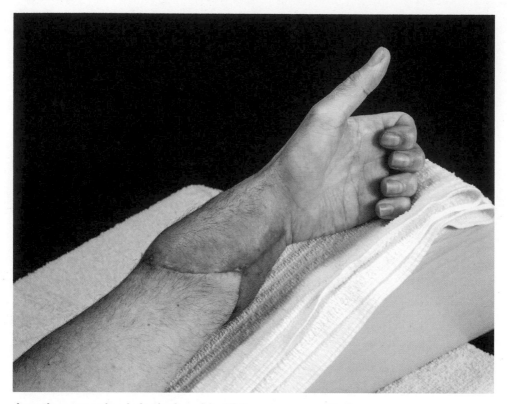

Jonathan wasn't a lefty before his 17-hour surgery. He is now.

feel like concrete? he wondered. His eyes were beyond bloodshot. He stopped by Rite Aid for some Aleve, Clear Eyes and Extra Strength 5-hour Energy, then dragged himself to his first meeting. Midway through his second, Jonathan looked at a colleague and saw three of her. When he stumbled in the hallway a minute later, she insisted on taking her boss to the emergency room. "You've got work to do," Jonathan told her. "I can get there on my own." A taxi dropped him off at George Washington University Hospital around 11 a.m. His temperature was 102 degrees.

Other than a knee surgery and a history of kidney stones, Jonathan Koch's body had never failed him, and he'd always returned the favor. At 6 foot 1 and 225 pounds, the

49-year-old former wrestler was an exercise addict who led a daily pre-dawn workout for friends. One colleague called him Superman for his drive and relentless positivity. He didn't drink or smoke. He ate a high-protein diet and loved his sleep; he and his girlfriend, Jennifer Gunkel, were typically in bed by 9 p.m. Now doctors in D.C. wondered if he had pneumonia. Between all the tests, the blood draws and the pain that surged through his limbs, he texted Jennifer: "They are killing me in here, baby."

Tuesday night fell, and the hospital admitted Jonathan to the ICU. His condition remained a mystery, and the pain was beyond debilitating. His circulation slowed; his hands and feet were turning blue as his body pulled blood from his limbs to protect his vital organs. Around 2 a.m., Dr. Lynn Abell leveled with Jonathan. "Text everyone you love," she said. "You're probably going to die tonight."

By the time Jennifer arrived in D.C. Wednesday night, doctors had put her partner into a propofol-induced coma. The next day, he was in full-blown septic shock. With his outer extremities deprived of oxygenated blood, gangrene set in. Despite huge doses of antibiotics, Jonathan's body "was getting ready to die." Chance of survival: 10%.

❖   ❖   ❖

Most of us think that patients who are put into a medically induced coma fall into a peaceful sleep. In fact, many people who've been "put under" have terrifying hallucinations or nightmares. As Jonathan lay unconscious over the following weeks, he had both. He believed he was being held hostage by a family of ghouls with giant faces and jagged teeth. Lashed to a wood bench, he was bitten repeatedly by snakes. He sensed the presence of his 15-year-old daughter, Ariana, despite her being nearly 3,000 miles away. (With Jonathan's condition so uncertain, Ariana, who had bronchitis, stayed home with her mom.) Jonathan and his daughter had a tight bond. Each February since prekindergarten, they'd attended her school's father-daughter dance—once they'd even crashed another school's. Now he was missing the dance for the first time.

On the final day of his 2½-week coma, Jonathan saw himself in an empty, misty room with two doors. He understood that one door was the way back to existence; the other, the way out. Then he heard a deep voice. "If you choose to live, there will be a price that is so heavy that at times you'll regret it," the voice said. "If you decide to go back, it will be the fight of your life." Jonathan knew his answer. *A fight? Bring it.*

In an instant, he was propelled upward like a torpedo through dark water that grew lighter and lighter. Finally he burst through. His first words were "How did I get here?" Then he looked down at his feet, which were strangely black and beginning to shrivel. "Wow," he said. "Impressive."

❖ ❖ ❖

During Jonathan's 39 days at George Washington, his hands and feet became necrotic, or as he put it, downright "Egyptian"—leathery, mummified, charcoal black. Doctors sought to discover what had thrown his system into chaos, ruling out candidates one by one. He didn't have measles or Lyme disease. There was evidence that he had antibodies to the Epstein-Barr virus, which can result in chronic fatigue syndrome, but 95% of adults have the virus and do not develop complications. For a while, doctors thought he might have a rare bone marrow cancer and started him on chemotherapy. Their strategy: Treat every possibility at the same time. And it worked; he survived.

That March, hoping to discover what had caused his illness, Jonathan made the difficult decision to leave GW to travel to the Mayo Clinic in Rochester, Minnesota. "The one thing I don't understand," he admitted to Dr. Abell on his last day at GW, "is, why did this happen?" Dr. Abell said, "Jonathan, the reason you took such great care of yourself was not to *avoid* this. It was to *survive* this."

A Race Against the Clock

"Hand transplants throw you curveballs," says Dr. Kodi Azari, who performs the surgeries at UCLA. No matter what happens, though, doctors must work quickly to preserve the new limb. Here, a bit about what's involved:

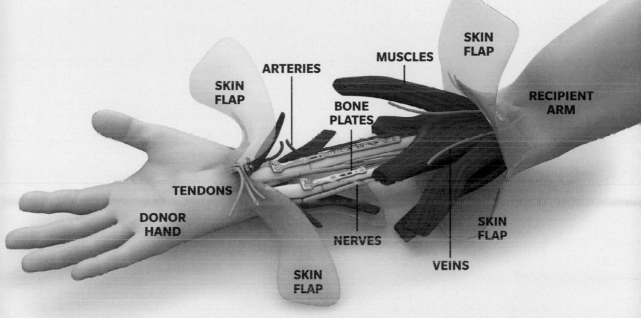

SKIN FLAP

ARTERIES

MUSCLES

SKIN FLAP

BONE PLATES

RECIPIENT ARM

SKIN FLAP

TENDONS

DONOR HAND

SKIN FLAP

NERVES

VEINS

SKIN FLAP

INSIDE OUT
As with building a house, structure comes first. Doctors start by precisely attaching the radius and ulna bones, or one arm will be longer than the other.

TINY VESSELS
Veins and arteries, some as slender as blades of grass,

must be sutured together one by one. Too few sutures and there may be leaks.

23 TENDONS
Again, precision is key: The extensor and flexor tendons on each finger must match, or their function will be impaired.

HOOKING UP
Nerves are to the hand as a coaxial cable is to a TV—an essential pathway for information. The trick is attaching like with like.

STITCH FIX
For Jonathan Koch, surgeons went through

about 300 feet of suturing filament, which is a fraction of the width of a human hair.

DEEP FREEZE
All this must be done in an operating room kept freezing cold in order to preserve tissue.

Still, Jonathan's time at Mayo was rough; his limbs were in constant, unspeakable pain. He'd lost 40 pounds. His hands and feet, wrapped in gauze, looked like paws. Doctors at Mayo began to discuss the possibility of amputations and, perhaps eventually, a transplant for his ruined left hand. Mayo had a division devoted to the procedure but had yet to perform one.

Jonathan (left) is "one of those guys you have to kill to beat," a colleague said.

On April 20, 2015, 85 days after Jonathan was admitted to GW, he and Jennifer told Mayo they wanted to return to Los Angeles for Ariana's 16th birthday. That was when someone mentioned a surgeon whose name they'd never heard before: Kodi Azari.

❖　❖　❖

Dr. Azari, 48, is the surgical director of the Hand Transplant Program at UCLA. The field is still relatively new. The first hand transplant to achieve prolonged success was performed 18 years ago in Louisville, Kentucky; by 2015, fewer than 85 procedures had been undertaken worldwide. But Dr. Azari is at the forefront. He has traveled the country as a lead surgeon in five hand transplants, including the first double-hand transplant and the first arm transplant in the United States.

The doctor had some hypotheses he wanted to test, provided he could find a patient with the ideal requirements: excellent health, enormous self-discipline and—rarest of all—a limb that needed to be replaced but had not yet been amputated. Most hand-transplant candidates have been injured in accidents or in battle, when a catastrophic event forces an emergency amputation to minimize suffering. Generally that means the arm is severed closer to the elbow than to the wrist, and the nerves and tendons are trimmed and tucked inward to lessen discomfort. All those tucked-in nerves and tendons tend to merge over time into a jumble that is difficult to connect to a new hand with precision.

Wouldn't it be great, Dr. Azari thought, if a transplant recipient's arm could be amputated in a way that prepped it specifically to receive a new limb? How much more quickly would a patient recover if each tendon, nerve, artery and vein were left in place and marked like so many colored speaker wires to be hooked up to a matching apparatus? Dr. Azari believed this fantasy patient would awaken post-op, look at the new hand and be able to move the fingers right away. Now all he needed was the right patient.

And then he met Jonathan. Dr. Azari set about examining his patient, body and mind, a week after his return from Minnesota. He started with Jonathan's left hand, which was completely ruined, with a charred-looking exterior except for a tiny patch of palm. The right hand was better off; while the fingers and thumb were blackened, the rest could be saved.

His right foot looked as if it had been fashioned out of charcoal briquettes.

Damage to the left foot was mostly confined to the toes, but the right looked as if it had been fashioned wholly out of charcoal briquettes. "Get rid of it," Dr. Azari said. "It's a no-brainer." Something about his affect—direct, gentle, kind around the eyes—calmed Jonathan and Jennifer. "I will make you this promise," Dr. Azari said. "I will not do anything to make you worse."

On June 23, determined to save as much healthy tissue as possible, Dr. Azari amputated Jonathan's left hand and about half of each finger on his right. Severing the left hand closer to the wrist than to the elbow, Dr. Azari kept all the nerves and tendons long and extended, which would give him plenty to work with later.

> ## "The hardest part has been the period of subtraction. This is the beginning of the addition."

Oddly, losing his left hand didn't faze Jonathan. It had been such a source of pain, its absence brought only relief.

❖   ❖   ❖

There was much to prepare for the chance at a perfect hand transplant. UCLA, where Dr. Azari hoped to perform the surgery, required Jonathan to undergo myriad physical and psychological tests.

Then came the challenge of matching a donor's left hand with Jonathan's in terms of size, skin tone and hair pattern. The closer the match, the easier it would be to incorporate into his life.

While he waited, Jonathan tried to "scrape back" something each day, reassuming responsibility for tasks that he'd once taken for granted. He taught himself to hold a fork using the stubs of the fingers that remained on his right hand and mastered grabbing a stylus to type texts and emails on his phone.

On Aug. 17, 2015, Jonathan and Jennifer were married in a tiny ceremony in their backyard. The next day, doctors amputated Jonathan's right leg midway between his knee and his ankle and snipped off the necrotic toes on his left foot. Jonathan tried to joke about the horror of watching parts of himself disappear, calling himself Mr. Potato Head. But the loss of his foot hit hard. "The hardest part for me has been in the period of subtraction," he said. "This is the beginning of the period of addition."

Eight weeks after his foot surgery, Jonathan was fitted for his first prosthesis; he walked right away. Soon he would upgrade to a Triton smart ankle, a bionic contraption he could adjust for whatever type of movement he needed to do. He'd also have a prosthesis for running called a Rush foot. "Eventually I'll have a special tuxedo leg for the Emmys," he joked.

Dr. Azari was less at ease. "The clock is your enemy," he says. "Hand transplants throw you curveballs. And there is no cookbook on how to do it." So like a chef trying out a dish before serving it, Dr. Azari and his team practiced Jonathan's surgery several times in the anatomy lab.

After Jonathan's name was formally added to the transplant recipient list, he and Jennifer waited seven months to get the call. On Oct. 24, 2016, a donor candidate was found who shared Jonathan's blood type and had a hand that matched his.

The next morning, Jonathan walked into the Ronald Reagan

Moments after Jonathan awoke from his coma, he asked Jennifer to marry him.

UCLA Medical Center at 9:45. Dr. Azari met him at intake with a hug and a promise: "We're going to do this." As Jonathan went to be prepped for surgery, Dr. Azari hit the road, heading to another Southern California hospital. It was time to pick up Jonathan's new hand.

When Dr. Azari arrived, the donor was on life support, and the doctor had the rare opportunity to meet the donor's brother and pastor. In the operating room, where the hand and other organs were to be removed by several

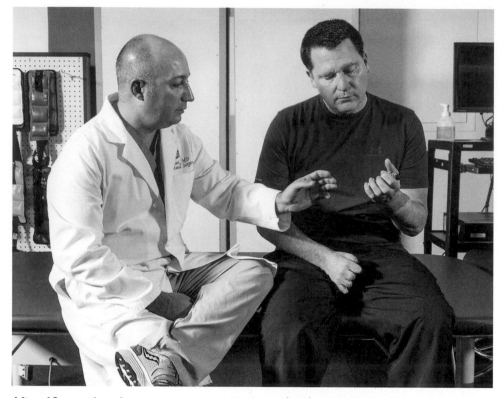

After 19 months of constant contact, Dr. Azari (left) considered Jonathan family.

surgical teams, the entire staff took a moment to say a prayer of gratitude. Across town, Jonathan was started on an anesthetic drip, and Jennifer prepared to wrap her husband in one more embrace before saying goodbye.

At 3:32 p.m., the first cut was made to prepare Jonathan's arm. Dr. Azari arrived within the hour and joined his team. The first curveball came right away. The doctors had planned to sever the radius and ulna bones at about 11 centimeters above the wrist. But after opening up Jonathan's arm, preserving more bone seemed possible. This approach might enable the arm to heal better and have more range of motion, but there were no guarantees. The surgeons went around the room and came to a unanimous decision: Preserve another 7 centimeters of each bone, affixing the hand just 4 centimeters above the wrist.

Tick, tick, tick. They were only a few hours in, with at least a dozen more to go. The team sutured a few key tendons together. Then the doctors moved on to the arteries and veins. Here came the second curveball. Because of the gangrene and the lack of use, Jonathan's veins and arteries were very small—"like chives," Dr. Azari says. They were also tough with scar tissue, which made suturing them exponentially more difficult. As the team continued repairing the musculature of the arm, pulling it more tightly together, the arteries and veins they'd attached early on began to protrude, like a loop of extra yarn. The surgeons had expected this. Plastic surgeons always leave more of everything than they think they'll need on the first pass because the excess can always be trimmed. Those vessels were shortened and resutured.

Various tendons were similarly tightened, particularly in Jonathan's pointer, middle and ring fingers. "We went back and did these three tendons many times until we got them right," Dr. Azari says. The tendons of the forearm, meanwhile, were woven into one another over a 3-inch span to maximize strength and resist tearing. The resulting bulge is permanent.

Jonathan's new hand went from white to pink to red. The pulse began to pound.

———

At 11:01 p.m., after the doctors removed the tourniquets and clamps, Jonathan's new hand went from white to pink to red. The fullness returned to the tissue, and the pulse began to pound. It was exhilarating.

For several hours, the surgeons worked to complete repairs on the remaining tendons. At 7:07 a.m., the hospital called Jennifer to tell her that the team was closing and suturing. The procedure's official stop time:

9:09 a.m. They'd been at it for 17 hours and 37 minutes.

Jonathan's first words after emerging from the anesthesia were "Did you do it?" When Dr. Azari answered yes, Jonathan looked down at his new hand and started singing the theme song from *Rocky*. Jennifer arrived at the hospital about an hour later. It was her birthday, and she was ready for her gift. "Move your thumb," she told Jonathan. And he did.

❖ ❖ ❖

The total cost of Jonathan's transplant and follow-up care is impossible to measure, but some past procedures have cost about $1 million.

So what made him sick? He will never know for sure. Jonathan says the consensus is that exposure to the Epstein-Barr virus, combined with stress, may have triggered "a one-in-20-million event."

Now he is focused on what's ahead. At the crack of dawn every day, Jonathan goes to UCLA for occupational therapy to improve his motor skills and flexibility. Just five

months postsurgery, he was already dribbling a basketball, jumping rope and teaching himself how to play tennis again, holding the racket with his new left hand. He is back to leading intense "insanity" workouts for friends, and he's learning to use a set of prosthetic fingers fitted to his right hand. At some point, a tattoo artist will disguise the slight difference in skin tone between Jonathan and his new hand with a bit of well-placed ink.

Meanwhile, there is life to enjoy. Recently Jonathan put on a dark suit and tie, a crisp white shirt, his Triton smart ankle, and a pair of shiny black leather high-tops and took Ariana, a high school senior, to their final father-daughter dance. Fourteen red hearts decorated his lapel—one for each dance they'd attended together. Few people other than Ariana knew that his attendance itself was a miracle.

I'm Letting Myself Go

How to relax—in a few uneasy lessons

—

BY **COREY FORD**

Originally published in May 1960

Who says I'm tense? I'm perfectly calm, I tell you. I'm as cool as a cubercum. I mean a cucumber. I can lift a cup of coffee without spilling it, provided I hold on to my wrist with the other hand, and when I go to bed I sleep like a top. (Sometimes I spin all night.) I've been reading a book on how to relax, and I'm completely cucumbered I mean cured.

It's this undo-it-yourself fad that's sweeping the country these days. We're all wound up tight, the doctors warn. The accelerated pace of modern living and the effects of the war (all those sergeants yelling "'Tension!") are causing people's nerves to snap like garters. The way to get hold of yourself is to let yourself go. Don't worry about being worried. Be loose.

The trouble is that the looser I try to be, the tighter I get. I've taken all the doctors' cures to give me peace of mind, and now I'd like to give them a piece of my own. It isn't the tension that makes people tense. It's this effort to relax that's tying us all in knots.

My friends got me started. Not that I really had anything to be alarmed about, they assured me. It was just that several of my classmates had keeled over recently without warning and, after all, a person my age shouldn't push too hard. I ought to have a few good years left in me yet, if I was careful.

"Take it easy," they suggested. "Stop thinking about your work, or you'll get ulcers."

So I stopped thinking about my work and started thinking about ulcers instead. The more I thought, the more I became aware of certain little symptoms I'd never noticed before. There was a fluttering sensation in the pit of my stomach, for instance, and my pulse sounded funny. The following morning I nicked myself while shaving. My friends couldn't have been more pleased if I'd cut my throat.

"Better take a day off," they advised. "Stay home and read the papers, and don't even answer the phone. Put everything out of your mind."

I finished the papers, and it was only 8:30. I read them a second time, including the society notes and want ads, and looked at my watch again. Nine o'clock. Everybody else would be getting to work about now. I wandered aimlessly around the room, emptying ash trays, straightening pictures, then stole another glance at my watch. Nine-thirty. Might

be a good chance to catch up on some correspondence. But that would be too much like working. Still 9:30.

The phone rang suddenly. I started to reach for it, then gritted my teeth and counted the rings: six, seven, eight. Suppose someone was sick, or the building was on fire? The phone stopped ringing just as I snatched up the receiver. All I got was the dial tone.

I began to circle the room faster and faster, snapping my fingers and waiting for the phone to ring again. "Relax," I muttered to myself. Maybe a breath of fresh air would help. "Relax!" I yelled at the elevator boy, and I set off down the street at a brisk stride, gradually increasing to a dogtrot. My knees were knocking as I galloped into the club, and I had to brace both elbows on the bar.

"What you need," my friends told me, "is to relax. You're nothing but a bundle of nerves. Look how you're gripping that glass."

I loosened my grip, and the glass shattered on the floor. They glanced at one another significantly.

"A clear case of nervous tension," one said. "Now. here's a little book that cucumbered me. It's called *How to Relax*." I noticed that he kept getting up and sitting down, and drumming his fingers as he talked. "Before I read it, I'd jump 3 feet in the air if someone said 'Boo!'" I said "Boo!" and he jumped 4 feet in the air. "I've gained a whole foot," he said delightedly, "since I read that book."

The jacket blurb was unnerving enough. "How close to the BREAKING POINT are you?" it demanded in large black type. My fingers fairly flew as I opened the book to the first chapter, titled "Passive Relaxation: The Secret of

Mental Peace." Passive relaxation, the explanation explained, is not what you *do*. It is what you *don't* do when you stop doing something.

To make the whole thing even clearer, there was a drawing of a very thin man, wearing only a pair of polka-dot shorts, lying on five sofa pillows in an attitude which seemed to me about as relaxed as

I clenched my fists and forced the air up up up until it was crammed under my collarbone.

---

that of a shady banker awaiting the arrival of the federal examiners. "You *too* can find Mental Peace," the caption urged, "if you will learn to Let Your Muscles OUT."

I had a little trouble locating enough pillows, but I added a copy of *Who's Who* and a telephone directory, and arranged myself on top of them, holding the book overhead in order to follow the instructions. "First, unlock the

forehead." I smoothed the furrows in my brow. "Now the ears." I let my ears out. "Now the jaw." I unlocked my jaw. "Now the back." My spine was as limp as a lily—but along about this point I discovered that my jaw was locked again, and in addition I had developed such a crick in my neck that I had to bang on the floor for my wife to come help me up. "What are you doing?" she asked, opening the door. "I'm *not* doing," I explained. She shut the door quietly.

The next chapter was called "How to Woo Sleep." "Put everything out of the mind," the book said, "by closing the eyes and concentrating on a small, black object, such as a punctuation mark." Well, I shut my eyes and concentrated on a period (.). The trouble was that I kept thinking of other periods until I had a whole row of them (.....), which reminded me of my income-tax form, which made me think of a dollar sign ($)—and there I was, wide-awake again.

I tried to concentrate on a comma (,) instead, but for some

reason it hopped up and turned into an apostrophe ('). Meanwhile, the period kept wandering back and forth in my mind until suddenly it halted under the apostrophe and made an exclamation point (!). I sat bolt upright, shouting "What!"

"Everyone should learn to breathe," the final chapter stated. This seemed like pretty good advice, because there are lots of times when breathing comes in handy. "The proper method," the lesson began, "is to inhale *all the way*!" This was vividly illustrated by the same man in polka-dot shorts following Step One: "Bend over from the waist with the arms dangling loosely between the thighs, fill the lungs with air and *ho-o-old* it." I propped the open book on the bureau, filled my lungs with air and he-e-eld it.

"Step Two: Force the air up UP UP out of the diaphragm into the upper chest." I clenched my fists and forced the air up up up until it was crammed under my collarbone.

"Step Three: Still holding your breath, go into a slump. Sag for all you're worth. Relax the muscles completely." I could practically feel my tension slipping away. My face was growing black, my knees sagged lower and lower, my body slumped forward and my head collided with the corner of the bureau as I toppled onto my face …

The doctor said later that there was nothing to be alarmed about. My stitches should be out in a couple of weeks, and what I really needed was a nice long rest. "Relax, that's all," he told me. "Put everything out of your mind. Just let yourself go."

The Folks at Moe's Diner

A roomful of people I didn't know taught me about patriotism, gratitude and love

BY **RU FREEMAN**

Originally published in June 2014

n the late spring of my freshman year in college, I, a nondrinking but hard-dancing international student from Sri Lanka, was high on two things: enjoying the freedom of being nearly 10,000 miles away from home, and my very handsome American boyfriend.

Mark, a true-blue Connecticut Yankee, introduced me to all things American. He took me to the top of the press box in the college football bleachers and to the crown of the Statue of Liberty. He got me hooked on movies at the college library and eggs over easy with sausage on the side at Denny's on Main Street. He took me for walks around the campus and drives to the state parks of Maine, where we slept in the back of his Ford pickup truck and I tasted my first vaguely smoky hot dogs and s'mores. Like I said, American life.

It stood to reason, then, that I would want to share something that he didn't know about. I had been teaching dance for a month during what was called short-term, a time for students to take just one more intensive class instead of leaving college for an early start on summer. Over the course of the class's travels to public elementary

and middle schools, I had taken in the areas surrounding our campus, the land rolling away into farms and mill towns. So one night when Mark suggested that we drive to an open area where we could see the stars, I announced that I knew just the place.

I did know. Sort of. I had seen a path leading to a clearing off the

I have never sung any song with more heart than when I finished that anthem.

main road earlier that afternoon from the bus. Where, exactly, that clearing was I didn't know. I have always just felt places. I travel by intuition and implicit trust that "something in my bones" will help me navigate roads, people, places and life itself.

Late at night, though, in semi-rural Maine, with no streetlights and few houses, we were easily lost. Not simply lost, we were stuck in a mud bog. There I sat,

ladylike in my very light cream sweater, while Mark attempted to get the front wheels of the pickup out of the swamp. I helped, eventually, but only when repeated suggestions that we "just ask the nice people who probably live in the house up the hill to help us" fell on deaf, obdurate ears. The farmer did help us in the end, when he strolled out in the first pink-gray light of the morning. It was a small but sweet victory to hear him inquire why we hadn't asked for help in the first place, all night long as he had lain in his bed wondering about the engine revving across the street. "There's an abandoned railway line at the far end of my farm," he said, pointing as we said our goodbyes, after he had invited us in to wash up. "You can come and park there anytime." He smiled as he said this, and Mark had the good sense to blush.

It was in that mood that we set off for home, which was back to our dorms, a little contrite on his part, a little jazzed up on mine, never mind that it was I who had gotten us into the mess in the first place.

By the time we stopped at Uncle Moe's Diner, a place we now visit whenever we are back in Lewiston, but which we had never heard of until that morning, Mark was a little tired of my crowing, and I was just getting started.

The diner was crowded that Sunday morning, old-timers filling up the tables, the waitresses busy. We got a table off to the side of the main room. For no good reason that I can recall, I started humming a song my mother had taught me when I was about 7 years old: "The Star-Spangled Banner."

"Why don't you just sing the words?" Mark taunted.

I did.

"Why don't you sing it even louder?" he challenged me.

I did.

"I dare you to stand up by this table and sing it," he said.

"I will," I said, and made a move to stand.

He said, "I bet you wouldn't go to the front of this diner and sing it there."

The waitress came by to take our order. When she left, I followed her to the counter, which sat just to the left of the front door, open to the room and its diners. I spoke to the older woman standing there, told her I'd like to sing the national anthem. You've got to love Mainers, unfazed by just about anything. She asked me to wait a minute; she'd need to ask Moe.

"You want to sing the national anthem?" Uncle Moe asked me, a little furrow in his brow. "Why?"

I don't know how this fragment of information came to me, but it sprang to my lips with ease: "Because the troops are coming home."

Uncle Moe walked around that counter and stood beside me. "Excuse me, everybody," he said to his customers. "This young lady would like to sing the national anthem in honor of the troops coming home today." He turned to me and said, "Go ahead."

I began, glancing over with triumph at Mark, who sat with his fingers interlaced, utterly shocked. It was not the triumphant song my mother had taught me that rose to my lips but a song-on-a-dare, the kind of song that could be any song. But when my eyes moved away from Mark and returned to the people in front of me, I saw that several of them had stood up and had their palms over their hearts. I would earn my American citizenship more than a decade later, but I believe that I learned my love for this country in that moment. I could see so clearly what this anthem meant to each person there, the stooped veterans, the women and men on their way to church, the ones for whom the stop at this diner was a Sunday ritual. I saw people for whom the words meant just as much as the words of my home country's anthem meant to me. I don't believe I have ever sung any song with more heart than when I finished that anthem.

It isn't the applause that has stayed with me or the "thank you for singing the anthem" that I heard from a few people or the fact that Uncle Moe and his wife remembered me—when Mark and I, now married, went back years later—and said, "Aren't you the young woman who sang the anthem here?" What has stayed with me is the grace I learned in understanding that my song was a much smaller gift to those people than their gratitude was to me. For in that gratitude I saw a bridge, the one I walk on toward people I don't know, the one I lay down for them to walk toward me. It has no political stripe, no class, no gender, no agendas. It is itself: a bridge built of that grace and recognition of each other's essential, deep, vulnerable humanity.

The Priceless Car Loan

A wonderful gesture—call it a slice of nice—in tiny Wild Rose, Wisconsin, helps soften the sadness on a lousy day

BY **MARISSA LALIBERTE AND ASHLEY LEWIS**

Originally published in June 2017

fter a long drive and precious little sleep, Todd Steinkamp left his Wisconsin motel around 5:30 a.m. to make it to a funeral near Green Bay. Not long after, he started to hear a grinding sound coming from his front tire, and it kept getting louder. He finally pulled into Lauritzens BP & Sports shop in Wild Rose, Wisconsin, hoping to find help. It was only 7 a.m., and he still had 75 miles to go.

As luck would have it, Steinkamp found Glenn Geib stocking oil on the shelves. The mechanic checked out the car and gave Steinkamp some bad news: The wheel bearing was failing and needed to be repaired right away. Fixing it would take a few hours. Geib then looked Steinkamp up and down and asked why he was so dressed up. Steinkamp explained that he was going to the funeral of his boss's wife.

Geib checked the one rental car agency in town, but it was sold out (it has only one rental car in its fleet). The next closest rental agency was 40 miles away. "I must have looked pretty stressed out at this time," Steinkamp wrote later on Facebook. Geib noticed, and he was determined to help.

Todd Steinkamp (right) snaps a selfie with his selfless new pal, Glenn Geib, in his service station.

With a population of 699, close-knit Wild Rose has a reputation in central Wisconsin for kindness. Seniors gather at the Wild Rose Community Center for free midday meals. The local Lions Club chapter collects used eyeglasses for folks who can't afford them, part of the Lions Recycle for Sight Program.

But kindness in Wild Rose doesn't come just from organizations. Kent Barnard, the town library director, remembers a high school kid who walked into Patterson Memorial Library needing gas money. Barnard happily gave it to him, and the guy went on his way. A couple of years later, that man came back. "You gave me $10 for gas when I was in high school," he said, and Barnard was repaid.

"People are not well-off, but they're taking care of each other," says Jerry Apps, a local author who lets the library sell his books and DVDs and keep some of the proceeds to fund its programs.

So, faced with a stranger in need at the service station, Glenn Geib did what came naturally. He reached into his pocket, pulled out his keys and said, "Take my truck. Fill it up with gas, and get going." With a smile, Geib added that the truck could go 120 miles per hour if needed.

The men had met just 10 minutes ago. They didn't even know each other's names. But Geib insisted. Steinkamp hopped into the 1999 Chevrolet Silverado, with Geib's tools and piles of split wood in the back, and made it to the funeral. He came back to the garage seven hours later with a heavy but thankful heart.

"The 74-year-old mechanic with a grip of steel turned a terrible day into a good one, with a great lesson," Steinkamp wrote on Facebook. The lesson could be the Wild Rose motto: "Just be kind, and help if you can."

Remembering Stephen Hawking: Brilliant and Funny

Physics and humor may be more closely related than you'd think

———

BY **MARC PEYSER**

Originally published in September 2018

There's no rule that says a guy who spends his days formulating equations to explain black holes, unified field theory and other mind-bending mysteries of the universe can't also be a cutup. Still, it was always surprising when physicist Stephen Hawking showed up on TV and cracked a joke.

Hawking was perhaps the most famous scientist in the world when he died at age 76. His 1988 book,

A Brief History of Time, sold 10 million copies and made him an unlikely superstar even to people who sweated through high school science.

But humor was always a big part of Hawking's effort to bring physics to the masses. In his 2010 book, *The Grand Design*, for instance, he recounts how in 1277 the Catholic Church declared scientific laws such

Professor Stephen Hawking attends the gala screening of *Hawking* at the Cambridge Film Festival held at Emmanuel College in 2013.

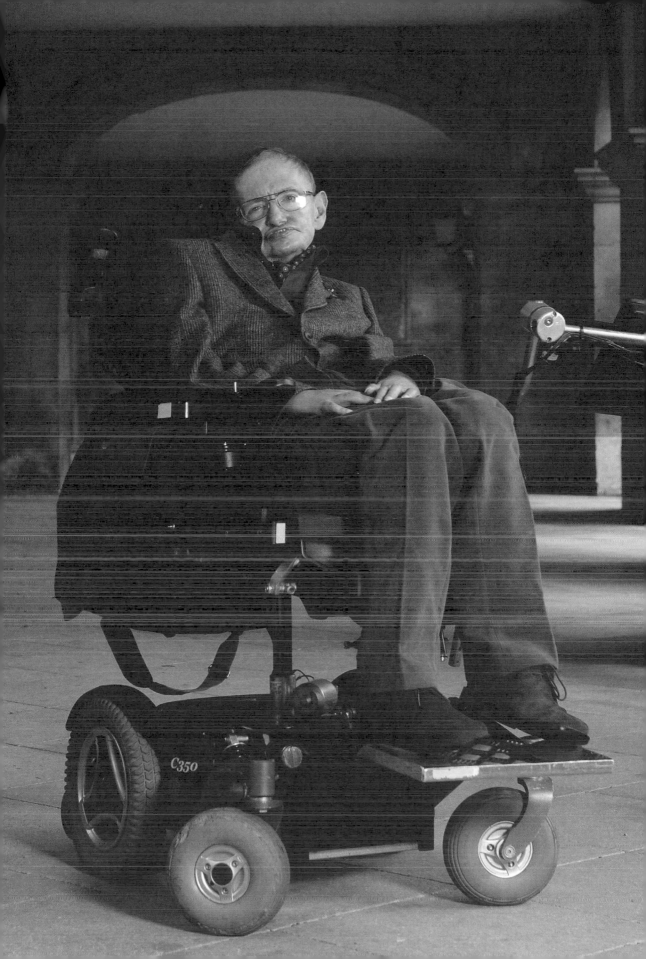

as gravity to be heretical, since they seemed to diminish God's omnipotence. "Interestingly," the text adds puckishly, "Pope John [XXI] was killed by the effects of the law of gravity a few months later when the roof of his palace fell in on him."

Leonard Mlodinow, Hawking's co-author on *The Grand Design*, points out that physics and humor are more closely related than you'd expect. "Humor often relies on looking at things in different ways or making odd or unexpected

Hawking enjoyed rolling over Jim Carrey's foot.

associations," says Mlodinow, who has published a book called *Elastic: Flexible Thinking in a Time of Change*. "In physics, the same thing happens."

In a sense, the element of the unexpected was Hawking's secret humor weapon. It wasn't only the absurdity of an egghead scientist shouting "If you are looking for trouble, you found it!" before punching a guy, which an animated Hawking did on *The Simpsons*. It was also that Hawking kept smiling even though he spent more than 50 years in a wheelchair.

He was only 21 when he was diagnosed with the degenerative motor neuron disease ALS. For most people, the condition would have been a calamity. But Hawking rolled over adversity as if it were just a pebble under his wheelchair. "Life would be tragic," he once said, "if it weren't funny."

And so he cracked jokes. There was the time when talk show host John Oliver asked him about parallel universes. "Does that mean there is a universe out there where I am smarter than you?" Oliver quipped. Hawking's dry reply (made all the funnier by the affectless timbre of his computer-generated voice): "Yes. And also a universe where you're funny."

Hawking liked physical humor too. He reportedly enjoyed wheeling his chair over the feet of people who annoyed him, including Prince Charles. "A malicious rumor,"

> ## *Hawking's greatest hit, humor-wise, was probably the cocktail party he threw in 2009.*

Hawking said. "I'll run over anyone who repeats it."

"He loved adventure and fun," says Mlodinow, who once took Hawking on a punt-boat trip down the river Cam in Cambridge, England, despite the obvious danger of the boat capsizing. "You know about when he went on the vomit comet? It's a plane that flies in a parabolic path so you are weightless, like you are in space. A lot of people barf, but he loved that sort of thing." And he was 65 at the time.

Hawking's greatest hit, humor-wise, was probably the cocktail party he threw in 2009. It was a "welcome reception for future time travelers," he said, so naturally he sent out the invitations the day after the party. No one showed up—yet. "Maybe one day someone living in the future will find the information and use a wormhole time machine to come back to my party, proving that time travel will one day be possible," Hawking explained. And if that happens, don't be surprised if Hawking is there too. After all, he never missed a chance to have fun.

Credits and Acknowledgments

"Wisdom of Bear Wood" by Michael Welzenbach, *Reader's Digest*, December 1994

"Heist" by Simon Worrall, *Reader's Digest*, December 2008
   Photo-Illustration page 6 by Andrew Brusso; photograph page 9 by Album/Alamy Stock Photo

"Sergeant Erwin and the Blazing Bomb" by Corey Ford, *Reader's Digest*, July 1965
   Photograph by Shawshots/Alamy Stock Photo

"The Lost Art of Doing Nothing" by Don Herold, *Reader's Digest*, October 1948

"Baby in the Stream" by Derek Burnett, *Reader's Digest*, December 2015/January 2016
   Photographs by Dustin Cohen

"He's Always Magnificently Wright" by Arch Oboler, *Reader's Digest*, February 1958
   Photograph by Underwood Archives/Getty Images

"The English Lesson" by Elsa K. Hummel, *Reader's Digest*, September 2017
   Illustration by Gerard Dubois; photograph courtesy Elsa Hummel

"The Hidden Message" by I.A.R. Wylie, *Reader's Digest*, January 1954

"'I Stared Down Death'" by Christopher W. Davis, *Reader's Digest*, March 2006
   Photograph page 49 ©2005 Kevin Horan; page 50 left, courtesy Ohio Department of Corrections; page 50 right, courtesy WRTV McGraw-Hill Broadcasting; page 55 by AP Photo/Michael Conroy

"The Flowers Will Be There" by James A. McCracken, *Reader's Digest*, July 1982
   Photograph by Ron Levine/Getty Images

"Oh, Behave!" by Lenore Skenazy, *Reader's Digest*, April 2016
   Illustrations by Edwin Fotheringham

"The Gold-and-Ivory Tablecloth" by Rev. Howard C. Schade, *Reader's Digest*, December 1954
   Illustrations by Katrinn Pelletier

"How I Learned a Lesson in Parenthood" by Danny Kaye, *Reader's Digest*, September 1959
   Photograph by Bettmann/Getty Images

"Old Ben Franklin and His Miserable Maxims" by Mark Twain (1872) from *Protection* (March 1965) by The Travelers Insurance Companies, Hartford, Connecticut, *Reader's Digest*, June 1965
   Illustration by CSA Images/Getty Images

"Trapped in a Sunken Ship" by Capt. Richard Miranda, *Reader's Digest*, December 1982

"The Ordeal of John Cali" by Gerald Moore, *Reader's Digest*, January 1975
   Photograph by Brian Koellish/Getty Images

"My Most Unforgettable Character" by Red Barber, *Reader's Digest*, May 1970

"They Brought Home the Wrong Baby" by Murray Teigh Bloom, *Reader's Digest*, June 1955

"The Man Who Willed Himself to Fly" by Jack Fincher, *Reader's Digest*, April 1982
   Photograph page 109 by aviation-images.com/Getty Images; page 110 courtesy Jennifer Pickering

"Why Mothers Don't Get Sick" by Joyce Lubold, *Reader's Digest*, February 1967

"The Day I Was Fired" by Eddie Cantor, *Reader's Digest*, October 1955

"The Killer Among Us" by Max Alexander, *Reader's Digest*, January 2004
   Photographs page 122, 129 by MediaNews Group/Boston Herald via Getty Images; page 125 by Aleksei

Lazukov/Shutterstock; page 126 by Gary D'Ercole/ Getty Images; page 130 by Portland Press Herald/Getty Images

"Goblins, Go Home!" by Will Stanton, *Reader's Digest*, October 1968

"'Can't Anyone Hear Me?'" by Tom Hallman, *Reader's Digest*, September 2017
Illustration by Jonathan Bartlett

"The Bear Who Came to Dinner" by Robert Franklin Leslie, *Reader's Digest*, December 1964
Photograph page 144 by mlorenzphotography/ Getty Images; page 149 by FrankHH/Shutterstock

"'Why Don't They Pick My Daddy Up?'" by Karl Detzer, *Reader's Digest*, August 1956

"Don't Do It Now!" by Corey Ford, *Reader's Digest*, February 1963
Photograph by biffspandex/Getty Images

"Amazon Adventure" by David Dodge, *Reader's Digest*, October 1955
Photograph by Ricardo Lima/Getty Images

"The Christmas Present" by James Michener, *Reader's Digest*, December 1967
Photograph by amnachphoto/Getty Images

"Down, Boy, Down, Blast You!" by Charlton Ogburn Jr., *Reader's Digest*, June 1966
Illustrations by CSA Images/Getty Images

"Don't Be Afraid of Your Feelings" by John Kord Lagemann, *Reader's Digest*, July 1967

"World's Dumbest Criminals," *Reader's Digest* International Edition, April 2018
Illustrations by Kirsten Ulve

"A Killer Is Loose" by Joseph P. Blank, *Reader's Digest*, December 1961

"Locked in the Lion's Jaws" by Arnold Shapiro, *Reader's Digest*, May 1977
Photograph page 197 by jacobcukman/Getty Images; page 201 by Chris Jackson/ Getty Images

"'Charlie Would Have Loved This'" by J.P. McEvoy, *Reader's Digest*, June 1954
Photograph by Jupiterimages/Getty Images

"Granddad" by Peggy Mapes Tate, *Reader's Digest*, October 1965

"Clams Are Not My Dish" by Don Herold, *Reader's Digest*, November 1960
Illustration by CSA Images/Getty Images

"An Army of Two" by Robert Kiener, *Reader's Digest*, April 2018

Illustrations page 217, 223 by Michael Byers; photograph page 218 courtesy Jud Esty-Kendall/ StoryCorps

"The Wreck of the *Guinevere*" by Rodney Strulo, *Reader's Digest*, July 1965
Photograph by HadelProductions/Getty Images

"Forget and Forgive" by Robert Zacks, *Reader's Digest*, October 1954

"The Most Nerve-Shattering Word in the Language" by H. Allen Smith, *Reader's Digest*, April 1967
Illustration by CSA Images/Getty Images

"One of America's Worst Disasters" by Jo Chamberlin from *The American Legion Magazine* (January 1942) copyright 1941 by The American Legion, *Reader's Digest*, January 1942
Illustrations by clu/Getty Images

"This Is What Friends Are For," *Reader's Digest*, May 2017
Photograph page 245 by Dr. Paul Wolff & Tritschler/ Getty Images; page 246 courtesy Meghan Simecek; page 249 courtesy Lorraine Morrow

"Anatomy of a Perfect Hand Transplant" by Amy Wallace from *Los Angeles*